JOHN NICKSON

OUR COMMON GOOD

IF THE STATE PROVIDES LESS, WHO WILL PROVIDE MORE?

Biteback Publishing

First published in Great Britain in 2017 by
Biteback Publishing Ltd
Westminster Tower
3 Albert Embankment
London SE1 7SP
Copyright © John Nickson 2017

ISBN 978-1-84954-803-8

10 9 8 7 6 5 4 3 2 1

A CIP catalogue record for this book is available from the British Library.

Set in Adobe Caslon Pro

Printed and bound in Great Britain by
CPI Group (UK) Ltd, Croydon CR0 4YY

MIX
Paper from
responsible sources
FSC
www.fsc.org   FSC® C020471

"The happiness or unhappiness of the society in which we live depends on ourselves as citizens, not only the instruments of political power we call the State."

WILLIAM BEVERIDGE, LIBERAL AND FOUNDING FATHER OF THE WELFARE STATE.

For Simon Rew
And Innocent Mugyenzi

IN MEMORIAM

O*ur Common Good* is also dedicated to the memory of three
friends:

Sir John Burgh

John Burgh was an immigrant. He arrived in London shortly
before the Second World War, an Austrian–Jewish refugee unable
to speak English. After three decades as a senior civil servant, he
became Director General of the British Council, which has taught
English to millions around the world. I was head of the press
office at the British Council in the 1980s when John did his best
to temper my rhetoric but not always successfully. John had a gift
for friendship. At his funeral, Shirley Williams, former Secretary of
State, talked of John's 'unquestioned integrity' and described him as
'irreplaceable'. I miss his curiosity, his encouragement, his wit and
his warmth. John died aged eighty-seven, so we had to let him go.

Dr John Cobb

John Cobb was a consultant psychiatrist. Following a heart attack
in my twenties, I became depressed and was referred to John. I
believed, wrongly, that this was the lowest point of my life. On
the contrary; the experience was illuminating. John led me out of
darkness into light and a new world of understanding. We became
friends and discussed the possibility of collaborating on a book.
Nine days later, John suddenly stopped speaking. His death was
unexpected and too soon.

Rebecca Williams

Becky worked for me at Tate where I was responsible for fundraising. I realised she should be my successor. Indeed, she took over running the department long before I retired. One of the main requirements of the job is to persuade those more senior than you to do what they know they should but would rather not. Becky was brilliant. She had the persistence of a terrier, well disguised by her eloquence and wit. Tate had a colossal fundraising target of more than £300 million and although we had made good progress by the time I retired in 2011, Becky led her team of trustees and staff to complete the restoration of Tate Britain and the building of the Switch House at Tate Modern. Becky was struck down by a particularly aggressive cancer and died age forty-five, two months before the opening of the Tate Modern's Switch House, and far, far too soon.

All three have been in my thoughts throughout the writing of *Our Common Good*. I shall be eternally grateful to them.

RIP. Carpe diem.

ACKNOWLEDGEMENTS

I am particularly grateful to the following for their encouragement and advice as well as their practical and moral support:

Rory Brooks, John Botts, Victoria Barnsley, Michael de Giorgio, Sir Simon Robertson, Lord (Dennis) Stevenson and John Studzinski.

Susan Sturrock gave me invaluable editorial advice and support and I could not have written *Our Common Good* without her.

I am indebted to Olivia Beattie, Laurie De Decker and their colleagues at Biteback Publishing for all their support, guidance and patience.

In addition to all those who appear in the book, I am grateful to the following who contributed in so many ways:

Andrea Bagg, Peter Bettley, Ian Blatchford, Dr Beth Breeze, Will Campbell-Gibson, Sam Carter, David Clark, Scott Colvin, Jonathan Cooper, Mary Cosgrave, Professor Brian Cox, Chris Cox, Rebecca Eastmond, Sheryl Forfaria, David Gordon, John Groves, Annie Harris, Professor Charles Harvey, Dr Philip Hopley, Talia Hull, Sir Peter Jonas, Paul Knox, Alice Memminger, Gina Miller, Robert Napier, Gábor Pál, David Parkinson, John Pepin, Professor Cathy Pharoah, Lois Pimentel, Christopher and Phillida Purves, Sir Simon Robey, Kath Russell, Zoe Sheppard, Anne de Silva, Katherine Smith, Paul Smith, Alexander Stevenson, Sally Tennant, Caroline Underwood, Joelle Warren, Rob Williamson and Raz Yunnus.

CONTENTS

Preface   XV

PART ONE
Surviving an age of irresponsibility   1
Chapter 1. Who is responsible?   3
Chapter 2. How unequal is Britain?   5
Chapter 3. The challenge of being young   15
Chapter 4. Trust and the threat to democracy   21
Chapter 5. Perspectives from academia   29
Chapter 6. Where will the children live?   59
Chapter 7. Equality and the law   75
Chapter 8. Investing in knowledge and intellectual capital   87
Chapter 9. Culture and the need to explain   103
Chapter 10. Health: a public service in crisis   125
Chapter 11. Who should pay for doing good?   143

PART TWO
Towards a new world of responsibility and enlightenment?   165
Chapter 12. Defining and achieving the common good   167
Chapter 13. How can great wealth respond to social need?   179
    Independent foundations and their contribution to the
    common good
Chapter 14. The woman and the dress: inequality in Surrey   195
    and Zambia
Chapter 15. Renaissance: a tale of two men and two towns   211

Chapter 16. Those were the days: why the rebirth   225
of a town matters

Chapter 17. Northern Ireland: how community, philanthropy   257
and social enterprise made peace possible

Chapter 18. Community First: a crusade for more local giving   277

Chapter 19. Pioneering new charities: the heroes   291
and heroines of twenty-first century Britain

Chapter 20. Are millennials 'nicer'?: new thinking   325
about giving

Chapter 21. Catch-22: charity's dilemma   349

Chapter 22. Community power: the regeneration   361
of east London

Chapter 23. From Oldham to the Universe: the path   377
to youth empowerment

Chapter 24. Conclusions: Observing eternal truths   393

Appendix   405

PREFACE

'We live in paradise.' So said my doctor when I gave her a copy of my first book, *Giving Is Good for You*. Her practice is in London's poorest ward. One might ask: paradise for whom?

We live in a paradox. The world has never been richer and billions have been lifted out of extreme poverty. A new middle class has been created in the developing world, transforming the global economy. Inequality between nations has decreased but inequality within some nations has increased greatly. The world is better connected than ever but many feel disconnected from society. Britain has emerged from the recent recession with a notable ability to create jobs, yet many of our fellow citizens are in receipt of benefits despite being in work.

Many in other countries regard Britain as paradise and want to live here. According to the United Nations Refugee Agency, we live in 'an age of unprecedented mass displacement'. The UN estimates that in 2015, one in every 122 people in the world was a refugee, internally displaced or seeking political asylum. The total number is estimated to be a record 65.3 million people, equivalent to the population of the UK and 60 per cent more than ten years ago.

More than a million refugees and migrants arrived in Europe in 2015, fleeing the destruction of their societies, challenging our notion of what society means, our sense of responsibility towards others, and our humanity.

There is evidence of rising xenophobia, racism, discontent, intolerance and anger in the so-called developed world, expressed in the rise of populism and parties of the extreme left and right. The politics of fear and blame are symptomatic of failure.

The disappointed and disaffected do not wish to consider the rights and needs of other people who come to be seen as less than human, to be excluded, expelled or worse. This is a dangerous road and we know where it leads.

Britain is divided between north and south, between Scotland and England, between metropolitan and non-metropolitan, between London and everywhere else, between pro- and anti-Brexit and between the 1 per cent and the 99 per cent.

As social bonds weaken, the role of the state is changing. The state is redefining its role and providing less. This is already increasing demand upon the voluntary sector, which is much smaller than the public and private sectors.

If the state provides less, who will provide more?

Being conscious of the debt of gratitude that my generation of baby boomers owes to previous generations who fought two world wars to defend our liberty, I am concerned about what we will bequeath to the young. Will they inherit a mountain of debt to add to the cost of their higher education in addition to the escalating cost of finding somewhere to live and of looking after my generation in old age? This will have profound implications for the future of our society because they will also inherit an increasingly unequal world where, according to Credit Suisse, 1 per cent of the world's population already owns almost half of global wealth. Will democracy become plutocracy?

My aim is to cast light upon a subject that is of fundamental importance to us all. Civil society, the voluntary sector and the philanthropy that funds it are not part of public discourse or a political priority. And yet, contemporary Britain is defined by the generosity of our predecessors. Our hospitals and hospices, social housing, medical and scientific research, museums, galleries, theatres, concert halls, public parks, many of our schools, universities and conservatoires were made possible and are sustained by philanthropy as well as the state. Much of the social progress achieved in the past 250 years, such as the abolition of slavery, votes for women, the decriminalisation of homosexuality and the preservation of our rural and cultural heritage would not have happened without campaigning charities funded by personal donations. Given a state that will provide less, we shall need more people to be more generous in future.

By more people, I mean you and me, not just the very rich.

Charitable giving has not grown in line with personal wealth since the 1970s, according to the Charities Aid Foundation (CAF). In 1995, there were five billionaires based in Britain. In 2015, there were estimated to be 117 billionaires living here. Only a minority of the wealthy is philanthropic. Without more giving, the voluntary sector is not equipped to meet extra demand, and this requires a practical as well as a moral response from all of us if we are to bequeath civil society to future generations.

Some define civil society as being synonymous with the voluntary sector or as that part of our national life that is distinct from and independent of government and business. I find these definitions unsatisfactory, as the idea that the government and the private and voluntary sectors are independent of each other is out of date. I believe that our future lies with greater partnership between the sectors but on very different terms from those that operate now.

My definition of civil society is broad, encompassing the values and essence of liberal democracy. In a civil society, all citizens have the right to enjoy freedom and the opportunity to live and to work in a culture of transparency, accountability and justice within the law. Accordingly, we all have a responsibility to support our civil society, by paying tax, by giving what and when we can and by volunteering.

The health of civil society depends upon the strength of our commitment to the common good. I define the common good as the sum of all the values, activities and services that sustain our liberal democracy. The common good is about collaboration, inclusivity and collective as well as personal responsibility.

My definition of philanthropy is also broad. For me, philanthropy is about the commitment of both time and money. Anyone can be philanthropic.

Our Common Good is an investigation into threats to our civil society and to our democracy and the role that we can play in sustaining it by giving, volunteering and investing in social enterprise. I talked to more than a hundred people in different parts of the country and was surprised and encouraged by what I learned.

I had not appreciated how much we depend upon the voluntary sector and upon those who give their time, their money, and often both. I did not know the role that philanthropy and social enterprise had played in the Northern Ireland peace process and that continues today bringing together and rebuilding communities in ways that could be replicated throughout the UK.

I had not realised how much medical research depends upon philanthropy, including human fertility and current advances in treatment of Alzheimer's.

I learned that the regeneration of some of the most deprived parts of east London has been driven by social enterprise. The lives and prospects of those who live there have been transformed.

I did not know that charity is pioneering new ways for more effective and compassionate delivery of some public services or that the Lancashire Police Constabulary has created a social enterprise to turn serial criminals into contributing members of society. Nor did I know that Air Ambulances are charities funded by an army of small donors.

If Britain is to adapt to the new reality of less state provision, significant cultural change will be required. Traditional notions of left and right need to be challenged. Government, local authorities, the private and voluntary sectors must pool resources, forge new partnerships based upon mutual interest, mutual understanding and mutual respect. This is easy to say but hard to deliver.

However, I have evidence that this is happening. I report on a charitable and philanthropic enterprise in the north of England supporting 20,000 disadvantaged young people via a new form of public and private sector partnership. The results are remarkable: falling unemployment, less crime and more fulfilling lives for the young. The return on local authority investment is six-fold.

Philanthropy is convening private and public resources at a local level to meet local need and this makes a great community effort possible. Moreover, the role of volunteers is critical.

Charities and voluntary organisations at their pioneering best can do what the state cannot. That is not to deny the importance of the state. However, we have social problems that the state is not capable of dealing with. That is why private wealth should be encouraged to invest in well-funded institutions that are independent of government.

An outstanding example is Sir Clive Cowdery, who established the Resolution Foundation to stimulate debate about the need to improve living standards for those on low incomes, including campaigning for a national living wage.

Philanthropy, however, will always be a matter of personal choice. Therein lie its strengths and its disadvantages. Necessarily, philanthropy reflects the interest and enthusiasm of the benefactor. By definition, it cannot be comprehensive. That is why we shall always need an enabling state.

I believe the future of our liberal democracy depends upon our commitment to the common good. There is a danger that commitment will wane if the gap between the 1 per cent and the 99 per cent continues to grow. Peasants and pitchforks may not be an immediate prospect but the lessons of history are salutary.

I also believe that philanthropy is a manifestation of a healthy society. We should be concerned that the long-term trend for giving by households and by those under thirty has been in decline for thirty years, according to CAF.

We lost our nineteenth-century culture of giving for understandable reasons as the state took on more responsibility and taxes on the wealthy increased. Now that the state is in retreat and top-rate tax is half what it was in the middle of the twentieth century, we need to create a new culture of giving fit for the twenty-first century.

I hope that the people and projects that I have written about will illustrate what is needed and show that a practical and moral response to current social challenges is possible. I hope that it will become clear that philanthropy is for everyone and not just the rich. I hope that you will be as moved as I was by the men and women I met and maybe inspired to follow their example. They understand that the common good is an essential part of our humanity.

November 2016, London

PART ONE

SURVIVING
AN AGE OF
IRRESPONSIBILITY

CHAPTER 1

WHO IS RESPONSIBLE?

In June 2015, Mark Carney, Governor of the Bank of England, issued a warning to the financial services industry by announcing the end of the 'Age of Irresponsibility'. We must hope that he is right. I believe, however, that a description of our Age of Irresponsibility should extend way beyond the excesses and misdeeds of the financial sector. The way our country has been run for decades is irresponsible, and significant numbers of people have little confidence in those who hold power.

My focus is upon one particular aspect of government policy that has implications for all of us and for the young in particular. The state will provide less, and more demand will fall upon the voluntary sector. In 2013, I asked a former Labour Party leader what plans the party had to strengthen the voluntary sector. There were none. The same appears to be true of the Conservatives and Liberal Democrats. We may deduce that the voluntary sector is not high on the political agenda.

In order to understand the problems we face and to find solutions to them, I asked myself, and those I interviewed, the following questions.

- As the state provides less, how will the voluntary sector meet increased demand when charitable giving is not growing despite a colossal increase in personal wealth?
- Is it realistic to assume that philanthropists and charities will be able to compensate for less state provision and is it desirable that they should?

- Is it true that future generations will be less well off?
- What are the facts about inequality and poverty in the UK? What are the implications for the future of civil society?
- If wealth and power continue to be held by the few, will future generations inherit a plutocracy rather than a liberal democracy? How do we uphold our liberal democratic values in a world where democracy may not be predominant?
- How do we ensure and respect human dignity in a more impersonal world? How do we defend liberty and encourage personal responsibility when authority has lost respect and power is unaccountable?
- Who will provide the moral leadership to persuade the rich and powerful to follow the example of their forbears by supporting human endeavour for the common good as well as for personal gain?
- How do we ensure that all of us, not just the rich and powerful, understand that we have a personal responsibility for the health and vitality of civil society?
- How are today's philanthropists and social entrepreneurs responding to current challenges and how do they see their role evolving in the future?
- What has been the impact of recession upon charities? Do they have the capacity to meet increased demand?
- Do charities need to adapt to meet the changing needs of society? If so, how?
- Should charities be providing public services and if not, why not?
- Do we need to redefine the role and responsibilities of the public, private and voluntary sectors and the citizen?
- Does the concept of the common good mean anything in an era of neoliberalism or is there an irreversible trend towards more inequality and social fragmentation?
- Is it possible to imagine a future in which all those who contribute to the common good work together? If so, what could partnerships between the public, private and voluntary sectors look like and what could they achieve?

CHAPTER 2

HOW UNEQUAL IS BRITAIN?

"Why should growing inequality concern us? This is a moral and a political question. It is increasingly recognised that, beyond a certain point, inequality will be a source of significant economic ills."
MARTIN WOLF, CHIEF ECONOMIC COMMENTATOR,
FINANCIAL TIMES.

* * *

The wealth of sixty-two of the world's richest billionaires equals that of the 3.5 billion poorest people who make up half the global population.

How shocking is that? The problem with such statistics is that they seem remote and become meaningless with repetition. We need, however, to pay attention because it seems that growing disparities between the super-rich and the rest of us could threaten both our prosperity and our liberty.

Some dispute the significance of inequality and claim it is not growing in Britain. Inequality poses questions about the social commitment of most of the very rich and this has implications for all the rest of us. All the evidence suggests that only a minority of the wealthy in Britain is significantly philanthropic and this is a problem when the wealthiest 1 per cent, and particularly the 0.1 per cent, are vastly wealthier than the 99 per cent.

I have no ideological or moral objection to personal wealth. My interest is in how wealth is used and how that impacts upon others.

I believe that more of the extraordinary wealth created in Britain since the 1980s could be used to create social capital, thereby mitigating some if not all of the most damaging effects of inequality.

The commitment of the rich and powerful to what was then defined as the common good goes back to ancient Greece and beyond. Human progress has depended upon the creation of wealth to provide security and employment, and our investment in social, cultural and intellectual capital defines our civilisation today. The road from Athens to twenty-first century Britain may be long, crooked, bumpy and bloody, but we are where we are because of a shared commitment to the common good funded variously by both taxation and philanthropy. That commitment, exemplified by our willingness to defend our freedom and defeat tyranny, has enabled us to live in a liberal democracy, made secure by the state and sustained by civil society.

The worry is that most of the fruits of recent economic growth are being enjoyed by a small minority of the wealthy. Evidence shows that global inequality is increasing and that there is reason for us to be concerned about what that implies for commitment to the common good and the exercise of power.

Data from Credit Suisse Research reveals that at the beginning of this decade, 388 billionaires owned as much as half the world's population. By 2011, that figure had fallen to 117, and in 2015, only sixty-two people owned half the world's wealth.

Based on figures from Credit Suisse, Oxfam estimates that more than a quarter of the wealth created in Britain over the past fifteen years has gone to the richest 1 per cent. Inequality is even more extreme in the US and the impact has been different but there are pointers to what could happen in Britain.

According to the Organisation for Economic Development (OECD), between 1975 and 2012, 47 per cent of total growth in pre-tax incomes in the US went to 1 per cent of the population.

According to research by Pew, the middle class in the US is shrinking. In 1971, there were 80 million households defined as middle class with a combined 52 million in the groups above and below. Although there are now 120 million middle-class families, they are outnumbered by a growing number of the poor and a small number of the very rich, totalling 121 million.

How is it possible for the British Government to claim that inequality is not growing and that it may even be falling when Britain has become a profoundly unequal country? The answer depends upon what you measure and when. Income inequality for all but those at the very top has not grown for some years because tax and benefits have minimised differentials. The net effect is that for the vast majority, income inequality has remained stable from the mid-1990s.

The Resolution Foundation was founded by Sir Clive Cowdery (see Chapter 13) in 2005 as an independent think tank to improve living standards for low- to middle-income families in Britain. I asked Gavin Kelly, Chief Executive of the Resolution Trust, for a view on inequality.

We first talked in the summer of 2015 before the government announced the introduction of a new national living wage from April 2016. I asked Kelly for his perspective on Britain post-recession and for a context in which we should consider inequality:

How would I describe the UK today? Well, the optimist in me would point to the record employment rate, continued GDP growth, a vibrant and healthy democracy and our diversity and openness as signs that the UK is a good place to be – a country to love, even.

But, of course, this sentiment isn't felt across the country. The view from London is very different from the view from a former mining town. And even in successful cities like Manchester the problems are visible; the child poverty rate in Manchester is just shy of 40 per cent.

As the UK economy continues to grow it's clear that one of the next big questions we need to answer is: how inclusive is this growth going to be? The jury is out but the case for optimism isn't particularly convincing. If the gains from a period of growth accrue more to the top of the income distribution, as many expect, then with the planned cuts to in-work government support in the pipeline, inequality may rise and low income families are likely to experience little improvement in their standard of living despite rising GDP.

As we hear from the current US political debate, incomes for middle-class Americans have been flat for decades. We have to ask ourselves if this could happen here, and what the impact of a sustained period of economic growth coupled with a sustained stagnation in living standards would be.

The big inequality story of recent decades in the UK is the large increase in the 1980s through to the mid 1990s. This was driven mainly by increases in pre-tax earnings at the top and reductions in the top rate of tax. In general, during this period, the higher your income the more your income increased. The 1980s also saw shifts in social norms about pay and the collapse of trade union power – two changes which will have continued to push up inequality.

Income inequality then levelled out on to a plateau. In the Labour years, the gap between the middle and the bottom was reduced, partly as a result of the minimum wage. At the same time incomes at the top increased very fast – the top 1 per cent saw their income grow twice as fast as the average. The growth in pay and incomes in the top 0.1 per cent means that they and the top 1 per cent are now, in short, on a different planet from the rest of us.

The evidence strongly suggests that flat-lining inequality will not last. Inequality is forecast to rise again as a result of reductions in in-work support for those at the bottom and the return of earnings growth for the majority. Add to this tax cuts tilted towards the rich and the continued racing away of the very top and the outlook is far from cheerful. For example, child poverty is forecast to return to levels last seen in the late 1990s by the end of the decade.

It's also worth thinking more broadly about the changing role of government. It has clearly retreated in a number of important areas – from the construction of social housing to provision of services through local government (e.g. community centres, libraries and social care). The prospect of this withdrawal being reversed by an influx of private money is limited and without meaningful changes in policy, the direction for quality of life in the UK for those at the bottom shows no signs of rising fast any time soon.

Whilst inequality of incomes for the majority has been broadly stable for twenty years, top pay has continued to soar. In 1998, FTSE 100 company chief executive pay was on average forty-seven times more than that of the average paid to their employees. The typical FTSE CEO now earns 183 times more than average. These figures reflect the average. Some are paid very much more. In 2015, Sir Martin Sorrell, founder and chief executive of WPP, the advertising company, was paid more than £63 million in cash and share awards.

Increase in top pay has not necessarily been accompanied by increasing profits and share prices. In 2015, Bob Dudley, chief executive of BP, was awarded a pay increase of 20 per cent from $16.4 million to $19.6 million, despite BP recording a record loss of $5.2 billion, despite a fall in the share price of 13.5 per cent, and despite a majority of shareholders voting against the award. Why are companies rewarding failure?

These kinds of pay awards are a prime example of what constitutes An Age of Irresponsibility. The reason given for paying CEOs salaries that seem unreal is that they are determined by the market. If so, then a correction is due.

That something is wrong is now becoming apparent even in the right-wing press. In January 2016, columnist, commentator and former Tory MP Matthew Parris wrote in *The Times* about top pay:

For some of us lifelong Conservatives, it is becoming painful. Is the free market distributing its spoils in a morally defensible way… capitalism is supposed to cascade wealth down so why does it cascade up? And why is the abuse getting worse? … How much longer can we market liberals shrug off the huge failures in the working examples we have of capitalism? If the free market is to be defended in the new century these inequities are no longer something from which the centre-right can turn away.

Financial Times has given considerable coverage to inequality its significance, including a number of articles by Martin Wolf, its chief economics commentator. Here is a digest of notable points made by Wolf in his *FT* column since 2014:

When should growing inequality concern us? This is a moral and political question. It is also an economic one. It is increasingly recognised that, beyond a certain point, inequality will be a source of significant economic ills...

The US – both the most important high-income economy and much the most unequal – is providing a test bed for the economic impact of inequality and the results are worrying...

This realisation has now spread to institutions that would not be normally accused of socialism. A report written by the Chief US economist of Standard and Poor's, and another from Morgan Stanley, agree that inequality is not only rising but also having damaging effects on the US economy. The Morgan Stanley study lists the causes of the rise in inequality: the growing proportion of poorly paid and insecure jobs and insecure low skilled jobs; the rising wage premium for educated people; and the fact that tax and spending policies are less distributive than they used to be a few years ago...

These reports bring out two economic consequences of rising inequality: weak demand and lagging process in raising educational levels...

Left with huge debts and unable to borrow more, people on low incomes have been forced to spend less. The effect has been an exceptionally weak recovery of consumption...

Children from poor backgrounds are handicapped from completing college. Yet without a college degree, the chances of upward mobility are now quite limited. As a result, children of prosperous families are likely to stay well off and children of poor families to remain poor...The failure to raise educational standards is also likely to impair the economy's long-term success.

To my surprise, the International Monetary Fund, the most staid of institutions... in a note entitled Redistribution, Inequality and

Growth, came to clear conclusions: lower net inequality (post interventions) drives faster and more durable growth: and redistribution
is generally benign in its impact on growth, with negative effects
only when taken to extremes...

The implication of this work is perhaps surprising. Not only does
inequality damage growth, but efforts to remedy it are, on the whole,
not harmful...

Less inequality is likely to make economies work better by increasing the ability of the entire population to participate on more
equal terms. An important condition for this, in turn, is that politics
not be unduly beholden to wealth...

The costs of rising inequality go further. To my mind, the greatest
costs are the erosion of the Republican ideal of shared citizenship.
Enormous divergences in wealth and power have hollowed out re-
publics before now. They could well do so in our age.

The rebellion against the elites is in full swing. The vital question
is whether (and how) western elites can be brought closer to the
people...

In the west, the idea of citizenship – that the public realm is the
property of all – is not only of ancient standing; it has been the
object of an ultimately successful strategy in recent centuries. An
essential attribute of the good life is that people enjoy not just a
range of personal freedoms but a voice in public affairs.

The outcome of individual economic freedom can be greater
inequality which hollows out realistic notions of democracy... we
already face the danger that the gulf between economic and tech-
nocratic elites on the one hand and the mass of people on the other,
becomes too vast to be bridged. At the limit, trust might break down
altogether. Thereupon, the electorate will turn to outsiders to clean
up the system. We are seeing such a shift to trust in outsiders not
only in the US but also in many European countries...

So what are the root causes of this divide in attitudes?... Perhaps
the most fundamental cause is a growing sense that elites are corrupt,
complacent and incompetent. Demagogues play on such sources of
anxiety and anger. That is what they do... Western politics are subject

to increasing stresses. Large numbers of people feel disrespected and dispossessed. This can no longer be ignored.

If income inequality has been stable in Britain for nearly twenty years and incomes are growing again after recession, are the concerns expressed by Martin Wolf somewhat exaggerated? They might be if inequality of incomes was to be our sole concern. However, a closer look at other forms of inequality is not reassuring.

The real story of inequality in Britain is about capital assets and who owns them. A study by the Institute of Fiscal Studies (IFS) published in November 2015 shows that Britain is a more unequal country when measured by wealth – the value of assets such as housing, pensions and shares – than when it is measured by income.

According to IFS, total household wealth between 2010 and 2012 was distributed very unequally. The wealth of the median household was £172,000. Nine per cent of households had no positive net wealth and 5 per cent of households had in excess of £1.2 million.

The Gini Coefficient is a commonly used measure of inequality in which 0 represents complete equality and 1 represents the most extreme inequality, when one person owns everything. According to IFS, in Britain, the Gini Coefficient for total household wealth is 0.65 compared to 0.40 for household net income. The Gini Coefficient for private pension wealth is 0.73.

Financial wealth, meaning bank balances and investments, has a Gini Coefficient of 0.91. This is the statistic that proves Britain is a profoundly unequal society.

The IFS study covered the periods 2006–08 and 2010–12 and found that, largely due to changes in pensions and increasing housing costs, younger households were on course to be less asset-rich than their parents.

Over the long term and despite fluctuating markets, those who hold well-invested capital may expect their wealth to increase in value faster than the rate of economic growth. This means that the commanding heights of the economy are dominated not just by wealth but also by inherited wealth, thus perpetuating and enhancing inequality.

Moreover, there are signs that income inequality may be return-ing to Britain. Despite the introduction of the Living Wage in April 2016 and the removal of planned cuts to tax credits in 2015 and to personal payments for the disabled in 2016, the IFS warns that welfare cuts and the introduction of Universal Credit (whereby six benefits are streamed into one payment) mean that an estimated 2.1 million working families will lose an average £1,600 a year whilst the top rate of income tax, capital gains tax and corporation taxes have been reduced, to the benefit of the most wealthy.

The Resolution Foundation published its seventh annual state of the nation report on living standards at the beginning of 2016. The report focuses on the experience of low- to middle-income Britain, 5.7 million primarily working households.

In summary, a recovery in incomes is underway, generated by the strength of the UK jobs market. The typical median household income in 2015 was roughly 3 per cent higher than in 2007–08, standing at £24,300. The report projected that median and mean incomes will continue to recover until 2020, supported by the in-troduction of the National Living Wage. The Foundation forecast reductions in incomes for the poorest 25 per cent of households between 2015 and 2020: 'This pattern is likely to reverse entirely the gains made on equality in the post-crisis period.'

My concern is not that the rich have too much but that those on lower and middle income have too little. And, if this trend continues, growing numbers of our children will be poorer than we are. That doesn't make economic sense, as demand will fall. More poverty and inequality also threatens to undermine many of the social gains we have made at great cost in the last 100 years. Moreover, inequal-ity in terms of opportunity, social mobility, health, access to housing and to the law should also be considered. So what are the challenges facing the young today, what are their prospects for the future and what are the implications for the common good?

CHAPTER 3

THE CHALLENGE OF
BEING YOUNG

"Now we fear, that despite the achievements of the Welfare State,
our society is becoming less cohesive and less mobile… We think
of haves and have-nots now. But what if the haves are us now and
the have-nots are our children and grandchildren in the future?"
DAVID WILLETTS, AUTHOR OF *THE PINCH: HOW THE BABY
BOOMERS TOOK THEIR CHILDREN'S FUTURE … AND WHY
THEY SHOULD GIVE IT BACK.*

*   *   *

Is this generation the most spoiled in human history or is it jinxed?
Is it true that they must expect to be poorer than their parents
and grandparents and if so, why would that matter?

Health and life expectancy have been transformed since the end
of the Second World War. Food is plentiful and cheap. We can travel
almost anywhere. Communication is instantaneous, information is
easily accessible and seemingly limitless. More young people are
able to enjoy the benefits of a higher education. Britain has become
a more tolerant society. Only those who volunteer need fight.

The lives of my parents' and grandparents' generations were
defined by two world wars. Millions died and every family suffered.
This generation of millennials (born between 1980 and 2000) must
be the healthiest, best educated and potentially the wealthiest ever.
Talking about austerity is a joke for those who experienced the real

thing. And even if there is evidence that youth unemployment remains high and growth in the incomes of the young is less than those of older people, surely money should not be the only measure of happiness and fulfilment?

Most people would agree with Gavin Kelly of the Resolution Trust who says there is much to love about Britain. However, there is evidence that future generations should not expect the political, social and economic progress that has been the experience of my generation.

In 2015, the Resolution Foundation published a report: *Securing A Pay Rise: The Path Back to Shared Pay Growth*. The facts are disturbing. The squeeze on pay between 2009 and 2014 has been tighter for some than others.

Young people were hit the hardest with a cumulative fall in median pay of nearly 13 per cent over five years for workers in their twenties. This compares with drops of around 10 per cent for workers in their thirties and forties and 7 per cent for those in their fifties. Hourly pay for 22- to 29-year-olds is now lower than at any time since 1998.

A Resolution Foundation report titled *The Generation Game* shows that university is not always the road to a well-paid job. New graduates who earned enough to start paying loans in 2011–12 were earning 12 per cent less in real terms than graduates at the same stage in their careers in 2007–08. Chris Giles reports:

> Wages are, of course, only one element of income so a wider analysis of living standards is necessary to see if something really has changed. The FT has shown what appears to be a jinxed generation – those born between 1985 and 1994 – who were the first who were not to be better off at the same stage of their lives than their forebears.

According to Giles, intergenerational inequalities are rising rapidly:

> Older generations are using the power of experience to defend

their status, pushing all the pain of recent years on younger, more inexperienced people. If so, then there is a genuine grievance that requires public policy action.

Without action, the consequences are almost all bad. If the young have been kept in jobs below their skill levels, the scarring is potentially worse than the long-term unemployment of the 1980s. The lack of owner-occupation is not much of a problem if wages and pensions enable secure renting in the private sector. But if housing costs are so high that renters will fall back on housing benefit in retirement, present calculations of future social security costs will be grossly underestimated.

Worst of all, there is every chance that the wealth that already exists in Britain will be passed on to future generations in a way that concentrates inequalities. It is not an exaggeration to say that the danger from wealth accumulation in the current older generations is a miserable future two-tier society. Having rich grandparents, who benefitted from rising house prices, will mean housing security in your childbearing years. If you don't have that good fortune, you will be lucky to escape a life of insecurity in which bringing up children seems a burden too far.

The good news is that intergenerational problems are easy to fix – if only society has the will. The bad news is that many of the suggestions which seek to redistribute power, wealth or amenity from the rich elderly will face fierce opposition from large groups with a high likelihood of voting.

These groups are baby boomers born between 1946 and 1964. Baby boomers were initially made uncomfortable by talk of intergenerational inequality and the burden we shall be upon younger generations. However, I have a better understanding having read *The Pinch: How The Baby Boomers Took Their Children's Future – And Why They Should Give It Back* (Atlantic Books, 2010). The author, David, now Lord, Willetts is a former Conservative MP, a former Minister for Universities and Sciences in the coalition government 2010–15, and now Executive Chairman of the Resolution Foundation.

Willetts tells us that, historically, England has had unusually small families and strong central government unlike other societies where social insurance was shared within larger families and clans. This encouraged small families to look for alternative networks and led to the development of what we now call civil society:

> This English political tradition emphasises the strength and importance of civil society, our country's historic freedoms, a legitimate role for government in providing equitable justice accessible to all, together with a faith in evolutionary social progress. It sustained a political programme – spreading the rights of citizenship widely... that still matters today... Now we fear, that despite the achievements of the welfare state, our society is becoming less cohesive and less mobile... Instead of thinking just of the horizontal obligations we have to fellow citizens now, we need to think about the vertical obligations we have to our children and grandchildren and future generations. We think of haves and have-nots now. But what if the haves are us now, and the have-nots are our children and grandchildren in the future?
>
> In 1974, the average 50- to 59-year-old earned about 4 per cent more than the 25- to 29-year-old... by 2008 it was 35 per cent more.

The problem of intergenerational inequality is further compounded by declining social mobility:

> As we go through stages of the life cycle so we build up social capital ... The only trouble is that our move through the life cycle is slower and messier than it used to be. If things carry on as they are we will become even more dependent on our families for longer. So parents with more money can afford to support you and then pay for you to go out into the big wide world. We do our best for our own children even whilst our society gives a raw deal to young people as a whole – this is a reason for the decline in social mobility.
>
> Whatever the exact pattern of cause and effect the conclusion is clear: Families powerfully transmit advantage from one generation

to the next. We are better at providing for our own children than looking after the interests of the next generation as a whole. We are indeed better parents than we are citizens...

We used to assume social mobility would steadily improve. That is why it was such a shock when in 2005 evidence came out that social mobility had declined ... This would suggest that young people were losing out in the jobs market even before the recession struck ... During the years from 1997 to 2007, which we now see was a debt-driven boom, youth unemployment was actually rising.

The central argument of this book [*The Pinch*] is that we are not attaching sufficient value to the claims of future generations. This is partly because a big disruptive generation of baby boomers has weakened many of the ties between generations. But it is also an intellectual failure: we have not got a clear way of thinking about the rights of future generations. We are allowing one very big generation to break the inter-generational contract because we do not fully understand it.

The modern condition is supposed to be the search for meaning in a world where unreflective obligation to institutions or ways of doing things are eroded. The link between generations past, present and future is a source of meaning as natural as could be. It is both cultural and economic, personal and ethical. We must understand and honour those ties which bind the generations.

Britain is an unequal country. In addition to significant inequality of the ownership of assets, there is intergenerational inequality in terms of income and social mobility. There are also inequalities in access to housing and to the law and inequality in health outcomes. Despite the progress made in limiting income inequality, do these inequalities pose a threat to the civil society and the liberal democracy we, perhaps, take for granted?

David Willetts says there has been a breakdown of trust between generations. Is there an even more significant breakdown of trust between the 1 per cent and the 99 per cent?

CHAPTER 4

TRUST AND THE THREAT TO DEMOCRACY

"Capitalism has survived the crash, but at the expense of a collapse
of trust in ruling elites."
PHILIP STEPHENS, *FINANCIAL TIMES*,
18 DECEMBER 2015.

*   *   *

Liberal democracy depends upon trust as well as consent. If trust collapses, democracy and our civil society are at risk.

Humanity has never before been so well connected and yet, in Britain, there is a disconnection between people, institutions and authority. There have been scandals and a subsequent lack of trust in almost every part of public life: in national and local politics, business, car manufacturing, banks and other financial services, the health, care and social services, the churches, the media, the police and, last but by no means least, sport.

The danger is that lack of trust on this scale will corrode the ties between us and undermine our confidence in government and belief in the common good. What does the evidence tell us?

In 2015, Ipsos Mori published a poll that showed the British public is less likely to trust politicians than estate agents, bankers or journalists. This may not be a surprise but the statistics are worrying nevertheless. Only 16 per cent of Britons trust politicians to tell the truth. Doctors head the list of the most trusted, with 90 per cent.

In the US in 1958, Pew Research reported that 75 per cent of Americans trusted the US federal government to do the right thing. In 2015, trust fell below 20 per cent.

British Social Attitudes reports that 90 per cent believed the banks to be well run in 1983, but this had fallen to 19 per cent in 2012.

Lack of trust is a global phenomenon. According to Edelman, an international communications business, trust inequality is linked to income inequality:

> There is deeply disturbing news in the Edelman Trust Barometer 2016: A yawning gap is emerging between elite and mass populations. The global survey asks respondents how much they trust the four institutions of government, business, non-governmental organisations, and the media to do what is right. The survey shows that trust is rising in the elite or 'informed public' group, those with a college education ... and [who] have an income in the top 20 per cent. However, in the 'mass population' (the remaining 80 per cent of our sample) trust levels have barely budged since the recession...
>
> We now observe the inequality of trust around the world ... There is a 'grand illusion at play' – a lingering notion that elites continue to lead and the masses will follow. This historic model of influence was predicated on the belief that elites have access to superior information, their interests are interconnected with those of the broader public and that becoming an 'elite' was open to all who work hard. Rising income inequality, high profile revelations of greed and misbehaviour and the democratisation of the media have flipped the classic pyramid of influence. The trust of the mass population can no longer be taken for granted...
>
> In more than 60 per cent of the countries surveyed, the trust levels of the mass population are below 50 per cent. By contrast, the trust levels of the elite population are at the highest level in the sixteen years of study. In three-fourths of the countries, trust levels in institutions are over 50 per cent amongst elites.

Inequality of trust has important consequences. The most obvious is growing receptivity to politicians who prey on fear instead of offering solutions. Examples include assertions that refugees are a major security threat and that unemployment can be addressed by stopping foreign trade. Trust inequality seems to be a major pillar in the campaigns of Donald Trump in the US and Marine Le Pen in France.

Polling confirms that lack of trust is real. We should not be surprised. The behaviour of the churches in trying to cover up sexual abuse and protect abusers is almost as scandalous as the abuse itself.

The torrent of media money pouring into sport must have contributed to greed, fraud and corruption at the highest levels. The tabloid press is rancid with prejudice and ruthless in its pursuit of profit at the expense of others, including the most vulnerable. In 2015, the main headline of an issue of the *Daily Express* read:

SONGS OF PRAISE FILMED IN MIGRANTS' CAMP: THIS IS HOW THE BBC SPENDS YOUR MONEY

This kind of propaganda is worthy of Dr Goebbels.

The financial scandals of mismanagement, misselling and market-rigging are well documented as are the failings of the NHS, retirement homes and social services to fulfil their duty of care. The failure of the police to investigate the sexual abuse of children, the covering up of their own misdeeds and the falsification of evidence in relation to the Hillsborough tragedy undermine confidence in justice. The self-indulgence, greed and disregard for the public interest of those politicians who fiddled their expenses make a mockery of public service.

Oggling the super rich has become a spectator sport in our age of celebrity and irresponsibility. Lord Mandelson was reported to have said that the New Labour government was intensely relaxed about the very rich 'as long as they paid their taxes'. The mood has changed. The key question is: who pays tax and how much do they pay?

It has been the policy of successive governments since the 1980s to reduce personal tax and to increase indirect taxes, sometimes by stealth. Whilst most of us are aware that the nation has a debt problem, politicians send out contradictory signals that do not amount to a clarion call to pay tax.

In 2014, Facebook paid £4,327 in corporation tax, less than those on a UK average salary of £26,500 who paid income tax of £5,392.

The news in 2016 that Google, the second most valuable brand in the world, would pay £130 million in back taxes was not well received, except by then Chancellor of the Exchequer who seemed to be out of touch with the mood of his parliamentary colleagues as well as the public. Google's UK revenue in 2013 was reported to be £3.8 billion.

Whilst tax avoidance is legal, it is legitimate to question the integrity of those businesses that pay so little tax. The Edelman Trust Barometer also indicates a shift in expectations that business should also have social obligations and responsibilities. Integrity is a form of capital. Smart companies will be those that invest in integrity and for social as well as financial return.

In this climate and in the absence of both political and moral leadership, it is no wonder that people and companies are reluctant taxpayers, to the detriment of the common good. The parliamentary Public Account Committee reports that the amount of tax evaded is estimated to be £16 billion.

The need for tax to support a healthy society was made clear by Dr Dan Poulter, Conservative MP for Central Suffolk and North Ipswich and a former health minister, in an extract from a newspaper article he wrote in 2016:

> I struggle to see much improvement in some of the most disadvantaged people in our society … Chronic underfunding of mental health and social care services, a shortage of social and appropriate sheltered housing, together with a benefits system that does not always adequately recognise the needs of people with severe and enduring mental illness do not help. The increasingly fragmented health and

care services landscape coupled with the loss of many vital specialist substance abuse services, has made the situation worse...

The government is rightly committed to balancing the books and eliminating the national deficit but ... the challenges facing tens of thousands of people makes it all the more important that financially responsible government also means compassionate government. Our first priority must be to look after and protect the most vulnerable, and the genuinely disadvantaged.

When there is still so much to be done to improve the life chances of the most vulnerable, it is difficult to justify putting middle class tax cuts before the needs of the working poor, and the socially disadvantaged...

Improving the plight of the most vulnerable requires a political debate that better values the state as an important force for good. Perhaps the fundamental truth is this: that truly governing for one nation also means caring about the state, and recognising its power to both protect and to transform the lives of the most disadvantaged for the better.

I believe that capitalism, like liberal democracy, is the least-worst option for the developed world but the current neo-liberal version of capitalism is creating wealth for the few rather than the many. There is no 'trickle down'. Moreover, there is no evidence that those made wealthy by globalisation, neo-liberal economic policies and lower taxation are being more philanthropic. If capitalism is to survive and to continue to create the wealth we need to sustain a healthy and democratic civil society, we need our political leaders to help bring this about. So far, we have heard nothing relevant or significant about the constructive reform of capitalism from any politician or party. Instead, politicians use language to divide rather than unite in the pursuit of votes.

Criticism of the so-called feckless poor has long been a tradition in Britain. The country is apparently made up of shirkers or strivers, the latter being made up of 'hard-working families'. We are encouraged to distinguish between the deserving and the undeserving poor.

The welfare state needs reform in order to reflect social and economic progress since 1945. Social need has changed over seventy years and spending may need to be constrained at times of economic difficulty. However, to cut the benefits of the poorest whilst reducing tax for the richest is plutocratic. To stigmatise the poor and vulnerable in order to win and exercise power is divisive, dangerous and immoral.

Stigma is immoral because it suggests that other people are in some way less than human. History tells us that stigma and demonisation of others leads to violence and genocide. The common good is perverted to represent the interests of the few who hold power rather than the many.

The worldview of my parents' and grandparents' generations, born between 1880 and 1920, was shaped by some of the worst atrocities in human history. It is estimated that up to 100 million people were killed in the two world wars.

Those of us who were children in the 1950s had our lives defined by the Second World War. We learned about the holocaust, the genocide of six million Jews and other 'aliens' (gypsies, homosexuals and anyone opposed to the regime) in the Nazi death camps. We reassured ourselves that the experience was so appalling that nothing like it would happen in Europe in our lifetimes and, in any case, we British would never have been capable of such barbarity towards other people.

Nevertheless, there was genocide in Europe between 1992 and 1995 during the war in former Yugoslavia. More than 140,000 died and four million people were displaced.

It is natural to turn away from the worst excesses of the human race. However, we should be honest with ourselves and acknowledge what we are capable of and to remember what we have done. There have been episodes in our past which should remind us that the British are or were capable of formulating a rational argument in favour of the most ruthless exploitation of others on the basis that they were not fully human.

Slavery was not finally abolished in Britain until 1833, within the lifetime of my grandparents' grandparents. In 2015, BBC television broadcast a documentary *Britain's Forgotten Slave Owners*, presented by the historian David Olusoga, and based on research provided by University College London and its database of slave owners. We learned the following.

At one point, 46,000 British people owned 800,000 slaves in the Caribbean region. The owners could be classified as 'ordinary' people and included clergymen and single women in all parts of Britain.

Slavery was a component part of the British economy for more than two centuries, involving violent and barbarous repression. British slave owners received compensation for abolition from the British government equivalent to £17 billion today.

Those days are long behind us but we know that ruthless and violent exploitation of others is rife today in other continents, and was practised in Europe within the lifetime of most people living in Britain. Can we be confident that liberal democracy will prevail in the future if the global trend continues towards the concentration of wealth and power in the hands of the few? Will the discontented return to narrow nationalism and vote for populist political leaders whose commitment to democracy and the common good is determined entirely by their self-interest?

It has happened before. Now, as refugees and migrants from Africa, the Middle East and Afghanistan flee to Europe in their millions, barbed wire and fences are being erected and borders are closed. Donald Trump, campaigning successfully for the US presidency, promised to build a wall along the border with Mexico. Extreme right-wing nationalist parties in Europe are recruiting more support and governments in Poland and Hungary have been elected with a questionable commitment to the rule of law and free speech.

The corrosion of trust in politicians and institutions opens the door to extremism. The gap between those who have wealth and power and the disadvantaged encourages negative rather than positive responses and populist politicians who offer the voters enemies as solutions.

CHAPTER 5

PERSPECTIVES FROM ACADEMIA

"Spending money on the community (in fifth century Greece)
was not an optional extra, it was part of the package
of being an elite citizen."

MARY BEARD.

*   *   *

Before embarking on a tour that would take me from Blackpool
to Bromley-by-Bow via Belfast, I turned to academia in order
to find my bearings and a sense of perspective about the relationship between citizen and society, now and in the past. What role has
giving played in the evolution of society? What are the prospects
for the future of civil society and liberal democracy? I talked to two
historians, a social scientist, a classicist and a philosopher.

LONDON: A philosopher's thoughts on social change
I met Professor A. C. Grayling, philosopher, broadcaster, founder and
Master of the New College of Humanities in London early in 2016.

The New College of Humanities opened as an independent,
primarily undergraduate college in 2012, offering tuition in economics, English, history, law, philosophy, politics and international
relations. The College charges fees of £18,000 a year. The decision
to charge fees that more accurately reflect the cost of teaching goes

to the heart of the dilemma facing us: if the state provides less, who will provide more? Professor Grayling began:

> It is always difficult when one is in the middle of social change to understand trends and what the ultimate destination is likely to be.
>
> The society we are changing from is one which has been coloured by a conceptual framework that was put in place by the Liberal Government just before World War One and which was completed after the Second World War. It produced a welfare society which had an admirable and honourable aim: that we should provide safety nets for people, that we should invest in what would give people equal opportunities – health and education – that society should express an equality of concern for all. So there emerged, to put it roughly, a welfare mindset. Aspects of this are admirable and honourable, but we have discovered over time that other aspects are less admirable. Some welfare measures have been disempowering: too much responsibility has been taken away from individuals and vested in social institutions on which some have come to rely and a few have taken a free ride.
>
> What is also significant is that this has been accompanied by a decline in philanthropy as it was practised before the welfare era. There was a culture of giving in which wealthy people donated opportunities for others in the form of housing, schools, libraries and hospitals. The move from a philanthropic to a welfare culture was a dramatic change. Think of Peabody and Henry Wellcome in the nineteenth century. Contrast that with the quality of housing that is now provided by local authorities for people who cannot afford to buy. We have moved away from the idealism of giving to – out of economic necessity – a lowest common denominator public provision.
>
> For almost a century, society was protector, provider, enhancer and safety net; the situation now is that welfare has become too expensive. This has created a lot of political tension. Arguments between the left and the right revolve around the tax burden. Expedients like the lottery offer one way of trying to fund the arts

and sport and other projects without reliance on taxation, but one criticism of the lottery is that it is indeed a tax, and a tax on the poor. The idea behind the lottery is well meaning and many have reason to be grateful for it, but it is less than ideal.

So we know what we are changing from, but it is not entirely clear what we are changing to. Our move away from state provision has not been accompanied by a return to the kind of philanthropy we had in the nineteenth century. We are in a very different position from the US where the very wealthy see it as a kind of duty to give.

I pointed out that our lack of giving was a cultural matter and asked who will provide the example and the moral leadership to encourage people who have more money than they need to demonstrate their commitment to society by being philanthropic.

That is a good question. If there were a Bill Gates and a Warren Buffet leading the way, that would give a signal that there is something profoundly honourable about engaging with society through generosity and philanthropy.

I am a great believer in the anti-Tolstoy point of view about the significance of individuals in society. His view is that Napoleon and Kutuzov had nothing whatever to do with the outcome of the battle of Borodino in 1812. You have only to look at Nelson Mandela to see how an individual can transform the outlook of an entire people by encouraging them to see things differently so that they behave differently. I believe that if there were a Mandela-like character on either side of the Israel–Palestine dispute, it would be resolved.

You are right in saying that we need that kind of inspirational leadership. What militates against it is that the very wealthy are operating in an unstable environment. We don't know from one election to the next what the levels of top rate taxation will be.

I pointed out that there is another aspect of top rate tax. When the tax rate was cut from 50 pence to 45 pence, my family became thousands of pounds a year better off at precisely the same time that the poorest people in Blackpool (where my family made its fortune by building the Tower) had their incomes reduced by up to £900 a year, in a town that is now amongst the most disadvantaged in Britain. Those with the most became better off and those with the least paid the price. This must be morally questionable. But is anyone interested?

They should be, and I agree that what you have described is indefensible.

The crux of the issue is this. The mindset we had was that if we were to pay high taxes and thought of that tax as redistribution to help people at the bottom, then we might be happier about that than being in a position of wondering 'what shall I do with the extra money I have as a result of a tax cut?' Let us say I benefit to the extent of £20,000. What proportion of it should I give away? To place this responsibility on the individual is exactly the dilemma we can see at the beginning of Jane Austen's *Sense and Sensibility*. On his father's death bed, the son is told by his father that he has to leave all the money to him and that the son must decide how much should go to his father's second wife and her daughters, that is the son's half sisters. The son tells his wife that he will give them £3,000, a lot of money then, and she says to him: 'Do they really need so much money, three women living together in a small cottage?' Eventually, he ends up giving them nothing.

And so he behaves like a brute. How many people end up being charitable when they are better off? Not enough.

So the dilemma is to choose between the collective and personal endeavour, and it is made more acute because there is no guarantee that this notional extra £20,000 if paid in tax would make such a difference given all the calls on the public purse. An argument could be made that in these circumstances, £20,000 donated could make more social impact than if it were spent by the government. The problem is that this action is voluntary and there is no guarantee that it will take place.

The problem with private philanthropy is that it is patchy,

unpredictable, indeed unreliable: it is at the whim of the donor, and overall insufficient to deal with large social problems such as housing, health and education.

I said I was trying to shine a light upon something that is important but is not recognised as such. If the state is to provide less, we must look elsewhere for investment in social, cultural and intellectual capital. Where is the money going to come from? This has implications for all of us who will have to dig deeper into our pockets whether to pay for more public services, to pay more tax, or to give. But how will ordinary people have the means to be more philanthropic if education, health and care cost more?

'This is perhaps *the* conundrum,' said Professor Grayling.

I asked him what his thoughts had been when establishing the New College of Humanities.

When I first thought about setting up the College my instinct was to create it as a charitable foundation. I soon realised that this would be very difficult and would take far too long. We would have needed at least £10 million just to get started and much more to be operational. Instead, I set up the tripartite institution we are. We have the college, a small commercial enterprise, and a trust which exists to build up an endowment and to receive donations that we use for annual funding and scholarships.

One of the two major motivations for setting up the College was the inevitability that the burden for paying for higher education, starting ... in 1998 when the Blair government introduced top up fees, would shift from the taxpayer to the beneficiary. It is inevitable that we are going to have to fund higher education differently. There seems to me to be a dramatic disjunction between the moral and political imperative to provide good quality and free primary and secondary education, not least as effective instruments of social mobility and providing something that is the essence of a good society.

Tertiary education is different. Most of those who go into it will benefit handsomely compared with those who don't. The argument is that funding this could be regarded as an investment choice that will bring considerable advantage.

A tipping point will be reached quite soon in the way that higher education is run and financed. The £9,000 fee is an artificial figure rather like a supermarket price of £9.99. This is too low because it does not represent the real cost of education and it is forcing the HE sector to become more entrepreneurial. More than 70 per cent of students at the London School of Economics are from outside the UK and EU, who pay much more than the standard fees, and this is reflected across the university sector. They are paying full fees and subsidising those who don't.

As a country, we are no longer able to finance higher education in the way that obtained when you and I went to university. Then, only 8 per cent of school leavers went to university. It is a different matter finding funding for 45 per cent of school leavers. The shift to direct beneficiaries paying the cost of higher education is inevitable.

That is why we need new models. My view is that we have to accept this is the future. So that is why at the very beginning of our enterprise here we realised that we must start raising an endowment to help us offer places to those unable to pay fees. This will take us a long time because you need alumni to build up an endowment and it takes time to build up the case for support based upon your achievements and to persuade donors that you are worth supporting.

Our headline fees are £18,000 a year but some students don't pay anything at all, and the average fee paid is £7,000, considerably cheaper than mainstream universities. We would like to be able to offer more free scholarships but we do not yet have the resources. When I have Harvard's endowment of $35 billion, everyone can come for free.

I asked how British students could pay full fees in the absence of these kinds of endowments.

We need to look across the Atlantic. There are howls of pain from people who have built up enormous debts. The debt burden is now beginning to cause some difficulty.

I think there is an unanswerable case that investment in social capital should be the responsibility of the community via tax. I do think that the government should think about this again. The case for public funding for primary and secondary is accepted by all parts of the political spectrum but there is a problem with tertiary education. My own view is that the tertiary level needs its fully funded universities but the sector needs to be open also to independent and alternative providers that have different ideas.

Government should be prepared to invest more in intellectual capital in the tertiary sector because it is in the national interest to do so.

What might and could happen is that we get into a situation where we become like America – a university sector dramatically divided between rich and poor institutions – but without the philanthropic assistance that they have. So we have to recreate a culture of giving. But how likely is it that philanthropy will respond to the need?

Navigating through this is like being in a jungle with a python here and an alligator there. If we start to charge what university education really costs, the 'customer' will demand more. We are seeing this happening in the US where these kinds of pressures act on providers and make them modify the offer. Here, we say that it is our responsibility to inform our students that this is what we think it will take for you to become an educated and thoughtful person, and this is how we propose to challenge you. The more expensive education is, the better it needs to be. The key thing we have to create is the right ethos, the right provision for our students entering adult life in a very complicated century: and we cannot duck the fact that to do this well cannot be done for nothing.

*   *   *

CAMBRIDGE: The common good in classical Greece and Rome

There is a commonly held view that we inherited democracy and philanthropy from the ancient Greeks, but I was soon to learn that this is overly simplistic.

Mary Beard is Professor of Classics at the University of Cambridge, a fellow of Newnham College and Royal Academy of Arts Professor of Ancient Literature. We met at the Royal Academy in 2015, shortly after the publication of her most recent book (*SPQR: A History of Ancient Rome*, W.W. Norton & Co).

I told Professor Beard that I had referred briefly to philanthropy in classical Greece in my first book with a reference to tax exemption being offered for donations to hospitals. An eyebrow was raised at the very idea of a hospital in the sixth century BC. I was not wrong to talk about philanthropy in classical times but only with an important qualification:

Talking about philanthropy is a little awkward because the word means, literally, 'love of fellow men' and that is an elusive concept in ancient times. Philanthropy in the ancient world was very different from what it is now. There was no sense of charity in our sense and this did not begin to appear until the influence of Judaism and Christianity spread. There was no charitable giving to the poorest in Greco-Roman pagan culture.

However, there was something that is known as euergetism and that means an obligation on the part of the wealthy to give to the community. This began in fifth-century classical Greece and ran right through the Roman Empire. Euergetism has nothing to do with alleviating poverty and poor relief. It's something much more hierarchical.

For example, one of the ways the rich contributed was by giving handouts of corn. However, it was done in such a way that the rich got more than the poor! The handout reflected the existing social structure of the city. This was very much in the interests of the powerful and contributed to maintaining the social structure and keeping society together.

These donors would boast about their giving and there was a trade-off between honour and respect. These were 'Mr Bigs' and they were much feted. Some of these gifts were in support of building projects and there was some competition between the wealthy.

The Emperor might have wished to be the greatest euergetist of them all and have a monopoly of generosity, benefaction and display in Rome and this would encourage the second rank of the wealthy to give elsewhere in the towns of Italy.

They would build libraries and concert halls. This was one of the ways that the Greco-Roman elite defined themselves. The word that the Romans would have used is 'benefaction' and this was not unlike the Victorian philanthropists but without the charitable aspect that was often a feature of giving in the nineteenth century. There was an interesting trade-off between the prestige of benefaction and the benefit seen by the community.

In classical Greece, by which we really mean Athens, there were two sides to giving. Firstly, there was the euergetistical approach. This was, in a way, voluntary. One way of being 'Big' was to use your money for the benefit of the community, and it was part of a social contract between citizen and society. Secondly, there was a system called liturgies. These were almost compulsory demands upon the rich to support the public good. Support was needed for public buildings, theatrical displays and theatre prizes. This was more or less mandatory, unlike the offering of corn to every citizen. Liturgies were akin to a form of high taxation and they became quite competitive in terms of display.

Spending money on the community was not an optional extra, it was part of the package of being an elite citizen. There was no idea that poverty was a virtue. Giving was about politics, status and citizenship. The idea was that you did not go down to the Bay of Naples and spend all your cash on the equivalent of the Riviera. You only did that if you opted out of the basic political and civic contract.

There is no social contract now, which is why the government's idea that universities should raise money from the private sector is difficult and in a sense counter-cultural. It may well be that in fifty years' time the class of 2015 is funding a chair in Classics, but doing that now is a challenge. Most of our alumni came through when university tuition was free. Nobody thought about this when fees were substituted for grants.

Persuading my colleagues that fundraising for classics is a priority has been a challenge. It is much easier to raise money for dying
babies and liver transplants.

Why is studying the classics important? For better or for worse,
the traditions of the classical world are embedded in western
culture. You cannot begin to understand our culture without an
understanding of classical times. You cannot understand art and
literature. Without the classical tradition, the building blocks of our
modern culture are incomprehensible.

That doesn't mean that everyone needs to be an expert in Virgil.
But somebody needs to know.

And more people need to know that in civilised countries in the
past, there was an obligation to share your surplus wealth.

*   *   *

BERLIN: A German perspective on the common good
How have damaged or destroyed civil societies been restored?
Communist states did not have civil societies. In the 1980s, I visited
almost every country behind the Iron Curtain, including Albania. I
remember well the smell of fear on the streets of Bucharest only a
few months before Ceauşescu was deposed in 1989.

How has Germany been able to become a rock of democratic
stability and prosperity after most of the country was smashed to
pieces in the Second World War? Why are 21st-century Germany
and Britain so different despite both being liberal democracies? Is
there a different view of the common good in Germany? I put these
questions to Professor Dr Steffen Huck, Director of the Research
Unit, Economics of Change, WZB, Berlin Social Science Center
and Professor of Economics at University College London, when I
visited Berlin in December 2015:

The question to ask about Germany is how big was the discontinuity
after 1945? If you look at the public sector and look at all the judges,

most of them were implicated in the Nazi regime. Hans Globke, Konrad Adenauer's right-hand man, had helped draft the infamous Nuremberg laws. The Gehlen Organization which morphed into the BND, Germany's Federal Intelligence Service, employed hundreds of Nazis and war criminals and, of course, many of the important business leaders were also implicated in the regime and had made money out of slave labour. The Allies had decided that, for better or for worse, these were the people that were needed.

The physical structure was largely destroyed but society was not; there was much continuity and the left-wing terror in the seventies was a direct a response to this Nazi heritage.

One of the most significant phenomena about twentieth-century Germany is the importance of clubs. These are not just football clubs. There are clubs for a whole range of sports and social activity, and not just for competition. The smaller towns do not have a professional fire service so they have a club of volunteer firefighters. Our choirs are clubs and they have been an important feature of our civil society since the nineteenth century. The Nazis understood the importance of clubs and took over their leadership through the process of *Gleichschaltung*, which typically was not met with much resistance, and again you will find a lot of continuity after 1945. To this day it is hard to find many examples of German clubs examining their Nazi past. Now these clubs are crumbling. The new generation is not so interested as more and more of the younger people are moving into cities where clubs never had the same importance. This mirrors the decline of the church. Maybe it's the ultimate triumph of consumerism.

Nevertheless, we have a much more consensual society than Britain. We like the idea of the collective. The British, on the other hand, celebrate individualism. The whole notion of eccentricity as something valuable strikes me as very English. As Peter Ackroyd says in his piece on the Englishness of English Literature, you will only understand it if you understand the importance of cross-dressing. And, sure, it is perfectly acceptable to be a cross-dresser in London. In Berlin? Well, not so much.

We are both thinking about Wagner's Die Meistersinger von Nürnberg at this point! Yes, you can trace this sense of the self as part of the community all the way back to the sixteenth century in the states that are now Germany. The guilds were the fabric of the economy in the middle ages and for a long time thereafter. At the end of Die Meistersinger, Hans Sachs, the poet, playwright, shoemaker and moral centre of both the opera and the Nürnberg community, renounces personal and individual desires.

Unlike the UK, we have accepted more than a million refugees since 2015. It has been touching to see how many have been offering support. There is a lot of grass-roots willingness to help. About half the population supports what we are doing. The other half is almost violently opposed. There is a very depressing constant flow of despicable right-wing comment on social media and there were over 1,000 attacks on refugee homes last year and 100 cases of arson.

Now, with Brexit, you get racist attacks even on the streets of London which I always saw as the most cosmopolitan town on the planet. I lived there for fourteen years and not once did I feel like a foreigner because everybody appeared to be one. That this is gambled away now I find very depressing.

In Germany, the state has always played a significant role in the provision of social benefits, at least since Bismarck, which meant we had no need for much of the philanthropy that was such a feature in Britain, particularly in Victorian times. We never had the same culture of giving in Germany.

You have the *Sunday Times* Rich List and so everyone knows who the wealthiest 1,000 people are and have a sense about the extraordinary amounts of wealth created in the last thirty years. In Germany, there is a top ten list but it always has the same names on it. We do not know much about the rich who do not appear on this list. Everything is very discreet. In Britain, there are no secrets about the elite.

There is no wealth tax in Germany and so there is no data available on how much wealth has been created and who owns it and there is, of course, an interest in keeping this as it is. Many people are reluctant to be philanthropic because they don't want to draw attention to their wealth.

We also have one of the lowest rates of inheritance tax of all OECD countries. The majority of wealth is tied up in companies, rather than in houses and personally owned properties, so it is not taxed on death as is the case in most other countries. None of the political parties are willing to consider raising inheritance tax because of a rhetoric of fear that small and medium enterprises will suffer, which are the backbone of the economy.

The secrecy of wealth or any kind of elitism has an effect on the behaviour of people who have made money. They are hesitant about buying a flashy new sports car for fear of a negative reaction from the neighbours. That would be unthinkable in Britain. In any case, the real elites are happy because a consensus about a lack of ostentation means that they remain hidden.

Angela Merkel is leading what is effectively a social democratic government. The Christian Democrats are now the new Social Democrats and this is a crisis for the SPD, particularly in the former east Germany. There is no serious party that wants a smaller state to spend less. We do seem to have a greater sense of society and of belonging to a society than the British do.

At the time of the London riots in 2011, we were living in London. I found David Cameron's account telling. He said there was a sickness in 'parts' of our society. It seems to me that Cameron does not understand what a society is. It's like having liver cancer saying a part of my body is sick. The reality is that the entire body is sick. But, admittedly, in 2011, even as a sceptic I had no idea how sick British society really was. Now we see the full-blown disease and when I'm in London it's depressing to speak to my friends who don't feel at home there anymore.

When the riots broke out I initially wondered if they were a counter-reaction to the bank bail-outs or the big bonuses that were paid again, but they weren't. This was just looting. They were about getting trainers for free. They were about sheer greed. Yes, a majority of looters may have been the young unemployed but setting your

neighbour's shop on fire? This was a symptom of a sick society and
I still believe that anything like this would be unthinkable in Germany, where there is a much greater sense of belonging together.

It is true that there is not the same notion of class in Germany as
there is in Britain. Because the elite is largely hidden, people are not
bothered about them. People are also not so obsessed about making
money. It's just not very good for you if money and making money
is uppermost in your mind but this is what happens to everybody in
London and probably most parts of the UK where the idea of getting onto the housing ladder has become the single most important
concept for how to live a good life.

Maybe this is the one thing that contributes to our functioning
society and having a broad consensus about the things that matter
to us, namely that the majority of us are renters rather than people
who become entrepreneurs buying and selling houses and investing
in buy-to-lets. Over half the population lives in rented accommodation. Most landlords are not small buy-to-let capitalists but are
mostly institutional investors. We also have a lot of security and
safety as a tenant. We feel much safer as citizens in Germany because we cannot be kicked out of our homes.

Germany is a wealthy country but it depends how you measure
wealth. Personal wealth is not as great as it is in other countries, particularly the UK and the US, because we don't have the same levels
of home ownership. We do have generous pensions. We are certainly wealthy as a country and as a society in that the state coffers
are full.

These things function better here than in the UK not because we
are a better people. I do think we are slightly less concerned about
getting ahead and I do think that property ownership is a key point.

My wife and I lived in London for over ten years and at the end
we had more than doubled our joint income but still we felt poor
simply because of the cost of housing. I was advised by a good friend
of mine that I should take a job in Berlin so that I could stop thinking about money. And he was right! We are paying an affordable
rent close to the centre of Berlin. The rent goes up by 1.3 per cent

a year for six years and after that it stays constant. I don't have to worry or think about housing.

In London, there is an element of fear. We were renting a Georgian house in what has become a prized part of east London and, without warning, the landlord told us she would increase the rent up by 70 per cent. Fortunately, we were planning to leave London but we were being kicked out of our home. This kind of thing creates an existential fear. In Germany, we don't have that kind of fear and it makes a difference.

The idea that markets serve social ends through an invisible hand has never been accepted in Germany. We have a different social ethos. It was this, in addition to American aid after World War Two, that enabled us to pull through and rebuild our civil society and our country.

*   *   *

OXFORD: Learning from the Victorians

Dr Frank Prochaska is an American historian based at Somerville College, Oxford. He has a particular interest in philanthropy and nineteenth century Britain. Here is a passage from a lecture he gave in 2012, comparing the nineteenth and the twentieth centuries:

Paradoxically, there was more social connectedness in the age of Queen Victoria, with all its class distinctions and fear of representative democracy, than in modern Britain. Those very distinctions and fears made social contact within and between classes essential. Self-governing institutions, from lowly mothers' meetings to the mighty voluntary hospitals, had connected citizens to their communities and gave them a measure of direct control over their own affairs. In an era of religious commitment, limited government and strong local allegiances, social responsibility was not simply a corollary of privilege but a corollary of citizenship.

Dr Prochaska reminded me that philanthropy was practised by all classes in Victorian times, not just by the wealthy, and that

charitable giving was often used to further the interests and needs
of one's own class.

> Although the British government has announced its intention to
> shrink the size of the state to 36 per cent of GDP by 2020, gov-
> ernment will remain very much larger than it was in Victorian
> times, and having a strong state relieves philanthropists from the
> need to address inequality. Moreover, the problem with a fixation on
> wealthy donors is that it reinforces a view that charity is about the
> rich giving to the poor and that is not always the case.
>
>   The priority must be social stability. Threats to social stability
> can damage all classes. Britain remains one of the most centralised
> states in the world but centralised states tend not to be effective at
> addressing issues far from the centre. That is why we need to develop
> a more charitable civil society that is able to address local needs.

Dr Prochaska reminded me that much of the growth in charitable
activity in the last twenty years has been funded by the state. This becomes a problem if government subsequently reduces its funding of
charities, as it has done. Moreover, funding charities to deliver public
services makes it increasingly difficult to understand what a charity
is in the twenty-first century. Is there an acceptable halfway solution
between the current civil society model and the state model?

> The decline in local government since Victorian times is a serious
> problem, not least in the quality of local politicians and those who
> work for local authorities. Manchester is a notable exception. The
> failure to tackle acute social problems such as child abuse and or-
> ganised paedophilia are only one example.
>
>   The quality of Westminster politicians is also a matter of concern.
> Why do we need a Minister of Civil Society whose role seems to
> be to advise charities how to raise more public funding? A previous
> Civil Society minister advised charities to stick to their knitting
> thus demonstrating ignorance about what charities are for and how
> they should operate.

Dr Prochaska's concern about the role and independence of charities goes to the heart of the conundrum about who should be responsible for what and, with his permission, I quote extracts from his lecture to the Charity Commission in 2014:

> The twentieth century witnessed an historic, often bitter contest between the individualist and collectivist traditions in the pursuit of social progress. By the 1950s, it resulted in the state reigning supreme in health and welfare provision, with charities reduced to the periphery. Things have moved on in recent decades with something of a charitable revival.
>
> In the ambiguous welfare world of today, it has become necessary to use the word independent before the name of a non-governmental charity, for it is no longer obvious that a charitable institution is not a government agency … In an era of partnerships and public service contracts, the state and many voluntary bodies have become so intertwined that it is rather fanciful to think of them as representing two distinct sectors…
>
> The boundaries between state assistance and charitable assistance were much clearer in the past. In the nineteenth century, a general guideline was that charity dealt with deserving cases and the state with the undeserving…
>
> Victorian philanthropists could boast of remarkable achievements. In 1885 the charitable receipts for London alone exceeded the budgets of several European states. But in the late nineteenth century, attitudes to poverty began to change … in an industrial economy under strain, people began to take the view that poverty was not simply a product of individual breakdown, as charity's advocates had long assumed, but of faults of the economy and the structure of society…
>
> The story in the twentieth century is a familiar one … in time, a less personal approach to welfare, the belief in the efficacy of legislation and state intervention, became as compelling to its advocates as Christian service had been to the Victorians … The creation of the welfare state signalled that there was a decisive winner in the debate over social policy.

It was perhaps not surprising that politicians did not much encourage popular participation in their reforms. Social laws offered a blueprint for the reconstruction of society that did not require the participation of volunteers or summonses to self-help ... Ironically, the inheritance that politicians and civil servant mandarins welcomed, and built upon, was a systematic paternalism that far exceeded that of the voluntarists they often disavowed...

Crossman [Richard Crossman, Labour MP and Secretary of State for Health and Social Services in the 1960s] observed that to many on the left philanthropy was 'an odious expression of social oligarchy and churchy bourgeois attitudes' and 'do-gooding a word as dirty as philanthropy'. Barbara Castle, as Labour Minister of Health, believed that a proper social democracy should show a 'toughness about the battle for equality rather than do-goodery'. The use of 'do-gooder' as a term of abuse encapsulated the transformation of values that had taken place...

After the oil crisis in the mid-1970s, the spending limits of the state social services propelled a revival of interest in charitable provision. The new right, with its reversion to the language of the minimal state, echoed sentiments that had been little commended since the heyday of Victorian liberalism. But such sentiments were being voiced in a world that had lost its Christian underpinnings and in which more and more women went out to work, leaving them less time for volunteering. Mrs Thatcher, an admirer of Victorian values, often spoke in glowing terms of voluntarism, but her Victorian values were highly selective. She had a need for political control that expressed itself in greater centralisation, not less, and carried forward the collectivist agenda she disavowed...

The decline of world socialism after the collapse of the Soviet Empire in 1989 had more positive repercussions for voluntary traditions than Mrs Thatcher and the new right ... The challenges to collectivism effectively changed the language of politics, reshaping the context in which charity was understood. In the 1990s, charity came to be elided with notions of civil society or community service. The Labour Party under Tony Blair ... felt obliged to cast aside the dogmas of the past and embrace charitable institutions.

For all the talk about welfare pluralism and a fresh role for voluntary institutions in the 1990s, there was an assumption that the state was still in charge, but it should offer charities a more prominent role in social provision. For centuries, the standard definition of charity was 'Christian love' or 'love of one's fellow man', or simply 'kindness'. But as Britain moved from being a voluntary society to a collectivist one, such definitions looked decidedly old-fashioned ... An important update on offer came with the Charities Act of 2006, which defined charity as 'public benefit'...

As the state insinuated itself in the folds of charity, the government, not the voluntary citizen, has become the presiding judge of what constitutes charity or public benefit.

In recent decades, the balance has been further complicated by the so-called 'contract culture' ... As charities are brought into the orbit of government, they are encouraged to take on board a view of welfare that is favoured by the state ... The appetite for state contracts and grants has grown to the point where the question is being asked how institutions paid for out of compulsory taxation, which would not exist without state subsidies, can be called voluntary ... Furthermore, as charitable agencies become increasingly accountable to government, they are prone to forfeit their role as critics of government policy...

In the late 1970s, about 10 per cent of overall charitable revenue came from the government. In 2010, figures compiled by the National Council for Voluntary Institutions put the overall proportion of state funding at 38 per cent, or £14 billion ... At present, about 41,000 charities, about a quarter of all registered charities, have a direct financial relationship with the state. The balance of power in the voluntary sector has tipped in favour of large, publicly funded institutions.

Neither charity nor the government has lived up to public expectations of social provision. The charge once levelled at Victorian charity, that it could not cope with the volume of social need, is now levelled at the government. Partnership between the state and charitable bodies seems likely to grow. But if the contract culture continues to expand it may have unhappy consequences, not least for many of the independent institutions that struggle to compete for individual donations.

The poor will always have us with them. Consequently, charity is as important to the givers as the receivers. Historically, it was not simply about the delivery of services to the needy, but also about civic participation, self-help and moral training. Recent government statements suggest they admire such principles. But if our politicians really believed in them they would clarify the boundaries between the state and charity, would lessen the unnecessary regulations on those institutions that do not receive state assistance, and would increase the tax incentives to giving. There has been little sign of support for such changes … for it would reduce government revenue and control.

*　　*　　*

OXFORD: A historian looks to the future

I returned to Oxford, to a man who teaches, writes and gives. Dr Peter Frankopan is a historian at Oxford University where he is a Senior Research Fellow at Worcester College and a Director of the Oxford Centre for Byzantine Research. His most recent book (*The Silk Roads: A New History of the World*, Bloomsbury, 2016) is an international best-seller.

Dr Frankopan and his wife own a number of businesses. He is also an investor and philanthropist, a trustee of several charitable foundations and chairman of the Frankopan Fund, which has awarded more than 240 scholarships and awards to PhD and Masters students from Croatia.

Frankopan started by warning me away from a rose-tinted view of the past. He reminded me that there was no legislation to protect the poor in Britain until 1601 in the reign of the first Queen Elizabeth, and that provision was rudimentary:

The current issue for philanthropy is that there has been a breakdown in the understanding of what community and family mean.

There are progressive reasons why the family does not exist in the way that it used to – though even that is important to qualify. Recent research suggests that there were probably more unmarried mothers in 1800 than there are today, which means one needs to be careful talking about the collapse of an idealised 'family life'.

But there can be no doubt that the rhythms and nature of what families and kinship groups mean have changed dramatically. Tens of thousands of elderly either do not have family, or receive no visits from them – which leaves them isolated and cut off from society. The large number of cases where younger generations do not look after their old, or devolve care to residential homes, is symptomatic of the greater tendency for individuals to look after themselves – even within a family context.

I am opposed to the Hobbesian idea that mankind is inherently violent and wants to kill competitors, or the brutal Darwinian view that the strongest should survive. Charity represents the exact opposite: helping those who most need it, often through no fault of their own. The desire to cooperate is what distinguishes humans from animals, not just our ability to communicate but to work together. That is how we rose to the top of the food chain: we built up communities because we learned how to divide labour and developed complex ways of sharing goods, services and ideas.

History teaches that it takes time for people who have become rich quickly to learn how to be charitable. For example, in the 1600s, the Dutch became very wealthy incredibly fast because they had a window where they recognised it was all or nothing: they would either remain a Spanish colony, and be milked for tax with limited political rights, or they would come out the other side by betting everything on building up trade with the east – and using those riches, first, to build up their armed forces. The first Dutch East India Company mission came back with a profit of 400 per cent. From there, things just got better and better. Over fifteen years, they went from living below sea level to being the wealthiest people in Europe.

As the scale of their wealth began to dawn on them, the Dutch began to wonder why they had been so lucky and what do with their good fortune. One of the things they did was to pioneer charitable works, led by local communities. It also prompted views about how to display wealth – not to be proud of it, but not to be ashamed either. Even now, there are few curtained windows because the Dutch believe that if you have a beautiful work of art you should share it. They have a real sense of community.

Becoming wealthy is often associated with feelings of guilt. You may have become wealthy because you saw a gap in the market. Or in high finance, you become very wealthy by not creating anything, but by spotting pricing issues that you can take advantage of. Or worse, by betting against a share price.

Not surprisingly, most religions are proscriptive about the role finance plays in their cosmology and the role of charitable giving. As God is killed off by Richard Dawkins and others, it just so happens that the primacy of the individual and the detachment of any rules about how you should live and behave in respect of your family have changed. In atheist societies – such as in the Soviet Union, but also increasingly in the West – families and communities have struggled to flourish. The individual's views and expressions count for everything, and that is now even mirrored in the competition between the individual and the state. I think that generates real problems, particularly where there is an absence of peer pressure. When everyone is free, then society quickly becomes a free for all.

In the 2015 general election, no other party than the Greens dared to propose radical tax changes. If you encourage people to vote out of self-interest then things can become very difficult. People believe, with reason, that governments are very bad at spending money. Rather than give to the central government, there is a logic in local tax-raising and spending, and that was how city states become so successful. It makes sense to give money to the local hospital rather than pay to a faraway government that then spends it on its own priorities, rather than local issues.

Before the election, I was appalled to learn that the government will be selling off social housing, that spending on education will be capped in real terms and that benefits will be capped for single parents. It is very unpleasant to see how nasty governments can be. It is always the poor that are victimised. And that has now widened to include migrants, refugees and indeed foreigners in general. I don't remember such a poisonous atmosphere as today. We seem to want to think only for ourselves, and not for others.

The poor are stigmatised and that makes it even more difficult for the wealthy to support the poor. The language of equality is all window dressing and the promotion of social inequality is seemingly endless. According to the World Bank Gini index, society in the UK is now less equal than it is in Sierra Leone, Niger and Kazakhstan. I find that pretty shocking.

Civil society is fragile. John, you were born into a civil society in 1947 but if you had been born a few hundred miles further east, you would have been brought up in the ruins of a society that had perpetrated the holocaust, a society that produced Goethe, Schiller, Kant, Beethoven and Wagner and turned to genocide. And anti-Semitism was not a German problem; it permeated to the very highest levels in Britain as well: Henry Ford even kept a picture of Hitler above his desk. We need to always remember the horrors that we are capable of perpetrating on each other, and keep safeguards to prevent that from happening.

My children are studying the holocaust and they ask why we are turning away refugees and migrants and whether we should have done the same with Jews fleeing Europe during the Second World War. They see the suffering in camps in France and on the fringes of the European Union and ask me why we are allowing people to suffer like this. I tell them we should be hanging our heads in shame. I tell them that on one day in 1914, Britain took in 16,000 refugees from Belgium. So far – after five years of civil war in Syria – we have settled forty-three refugees in London. Not 43,000. Forty-three.

We also forget that after the Second World War, we made great sacrifices to help Germany rebuild itself and its civil society. The US led the way, with Marshall Aid, taking a long view on what the dangers would be of allowing a failed state in the heart of Europe to fester. I think that this is one reason why the Germans have led the way on refugees – and indeed in Europe more generally: the sense of community, of helping others onto their own two feet is deeply ingrained in Germany, because the Germans recognise the help they themselves had. As 'victors' of the war, we forget the lessons of history and talk of the glory of the defeat of the tyranny of Hitler – rather than the pride in helping rebuild after 1945. We are better at destroying and breaking, rather than building – just look at Iraq; or Afghanistan. That is why our responses to Syria, Egypt, Libya, Ukraine have been so hopeless. We have no idea how to create functioning societies or foster community spirit. But we are pretty good at demanding – and even forcing – change.

There is a big reaction against the western values we take for granted. We think our liberal democracy is a benchmark to which everyone should aspire. But all around us, Russia, China, and the Islamic world are fundamentally rejecting our values. And the West does not have an ally anywhere east of Venice: a different world is emerging in front of our eyes – reacting to our way of life. It is no coincidence that the West is increasingly seen across Asia as acting only when it suits, and only in its own interest.

How do we defend our values? That depends upon what our values are. We tend to take a deeply tinted rose-pink view. We talk about gender equality. But 100 years ago, women could not even graduate from my own university. We talk about freedom from religious persecution – but see leading politicians make statements that are anti-Semitic or anti-Muslim; we talk about sexual tolerance, but homosexuality was only decriminalised in the UK in the late 1960s. Seeing ourselves as the beacons of freedom risks being blind to our weaknesses. This rosy view hides the deep suffering experienced by millions in this country. People were persecuted for their choices, their beliefs and orientation.

As a historian of different parts of the world, I take a more dispassionate and cynical view of our 'red meat' triumphalist story, that we are the heirs of Athens and Rome, that we came up with decency and fair play and that more people should be like us. That is a product of being in the sunshine of prosperity – as those who led the world before the ascendancy of Europe around 1600 would attest. If only we could recalibrate and have a greater degree of humility so that we ask ourselves: how do other people live and what is their attitude to charitable giving?

Charitable giving is not just seen positively in many religions, it is positively demanded. Consider alms giving. Helping the poor and the weak is fundamental to Christianity – and indeed, as the Bible puts it, fundamental to being human: after all one of the greatest philanthropists was the Good Samaritan. So too in Judaism, where the teaching of Tzedakah – giving for the common good – is not just a central part of what it means to be good; it is part of the process of administering justice, by giving the poor their due.

In Islam too, you have duty as a Muslim to protect the poor. This is repeated throughout the Qur'ān, partly because the age of the Prophet Muhammad was one of great inequality as wealth was passing out of the hands of the many into the hands of the few. War and ecological crisis had an impact too that exacerbated problems. One of the core messages of the first Muslims was about solidarity, putting aside differences, and focusing on the good of the whole community – the *umma* – rather than looking after the interests of the elites. That became crucial to Islam's appeal fourteen hundred years ago.

That gave the story of the Muslim world a very different arc from that of Western Europe. There were few cities in Europe until industrialisation (in contrast to the urban life of the Middle East). So agrarian society developed in a steep pyramid with the king and barons at the top, and peasants at the bottom. Aristocrats were incentivised and able to build up power bases, centralising assets within the family and protecting that jealously in the middle ages by building castles that were all but impregnable. The story of Europe – and especially Western Europe – has always been about the concentration of power, excluding women and younger sons to keep the family as strong as possible. Although many aspects of that system have been improved, we are again seeing a return of power and wealth controlled by the few, and rising levels of inequality.

As a historian, I am interested in seeing how empires flourished and lasted – and it's clear that keeping society from becoming static is crucial. Ironically, pioneers who were successful included many who today have 'bad' reputations – like the Mongols, for example. Or the Byzantines, whose empire was centred on the awareness that the very rich pose a threat to the ruler and to the state, and that meritocracy was crucial for survival and beyond. The empire lasted a thousand years and we should learn from that. The government in Constantinople was very keen on the idea of recycling wealth and stopping some families becoming too dominant. There was legislation to protect the poor and to stop too much wealth being built up in the hands of the few.

In Islamic societies too, historically, there isn't the same profile of huge discrepancy between top and bottom, even though oil wealth has changed that in the twentieth and early twenty-first century. Part of that was the result of a tribal system where there is constant rhythm of recycling wealth amongst large extended families and tribes; part stems from the importance of cities, where trade matters.

Was the liberal democratic world more tolerant? No, of course not. Life has got better for many of the persecuted but the poor are still being stigmatised and demonised. We have reached this stage after centuries of profound suffering. We must not kid ourselves into thinking that we are not part of a cycle of ups and downs. Western Europe led the world for 400 years but it did not for millennia before then, and it may well be that it does not do so in the future.

Our history is a story of fighting for a set of beliefs that should triumph over everyone else's. It was not the virtue of those ideas in themselves that made them successful though, however much we might think that was the case; it was that our empires meant that we could deliver all our lessons across the world.

Wealth gives you time to reflect, or at least it should. It would be depressing if the indulgence of an hour-and-a-half massage persuaded you to think more positively about your own well-being rather than do something more positive to make the world a better place. You reap what you sow and helping others is such a powerful expression of love. That's why it is called 'philanthropy': the love of fellow men and women. Those who do not show that support for others less fortunate than themselves bring dangers, because it is easy for the wealthy to become detached from reality. And at some point others will take things into their own hands.

When that happens, as was the case in the French Revolution, change is systemic and universal. No one bothered to evaluate who were 'good' landlords and who were 'bad'. Anger rose up with the way that the rich lived, and the way they treated the poor. That's why I don't understand the way some people behave in London. Do the rich wake up every morning and ever think or remember how lucky they are? It is a shock going into the capital from Oxford and see huge cars that almost look as though they are armoured glide over zebra crossings, never pausing for pedestrians or allowing in cars from side streets. At some point, when you never hear the words 'please' or 'thank you' said to waiters and waitresses, to shop staff or at schools, you wonder why bricks don't get thrown through the windows of Peter Jones. When you are disengaged, detached, obsessed with your basement extension, your holidays and your own troubles, it is hard to see how others see you. And as money is cycled through fewer and fewer hands, there will inevitably be a correction. That is why charitable giving is so important – to recognise one's good fortune; but also to help others. One day, the boot may well be on the other foot. We were all brought up to treat others as you would like to be treated yourself. Manners, kindness and generosity do not cost anything.

Charity is a very noisy space. Need is constant and overwhelming. There is never enough to support all the projects, people and ideas that you want. The key point as a donor is to focus on a set of your own priorities. That is the only way to cope.

There is, I think, a current awareness amongst those who give on a regular basis about how to work together, about how to share common interests and mandates. How do you make ethical investments? How should environmental sustainability be best addressed? Is there a cross over where you can magnify your effort by working with other people? Are there skills that you have, beyond giving money, that can be helpful – contacts, ideas, ways of looking at problems and trying to solve them? This is a similar way to how private equity and venture capital people think when it comes to investing and adding value. Charities can learn from that. How do you apply rigour to make maximum impact as a result of your investment in charity? Look at the disciplines that others use to make impact, and try to learn from them. One looks for risks and weaknesses; consider the strengths and skills, assess the management team, benchmark them and then decide what success would look like. You can learn a lot from this.

It's an approach we have taken for some time in the various trusts I am involved with. One project we admire was established by a family we know well in Europe who set up a company that collects food reaching the end of its shelf life in supermarkets. Supermarkets do not want to be seen giving away something valuable but they are prepared to sell it to this company who distribute it to those who need it most.

We have helped a few charities at their very beginning, in the hope that they would grow to become bigger and more wonderful. We became involved in a charity called Global Witness in the 1990s. [Global Witness exposes the hidden links between the demand for natural resources, corruption, armed conflict and environmental destruction.] Initially there were two people in an office in Hammersmith and now they have offices worldwide and have been nominated for a Nobel Prize. They have gone stratospheric and we could not be more proud of the work they do.

Philanthropy is so much more than giving money. How do you follow it up? How do you benchmark yourself? How do you assess what good you might have done by supporting women's refuges? Real philanthropy requires proper engagement. That was relatively straightforward when people gave to and supported their communities. You knew who you were helping, and could see the results with your own eyes. The collapse of communities is a real problem. In our digital world, our friends are no longer our neighbours, but can be tens, hundreds, even thousands of miles away. That is exciting in one way; but it is also a problem. A virtual world is just that: 'virtual'.

The UK and the US are now amongst the most socially stagnant societies in the world. That is a real shock given the extraordinary change in both countries in the twentieth century, where both became meritocracies and accidence of birth – or even gender – were constantly removed as impediments to advancement. That's changed in the last couple of decades, for lots of reasons. But here in the UK, it's certainly a problem that our education system creates 'winners' and 'losers'. You leave school as one or the other. Without a fair educational system, you cannot have social equality, equality of earnings or equality of respect. We should invest more in schools and university, especially in the state sector. We need to change what we teach children – and how we teach them: in the world of tomorrow, Russia, Iran, China, Arabic-speaking countries will be crucial, because they offer challenges, but also opportunities. We serve our children poorly by keeping on teaching them about the Romans in Britain, the Battle of Hastings and Henry VIII and his wives, rather than about parts of the world that they already need to understand today, and will certainly need to understand tomorrow.

It seems crazy to me that fewer people are studying Russian now than twenty-five years ago when the Berlin wall came down. We risk becoming tone deaf to other people's cultures. How do we understand the Russians?

As a historian, I am used to using evidence to look back at the past, rather than try to guess about the future. But it seems to me that the West is on a downward spiral.

We are living through an age of a great transfer of power, influence and wealth. Other countries are working out how to create a middle class, and it is no surprise that much investment is going into education. There are not one but two Haileyburys in Kazakhstan, for example, while in the Middle East, things have moved from sending the cleverest children to Harvard and to the best schools in the US, to setting up campuses of great universities at home: in the Persian Gulf, for example, Yale, Columbia and Northwestern universities all now have permanent campuses – and others for sure will follow. Gulf societies are increasingly self-confident and charitable. There is still a long way to go in terms of tolerances, treatment of women and openness, but that already is changing. There are more women MPs in Iran than cleric MPs. Many more women have university qualifications in the Arabic-speaking world than men. In China, 50 per cent of directors of big companies are women – more than double the number in the UK. Change will come as wealth cascades through society – because prosperity and tolerance go hand in hand.

In contrast, there is the real sense in this country that the pie is getting smaller rather than bigger as it is in countries along the old Silk Roads. It is highly likely that envy and class politics will become even more important in our country, and that politicians with populist ideas, snappy one-liners and the hopes of a return to past glories will garner support. That is a familiar process in history, and not one with pleasant outcomes. Charity will become more important as society comes under more and more pressure. ... Helping others will become more and more important; but it will also become more and more difficult as needs grow.

CHAPTER 6

WHERE WILL THE CHILDREN LIVE?

"The increase in the cost of housing since the early 1990s is equivalent to a 10 per cent increase in the basic rate of tax."
RESOLUTION FOUNDATION, 2016.

"Philanthropists have invested in academies because they understand the importance of education. Can we create the same sense of legacy and mission in terms of housing?"
LORD KESLAKE, CHAIRMAN, PEABODY.

* * *

Most young people on average earnings cannot afford to buy their own homes or afford escalating rents. The acute shortage of affordable homes in Britain must be the most serious social challenge facing our country. Is there a solution other than building more homes? Is there a role for philanthropy and social enterprise, given that philanthropy pioneered the provision of social housing in the nineteenth century?

According to a Resolution Foundation report in February 2016, in 1998, more than half of young people aged sixteen to thirty-four living in households with incomes between 10 per cent and 50 per cent of the national average were buying their own homes. That figure dropped from a half to a quarter in 2013–14 and is forecast to drop to 10 per cent across Britain by 2025.

In London, the forecast is that only 5 per cent of young people on lower than average incomes will be able to own their own homes. Nationally, nine out of ten young people under the age of thirty-five will no longer be able to own a home within a decade.

Any would-be homebuyer earning the national average of £26,500 will find that 91 per cent of properties in England and Wales are currently beyond their reach.

The Resolution Foundation study used data from the Family Resources Survey conducted by the Department for Work and Pensions. It found that in 1998, 22 per cent of those under thirty-five on modest incomes were renting, a figure that has now risen to 53 per cent. The number of families in the private rented sector has increased by almost a million in the last decade.

The Resolution Foundation issued a further report in April 2016 confirming that the high cost of housing is undermining living standards. The key finding is that the increase in annual housing costs since the early 1990s is equivalent to a 10 per cent increase in the basic rate of tax.

If a household comprising a couple with one child was paying the same proportion of their income in housing costs as they did in the 1990s, they would be £1,500 a year better off.

There are 3.2 million households spending more than one-third of their income on housing.

Before housing costs, median household income in London grew by 2.9 per cent in 2006–08 to 2013–15 but *fell* by 3.7 per cent after housing costs.

The Resolution Foundation estimates that with house prices continuing to rise, it would take a quarter of a century for low and middle-income households to accumulate a deposit if they set aside 5 per cent of their disposable income each year.

A consortium of charities published a report in 2015 under the heading 'Just Fair'. The group's members include Crisis, Oxfam, Amnesty International, Save the Children and Unicef UK. According to the report:

- Private rents were double those of council properties, at £163 a week, and a quarter of those renting rely on housing benefit to meet the cost.
- One third of homes in the private rented sector do not meet the basic standards of health, safety and habitability.
- Rough sleeping in London increased by more than one third between autumn 2013 and autumn 2014 while funding for shelters fell.
- At the end of 2014, almost 62,000 households in England were living in temporary accommodation and 280,000 households were at risk of homelessness.

The report warns of 'profound issues of lack of supply, increasing housing costs, lack of security of tenure and homes of such poor quality that they are unfit for human habitation'. Dr Jessie Hohmann, the report's author, said:

> It is possible to take policy steps to protect the most vulnerable and marginalised, but the UK government has decided not to do that. Since the 1980s, we have lost any concept of housing's social function. Without decent housing, you cannot experience an adequate life in society but now housing is a just seen as an asset.

According to the Office for Budget Responsibility, the UK spent more than £25 billion on rent and home ownership subsidies in 2014, equivalent to a quarter of the UK's total budget deficit.

The National Housing Federation (NHF) reported in 2013 that of every £1 of government expenditure on housing, 95 pence was spent on housing benefit and only five pence was spent on building new homes.

The NHF also reported that since 2010, there had been an 86 per cent increase in the number of working people relying on housing benefit to pay their rent. Benefit payments to private landlords have doubled to £9.3 billion in a decade. NHF estimates that if all who are in receipt of housing benefit were in social housing, the government would save £2.2 billion a year. According to David Orr, chief executive of NHF: 'It is madness to spend £9 billion of tax payers' money lining the pockets of private landlords rather than investing in affordable homes.'

Despite the government spending more than £25 billion a year on housing benefit and home ownership subsidies, public funding for social house building was cut from £2.3 billion to £1.1 billion a year between 2010 and 2015.

Solving the housing crisis is beyond the scope of this book. However, drawing attention to the impact that historic and current housing policy, or lack of it, has upon civil society, and upon the young in particular, should remind us of the role that philanthropy and the voluntary sector have played in the provision of social housing in the past, and to consider what role they could play in the future.

One hundred and fifty years ago, the most enlightened Victorian entrepreneurs acknowledged social need in a way that is conspicuously absent amongst a majority of the wealthy in the twenty-first century. They supported their employees by building homes and supporting their communities. In 1893, George Cadbury built a model village of 300 houses near Birmingham. Lord Leverhulme built Port Sunlight in Cheshire with the fortune he had made out of soap. Port Sunlight has 800 Arts and Crafts houses, a cottage hospital, schools, a church and an outdoor swimming pool. Other leading entrepreneurs of the age, including the Guinness family, the Wedgwoods and the Nuffields, were committed to significant social investment.

In 1862, George Peabody, an American banker living in Britain, donated the equivalent of £40 million to provide affordable housing in London. His trustees decided that the fund should be self-perpetuating and that the capital should produce a return of 3 per cent to fund further building. Over 150 years later, Peabody owns and manages 20,000 properties in London, housing more than 55,000 people. Many Peabody estates have community facilities that are shared with other local communities.

As Britain entered the First World War, social needs demanded state action, and Prime Minister David Lloyd George declared that the nation would build 'homes for heroes'. The policy continued in the 1920s and 1930s and after the Second World War.

The state and public money spent by local authorities dominated the provision of affordable and social housing until the 1970s and 1980s when housing associations became more prominent.

Most housing associations are either charities or social enterprises that reinvest profits and surpluses. The oldest are the descendants of medieval almshouses. Others were created in the 1800s to provide accommodation for factory workers. There was a further increase in the number of housing associations in the 1980s due to changes in council housing brought in by the Thatcher government. Local councils were prevented from subsidising their housing from local taxes. Grants of public money for constructing new social housing were given to housing associations and council tenants were allowed to buy their homes at a large discount. Combined with reductions in local government funding, this led many local authorities to transfer their housing stock to housing associations.

In total, housing associations are responsible for 2.5 million homes in England, housing more than 5 million people.

In 2016, the government is compelling housing associations to sell their housing stock under its right to buy policy. This means that the government is effectively nationalising charitable assets before selling them on the market.

Most people in Britain wish to own their home. The introduction of policies to encourage and enable more home ownership has been a centrepiece of successive government programmes for decades. The Conservative government elected in 2015 is no exception. Ministers are aiming to create more starter homes restricted to first-time buyers under forty, to be sold at a discount of at least 20 per cent of the market price for properties costing less than £250,000, or £450,000 in London. The government will donate public land and, according to the spending review in 2015, will provide funding from the taxpayer totalling £20 billion.

Shelter, the homeless charity, has estimated that starter homes will be unaffordable to people on low incomes in 98 per cent of the

UK and unaffordable to those on middle incomes in 58 per cent of the country. To buy a starter home in London will require an income of £77,000 and a deposit of £98,000, unaffordable to all but the richest one-third of Londoners.

These proposals are accompanied by measures to force housing associations to sell social housing to those who want to buy and for councils to charge 'market rents'. For example, a couple living in a council home who earn a total of £30,000 a year (£40,000 in London) will be moved up to market rents. If tenants leave because they cannot afford to pay market rents, the Treasury will then force local authorities to sell what are classified as high-value homes. This could spell the end of council housing in central London. The government says that the sale of housing association and council housing properties will create funding to provide more affordable housing for people to buy. Unfortunately, ministers' definition of affordable does not apply to those who cannot afford to buy or pay market rents.

Lord (Victor) Adebowale, a cross-bench peer and a former chief executive of Centre Point, a charity for the homeless, and chief executive of Turning Point, a social care enterprise, says:

> The dominant argument since 1979 has been in favour of the private sector. We are now post-recession and we have made choices to shrink the state. The current discourse says that the state is expensive and needs to be shrunk and, until recently, no other voice has been heard. Other countries have made different choices. There has been very little debate. The state is regarded as a burden on freedom, and on individuals through taxation.
>
> There is a widely accepted view on the right and in government that welfare ought to be delivered by charities and funded by philanthropy. There is nothing wrong with philanthropy and the concept of a Big Society and volunteering. The only problem with philanthropy and charity, assuming there is enough philanthropic funding, which is unlikely, is that it is not equitable.
>
> There is a misreading and a misunderstanding about the state and its history. In the era of the great Victorian philanthropists, they

gave in the belief that the state should take on what they established. They were social pioneers.

There is a deeply ingrained belief in both Labour and Conservative politicians that there is a deserving and an undeserving poor. In our rich country, the children of the undeserving poor grow up to cost each of us a disproportionate amount of money. At any one time, there are 60,000 children in care. If you look at the statistics for prison, mental health and other manifestations of generations afflicted with social diseases, the majority are adults who spent part of their childhood in care. Why haven't we solved this? We know who these people are and we know where they are going. You could send all these kids to Eton and get far better value for the money we are spending. Why aren't we doing it?

Social spending is now branded as welfare. People who receive welfare are branded as scroungers when most of them are claiming against what they put in.

Yet government is almost silent on philanthropy. We have not had a shift in social policy in relation to philanthropy in my lifetime. In the 1800s, we had the start of social housing and forerunners of the NHS with cooperatives of doctors. We have had nothing like this until the 1960s when Shelter and Centre Point developed as a result of philanthropists responding to shocking social need in terms of housing.

We have lost a notion of philanthropy as a social good. We should be thinking about contemporary philanthropy in terms of venture capitalism. George Peabody invested a great deal of money into housing and his return was social capital. People like him, the Rowntrees and the Cadburys were intelligent people who recognised that if they were going to employ people, it made no sense for them to live in abject poverty. This was enlightened capitalism.

Of course, there was a lot less then for the rich to spend their money on. We now have a class of wealthy people that is almost unprecedented in human history with 100 or more billionaires living or based here in the UK. They are treated like gods and they have access to power. They can also pay very little if any tax. We are turning into a plutocracy.

The very rich do not need to be philanthropic and very few are.

We have an underclass of about a million people. They will be an increasing drain on the NHS. The problem is that the rich have bought themselves out of society. The middle classes need to understand that the growing numbers of the poor will be a burden on their children. They do know that their children will struggle to afford to buy and even to rent.

We need a contribution of billions to reboot the social housing market in London. We also need to regulate private sector renting to ensure quality which is sometimes shocking. I met someone from overseas recently who had bought twenty-seven flats in one day in Stratford, east London. He will use them as a hedge against the price of gold and they will remain empty.

The role of charity and the voluntary sector needs to be examined. I believe that the future of services to the public, including social housing, does not lie with the private sector or with the public sector as we know it nor with the not-for-profit sector. The future must be that all three work together.

None of the sectors should predominate. The private sector is interested only in profit. The public sector cannot afford to engage with all the people who need its services. The not-for-profit sector is neither standardised nor big enough. They have to find a way to work together.

We also need to have a debate about what public service should be. The world has moved on since the creation of the welfare state. What you can live without now is very different from 1945. Try living without a mobile phone or Wi-Fi. Try living without a bank account. Banks are private companies but rely upon the public for their existence. If you are a private company that has 30 per cent of the market in food, insurance or technology, you move from being a private to a public concern. We cannot afford the banks to go bust. We have to bail them out, so we have passed the point where moral hazard applies to them. In return, companies have to show that they offer positive social value. You have to pay enough so that your employees do not have to rely on the state. You must be transparent with the public about how you operate and how you contribute to society.

We need more philanthropists with the integrity of Peabody who are willing to invest into a set of ideas that shake up the notion of public service and find new ways to generate a means of delivery. What Peabody did was invest in bricks and mortar not only to provide homes but also to change ideas about housing. This could be done now with a multi-billion philanthropic fund designed to create social capital.

The danger is that we will end up with a public sector like the US that is run for profit. That would mean the end of our liberal civil society

My next interviewee has chaired and served on private and public sector boards, has given distinguished public service and knows more about housing and the property sector than most. He asked to be anonymous. We spoke in December 2015:

During the last Labour government, grants of public money were made to housing associations to build homes with social rents, typically 35 per cent of market rent. The grants were 65 per cent to 70 per cent of the cost of the house. The balance came from the reserves and surpluses of housing associations. This was a very good model providing the social housing the country needed, charging social rents to people who were never going to be able to aspire to home ownership. I believe very strongly that we must provide social housing for those who cannot or are not motivated to buy. We must consider the desperate needs of the under privileged in a housing market that is in crisis.

Currently, the taxpayer provides government subsidy on the capital for new homes or subsidises rents through housing benefit. Subsidy has to come from somewhere. The Liberal Democrats were able to protect the poor in the coalition government. Otherwise, I suspect that the Tories would have canned all subsidies. Instead, the coalition launched an affordable rents programme which meant less capital subsidy but more pressure on housing benefit. Two thirds of rents paid to housing associations are funded by housing benefit.

Elements of this government in 2015 give the impression that the poor are not high on their agenda. They have never seemed to like housing associations and don't seem to care for the tenants or for the concept of social housing. All they are interested in is home ownership.

The reason we are not building enough houses is because local government is not building; housing associations also have limited finance because the government has reneged on a ten-year deal, and reduced the amount by which rents can be increased, actually requiring them to decrease.

The logic and implementation of the extension of the right to buy scheme was not thought through. The Tories never expected to have to implement this because they thought they would remain in coalition. The scheme requires housing associations to agree to give tenants the right to buy properties at a discount that will be paid for by local authorities selling high value stock. This is probably unworkable.

The big house builders don't really build houses to make money. They trade in land. It is difficult to see how we are going to build 200,000 new homes a year, which is government policy. The continuing shortage of houses leads to further increases in prices and that only benefits the house builders.

Providing social housing for people who are vulnerable and who have a range of problems is a form of rehabilitation that should reduce welfare costs to the state. These kinds of people are never going to buy. And housing associations are exactly what these people need as the best offer additional support services.

The best housing associations build a range of products from property to buy to shared ownership and affordable rents with cross-subsidy between these different tenures. Housing associations are charities or social enterprises but they don't behave like charities because they don't (with a few exceptions) fundraise.

The government's priority remains homeownership. Their starter homes programme aims to provide homes to buy at affordable prices discounted below market price and this will replace any affordable or social rent programme. The aim is to increase home ownership and not to provide new homes for sub market rent.

In my view, we must restart building homes for social rent. Perhaps in future, a more enlightened government might do this but in the meantime, philanthropy could be critical. The role of philanthropy could be two-fold. Whilst government remains fixated on home ownership, it is also interested in expanding private rentals following the US model. These are the kinds of good quality blocks you see in American cities. Philanthropists could take the lead and build apartment blocks (at a contractor's rather than house builder's margin) and subsidise social rents from lets at market rates.

The other possibility would be for some of the leading housing associations to follow the example of fundraising charities and seek philanthropic backing as an integral part of their business model.

The big long-term question for the next fifty years is this: how is society going to pay for social housing? Who is prepared to provide the subsidy? Is it the taxpayer, is it some form of philanthropy, or a combination of both?

In order to understand what role philanthropy and social investment might play today, I talked to Lord (Bob) Kerslake, Chair of Peabody, a former head of the Home Civil Service and a cross-bench peer. I asked Bob Kerslake what motivated George Peabody in the 1860s:

The key thing to remember is that Peabody's mission was to ameliorate the conditions of the poor and needy in London. His project was not just about bricks and mortar but the environment in which people live.

I think most people would agree that reasonable housing is a necessary condition to relieve poverty. What was recognised in the post-war settlement in 1945 was that the country needed a mix of public and private housing because the market was not going to be able to provide the housing that was needed. The idea was to put subsidy into buildings in order to get the rents down rather than to spend public money on welfare in order to enable people to pay high rents.

The problem was that we failed to build enough affordable housing to compensate for the loss sustained by right to buy. The other problem was that the mono-tenure estates built under direct public ownership encased the disadvantaged in one place. There is some truth that these estates made it harder for people to see how they might improve their lives.

We are dealing with a legacy problem. We haven't got enough market or social housing. The problem is now acute, particularly in London. Whether you are an aspiring professional or a new entrant in low-paid work, the state of housing in London in terms of its availability is now a disaster.

How might philanthropy contribute to a solution? Would a new Peabody – or a group of Peabodys – make a difference? It could, but it would be important to hang on to the tradition that providing housing is not just about bricks and mortar. The Peabody mission is about the ability to live a good life.

Any new Peabody initiative would be about excellent design, green spaces, access to good schools and public transport. And it might build in some revenue provision as well as capital.

At Peabody, we have been able to do some significant things beyond providing housing. We train a thousand apprentices a year, whether or not the young people live in a Peabody property. We put a lot of thought and effort into design. If I were a philanthropist now, I would want to address a range of issues to make life better for people in addition to putting a roof over their heads.

I told Lord Kerslake that I had witnessed the public and private sector working together in the north of England to provide pioneering new youth services with a striking social and financial return. This initiative (see Chapter 23) marks a shift in policy away from spending public money to achieve narrowly defined objectives set by the public sector towards achieving goals agreed in common between the private, voluntary and public sectors. Kerslake responded:

> Could there be a parallel model for housing? Some local author-ities own a lot of land. One third of all the land in Southwark is owned by the council. The local authority could donate the land, the private sector could build at lower margins and the philanthropist could fund the things that would not make sense in building for the market. These might include additional services, community programmes and the quality of the landscape.
>
> This could be a very attractive proposition. You could design a set of principles to make that work. The good thing about Peabody was that he started with a set of principles.
>
> What has shifted since the previous consensus on a mixed eco-nomy is that we have a crisis of home ownership, not a housing crisis. That is intentional. The clear ambition of the government is to increase home ownership. There has been a decline in home ownership over the years, particularly in London. Their view is that in a home owning democracy, more people are likely to vote Con-servative. Their ambition is to target that group.
>
> There is nothing wrong with encouraging home ownership but the problem with this policy means that no effort will be put into making available more accommodation with social rents. This has an impact on huge numbers of people. If you focus on home ownership in London, then you are focusing only on the top 15 per cent.
>
> I don't think we can go on expecting government to lead. Gov-ernment policy is getting in the way. However, we might have to ask government to change the powers of local government in order for local authorities to be able to participate in and contribute to a new model that includes philanthropy. What I am interested in is replicable models.
>
> Philanthropists have invested in academies because they un-derstand the importance of education and of the need to invest in it. Can we create that same sense of legacy and mission in terms of housing? The key is to get all the different investors, including

philanthropists, to align their objectives. You could say: here is some land, all investors sign up to a set of objectives, principles and ways of working, and the outcomes will be XYZ, some of which may not have much to do with housing. This could be the community equivalent of the academies.

If you are going to start a project, London would be the best place because that is where the problem is most acute. The word that is key for the wealthy is investment. Only a minority is philanthropic but the enlightened see their philanthropy as investment that creates social capital. It was this concept of socially responsible philanthropy that inspired Peabody.

We need more people now to emulate what Peabody did in the nineteenth century. Look at his legacy; an initial gift of £150,000 has created so much social capital in terms of homes, communities and improving the quality of people's lives and a balance sheet worth billions. We are going to need more institutions that are devoted to the common good and that are independent of government. They are essential for a healthy society.

*   *   *

Governments of all parties have failed to ensure that our country has the homes that are needed. Politicians are obsessed with the short term and find it difficult to take decisions needing a long-term view. Housing policies, it seems, are designed to secure political advantage rather than serve the interests of the common good. The wish to enable more people to own their own homes is commendable but not at the cost of those who struggle to live anywhere.

Compelling independent charitable organisations to sell social housing is a scandal. Surely government ministers can see that if they want the state to provide less, they should be supporting institutions that are independent so that they may provide more. By forcing independent housing associations to sell their assets, the government stands accused of destroying social capital.

Government policy to spend public money on encouraging more home ownership whilst reducing public spending on social housing for the most vulnerable will almost certainly exacerbate social problems at some cost to the nation. As the government fails to address the nation's housing needs, private landlords become rich at public expense by living off poor people's housing benefits.

Where will the children live? The answer is that it depends on whose children we are talking about. If home ownership continues to decline despite the government spending public and charitable funds to provide more privately owned homes, then more will have to rely upon renting, much of which will be unaffordable. What will this cost in additional housing benefit? Can this really be in the national interest?

Those I have interviewed say that we should reflect on what was achieved by our forebears and apply their best practice to current circumstances. The need for philanthropic and social investment in housing has never been stronger. Public sector investment will continue to be essential and I will demonstrate what has been achieved by a public and private sector partnership in creating social housing in east London in Chapter 22.

CHAPTER 7

EQUALITY AND THE LAW

"We are diminishing and undermining the legal service, the legal system and our reputation for justice. We are damaging something that we have always been proud of as a country. We are undermining one of the basic structures of civil society and our democracy: access to the law."

BARONESS HELENA KENNEDY QC.

*　*　*

I had assumed that the right to equality before the law, or equal protection under the law, is fundamental to any just or democratic society. I was wrong. Overall spending by the Ministry of Justice was reduced from £9.9 billion in 2010 to £6.4 billion in 2015 and this has led to further cuts in the provision of legal aid. I asked Baroness Helena Kennedy QC to explain the significance of reduced legal aid:

> When I was first in London, one of the first things I did was to set up a free legal advice centre in Waterloo, aimed at young and poor people who were scared of approaching a law firm. Is there a need for this today? Even more so because most law firms are not interested in people walking in off the street.
> High-street law firms are no longer in existence to help people with what might be described as low-level events that can be devastating to those who experience them. I practised in the golden

days when these sorts of firms existed. They don't exist because legal aid has gone. Legal aid paid for a thirty-minute consultation to establish whether there was a case to be pursued through the courts and what that would cost if they were entitled to legal aid.

The previous Labour government started cutting back on legal aid. This is a part of public expenditure that most people do not think is a priority because they have limited contact with lawyers. They cannot imagine why anyone would need legal aid.

Try saying that to a woman suddenly left by her husband with a family and no maintenance; tell that to someone knocked down and needing compensation because they are unable to work. When ordinary people need help, they are frightened to go to the law and through the courts.

After the Second World War, it was agreed that the state should ensure that all would have access to justice. Now legal aid is being cut because it does not have the same appeal to the public as education and health. You now cannot get legal aid for divorce so most of the hardship is borne by women. You can get legal aid for domestic violence but it does have to be particularly serious. There is no legal aid for immigration advice and none for welfare. So people cannot get free legal advice if there has been some unfair ruling about benefits.

The lawyers who specialised in legal aid never became rich but they did become experts in the field. This expertise is vanishing. Our judges are becoming concerned that people are coming into court unrepresented and they are effectively acting as advocates as well as judges by helping the unrepresented to present their case in the best possible way. This is adding to the costs of the court.

There is also an impact upon the legal profession. With cuts to legal aid, there are no longer the same starting points for young barristers at the beginning of their careers. This is bad for the legal profession and our international reputation for being a democracy based on the rule of law.

All this has a terrible impact upon the lives of the poor and underprivileged. There is also a cost in human misery and in an undermining of our collective values as a society. If justice means anything it has to be available to all.

Legal aid is still available for criminal cases but the quality of what is available is compromised because the high-street lawyer is no longer there. If you don't live in the right place, you may be un-lucky. The state of legal aid on offer can best be described as service for the poor. We are going down the American road because the provision of legal aid is becoming a form of charity provided by law firms.

Charity is wonderful and society would be lost without it, but charity cannot provide a comprehensive service. We are diminishing and undermining the legal service, the legal system and our repu-tation for justice. We are damaging something that we have always been proud of as a country. We are also undermining one of the basic structures of civil society and our democracy: access to the law.

This is particularly putting the young at a disadvantage. In any system, you need committed lawyers who put in the time and go the extra mile. It is much harder now for lawyers to do *pro bono* work.

Charities and philanthropists are becoming increasingly involved in trying to fill in the gaps or to support initiatives to prevent re-offending. I am fundraising for a charity called Circles UK, an or-ganisation working with paedophiles coming out of prison. These are people who say they do not want to reoffend but they find it very hard. They need support that is not available. That person has come out of prison and then what? They rely upon charity and the volun-teers that keep them going. These are trained people who work in groups to provide friendship for paedophiles who are often isolated.

Circles are also working with young women who joined Islamic State and who have returned realising they have made a mistake. This is charity operating at the edge...

Britain has been exemplary and perhaps leads the world in terms of social capital because it has a long history and tradition of volun-teering and philanthropy, people giving their time and their money to make our country a better place. We now seem to be withdrawing into our work and our homes, wishing to keep everything tight and close and not engaging socially in the way that we used to. We seem to be increasingly disconnected from each other.

*   *   *

Helena Kennedy is primarily known as a human rights lawyer and for her support of campaigns working to protect the vulnerable. These are the people we don't hear much about. These are 'the other' who, in our paradoxically disconnected and fragmented world, we ignore. 'The other' are often the young, and Helena Kennedy introduced me to Shauneen Lambe, a barrister in the UK and an attorney in the USA, who is also Executive Director of Just for Kids Law. Just for Kids Law would not exist without philanthropic support.

Lambe founded Just for Kids Law in 2006 with Aika Stephenson, a solicitor with the Westminster Youth Offending team. Their first donation was £15,000 from a young entrepreneur and philanthropist. I asked Lambe to describe the challenges the young have to overcome:

Looking at the shrinking state and the impact on civil society from the perspective of young people, there has been some interesting research by a body called Just Rights about the perception of the young regarding access to the law. They find it unintelligible. They are unaware that they might have legal problems, unaware what the solutions might be and easily dissuaded from taking things further.

As a young person, we go to school and we are in an environment where we are being parented or cared for by people who make decisions for us. That dynamic changes over time and we transition from being told to being taught and to learning. However, adults continue to make complicated decisions and the idea of challenging authority is difficult.

Under civil law, children cannot own property until they are eighteen. They rarely pay tax. And if they are involved in a court case, an adult has to take the case in their name. Under criminal law, as soon as a child becomes ten, they are supposedly a client in a criminal justice system who will instruct a lawyer on how to run their case. There is total hypocrisy in the law.

When young people are told by those in authority that they cannot have something, they believe that is the case. So our charity tries to empower young people to challenge the power that tells them they cannot do something. For most young people, the gap between them and those who have power over decision-making is huge. It is our job to bridge that gap and to enable them to be heard by those who have power.

We provide direct services to young people. We worked with one young woman aged sixteen who was being very badly abused at home. She is also the youngest diagnosed multiple sclerosis (MS) patient at the hospital where she is being treated. She went to her local authority because her relationship with her violent mother had broken down. This young woman with MS had been physically damaged by her mother. Social services said they had no duty of care because she was sixteen. They had an option to provide care but they said that her circumstances did not warrant it.

So many of these problems are about money, how to save it and how not to spend it. Child welfare budgets have been reduced. Much of social welfare spending is now directed at the very young after the Baby P case. Teenagers are seen as less of a priority because they are closer to independence.

This young woman was rejected by her local authority and went to a unit for the homeless. She was then sent to a hostel in south London and put in a room above the ground floor without access to a lift. When she had particularly bad MS attacks, she was unable to leave the building. The hostel staff were concerned about her welfare and called us.

We started legal proceedings against the local authority and they caved in before we got to court. She is now fully supported and will be until the age of twenty-five. She is also very bright and wants to go to university. So we were also able to help with education support when her MS was bad. We introduced her to some of the young people we work with at University College London (UCL) who supplemented her education with tutoring. UCL also has access to a justice course they run with us. We were also able to provide her with emotional support, particularly when she has to be in hospital and one of us here will visit her.

We try to support the young holistically because that is what they need. The majority of our cases are about a failure to fulfil statutory rights. We worked with about 800 young people last year covering thirty-one London boroughs. These are youngsters who fall through the cracks. We are holding the authorities to account to ensure they deliver statutory rights.

The number of young people who come to us needing legal aid is definitely increasing. We used to be able to claim legal aid, but that has been cut hugely. The funding now comes from trusts, foundations and individual donors.

We have also achieved a landmark legal ruling in the Supreme Court. We were approached about three years ago by a school in east London about a student who was head girl. She had won a national debating competition and had been given an opportunity to work on Obama's election campaign. She had a place at the London School of Economics (LSE) to study law but she discovered that she had no legitimate status here and so could not qualify for a student loan although she had lived and been educated here since she was six; she was brought into the country from Jamaica as a child and did not know that her status had not been regularised.

She could not take up her place at LSE. We gave her a job but could not pay her. We helped her get an immigration lawyer. LSE waived her fees and gave her a scholarship. The young woman discovers that there are hundreds of other young people with the same problem and starts a campaign group called 'Let Us Learn' with the slogan: Young, Gifted and Blocked.

We intervened in a Supreme Court case involving another young student in the same situation. In 2012, the Student Finance Company had stopped these prospective students getting loans. Lady Hale read out the judgment that the Finance Company had been discriminatory and that students who were not born here had as much right to loans as those who had. The courtroom was full of happy tears.

With our help and encouragement, young people (none of them having the right to vote) have collectively created the power to bring about a change in the law that has so far benefitted 600 young people. And that gives them the energy to keep going.

Why did I set up the charity? I believe in the potential of young people and the importance of helping them fulfil it. I have never met a young person who did not want a job. But too many young people don't have access to the networks they need and it is our job to help them. I look at the young people we work with and realise that whatever they end up doing in life, the most important thing that they have is the belief in their ability to overcome difficulty and seemingly hopeless challenges.

Acting as the voice of the child is at the heart of our ethos. If a child says I don't want to go back to school, it may be the best thing for them to return and it may not be the outcome they want, but whatever the final decision, we must ensure that their voice has been heard.

*   *   *

I talked to another lawyer about how philanthropy defends liberty by supporting those suffering from the abuse of their human rights. Clare Alger was in the final weeks of her seven years as Chief Executive of Reprieve when we met in October 2015. Reprieve was founded in 1999 by British human rights lawyer Clive Stafford Smith to provide free legal and investigative support to those facing execution, rendition, torture, extrajudicial imprisonment and extrajudicial killing. Clare had much enjoyed her time with Reprieve but felt that seven years of torture and death was probably enough.

Before Clare told me about Reprieve, we talked about threats to civil society, to liberty and to human rights:

I think we are heading for a very dangerous place. In the US, Americans are acutely conscious of their rights in relation to personal freedom and children are brought up to celebrate them. That doesn't happen in Britain. Germany also seems to have this respect for human rights, perhaps because of its history. There is extreme suspicion of government and surveillance because they understand what it means to lose their rights.

We don't have this in our country where there is a general assumption that because we are British everything will be alright. What is really worrying is that there are a number of things happening that appear to be unconnected but taken together, are very dangerous. The cuts to legal aid are the most worrying. They simply mean that there is no access to justice for a large number of people who don't have money.

Too often, it is the rights of the poor that are infringed and they are made more vulnerable by cuts in legal aid in criminal as well as civil cases. Most of us in the middle and professional classes do not have our rights infringed and those who do have the wherewithal to combat abuses of power.

The government is also looking at curtailing judicial review, which is the way it is held to account by its citizens; this is potentially terrifying. Then there is the introduction of secret courts, currently restricted to immigration and terror cases. That means that whoever is being tried is unable to see the evidence against them. This is astonishing and seems to be extremely un-British. And then teachers in primary schools are being asked to inform on children showing terrorist tendencies and I do wonder if we will wake up in ten years and people will ask, how did this happen?

There is, of course, much to celebrate about Britain today. Just look at the status of women, for example. Civil society, in the sense of a thriving non-governmental sector, is very strong and amongst the strongest in Europe. However, more recent generations are removed from the experience of conflict, unlike your generation and their parents and grandparents whose lives were shaped by war and the fight for liberty.

After studying at Cambridge University, Clare became a corporate lawyer specialising in intellectual property litigation. She heard Clive Stafford Smith, a lawyer campaigning against the death penalty, on the radio and went to work with him in Louisiana, USA, where she met all sixty prisoners facing the death penalty. They successfully proved that it was unconstitutional for those on Death Row not to have legal representation after trial and an appeal. Following her return to the UK, Clive Stafford Smith asked her to run Reprieve in the UK in 2008.

Seven years ago, we had a turn-over of £700,000 and now it is about £2.5 million. £1.3 million comes from trust and foundations and the European Commission and the balance comes from individual donors.

Our modus operandi is to find clients who can be an emblem for an issue and we then tell their story. We are lawyers and we operate in a court of law but we do that in a way that influences the court of world opinion.

We have a 'stop lethal injections' project that appeals to and is supported by people working in finance. In order to kill someone by injection, you have to use drugs. One of our people has spent the last five years meeting pharmaceutical companies to persuade them to stop supplying drugs to death rows in the US. She has been successful. There are now only three states in the US which can execute; the rest are unable to do so because they cannot find the drugs. We decided not to mount a legal challenge to the death penalty. Our approach was entirely practical.

The pharmaceutical companies were not making a lot of money out of death penalty drugs. Initially, they said it was too difficult to put distribution controls in place. We conducted a campaign against a company in Demark. We said they were making drugs to kill rather than heal people. The company's share price halved in a week. They capitulated and introduced distribution controls. Now every pharmaceutical company has distribution controls in place and executioners will have to find other ways to kill people.

All these other methods (shooting, hanging, gas chamber and the electric chair) are so unappetising and lead to massive litigation. We may be on the road to abolition in the US because not many states will be prepared to use the gas chamber. We have a number of Auschwitz survivors who will advocate against it. Some US states have not been executing people and the sky has not fallen in. More people are thinking that we do not need this very expensive nightmare.

This is a campaign that we are very proud of. Our donors are very pleased that the death penalty by injection has been stopped by one person who earns £38,000 a year. And there is now a small majority against the death penalty in Britain after years of large majorities in favour. This is significant.

Our work in Guantanamo has been important. Guantanamo has become a symbol of a lack of justice and democratic process. The US government has deliberately created this place offshore so that it is removed from the legal process. When 9/11 happened, it was understandable that something had to be done in response. At that point, intelligence in Pakistan and Afghanistan was poor. So the immediate response was to find al-Qaeda and huge bounties were offered and that led to people being handed over to the Americans and some of them were nothing to do with al-Qaeda. The intelligence that led to people being incarcerated was very sketchy, compounded by language problems and an inability to distinguish names properly. Many of these people were tortured and forced into giving wrong information. This simply perpetuated bad intelligence and made it worse.

This is not to say that everyone in Guantanamo was innocent but a surprising number were. Serious mistakes were made. Initially, Guantanamo prisoners were not entitled to legal representation. We were part of a trio of lawyers who got in. We had a problem in that we could not represent them because we did not know who was there and the Americans would not tell us. Eventually, we did get a ruling that lawyers had to be admitted and that prisoners could be legally represented.

Donors like to support us because we have had a number of 'wins' at the extreme end of human rights. The right not to be tortured and the right not to be killed should be fundamental rights. Sigrid Rausing has been a significant and generous donor. She is a visionary philanthropist. Grayson Perry, the artist, is a recent donor. Another very interesting donor is Stuart Wheeler, founder of the spread-betting firm IG Index. He is in favour of the death penalty but finds torture absolutely disgusting, not least because there is no due process. He has been brilliant at helping us raise money.

On the death penalty, we are also working in Pakistan, where they have started hanging people again after a moratorium. They have executed 260 people so far in 2015 and there are 9,000 on death row. We don't work in China because it seems to be counterproductive but we are active in regard to Saudi Arabia. Saudi Arabia is planning to crucify a seventeen-year-old after cutting his head off. The British were planning to build a prison there but have withdrawn.

We are also looking at the drones programme. When we were campaigning to get into Guantanamo, the US Attorney General told us that if they were unable to imprison and interrogate people they would just kill them. No one is going to Guantanamo anymore because people are being killed extrajudicially in their own countries by drone strikes.

When Guantanamo opened, a lot of people thought that was quite a good idea. We have been able to initiate a debate that has resulted in people thinking this is not a great idea. Many people welcomed the drone programme when it started. You kill the bad guys without needing boots on the ground. Now there is a greater realisation that there is collateral damage. Innocent people are being killed and those who are named as militants are 'killed' multiple times, which suggests the intelligence is not good.

There needs to be more regulation, oversight and transparency and that is what we are campaigning for. We have been working with a man from Yemen whose father-in-law and brother-in-law were killed in a drone attack. We have taken him to the US to talk to Congress and to speak to the security people at the White House. We are bringing together litigation on his behalf. These people were definitely not al-Qaeda or terrorists of any kind.

None of the access and power we are able to exercise would be possible without generous philanthropists and a supporter base of about 55,000 people. We are a charity but we behave more like a start-up company crossed with a law firm. There is a tendency in some larger charities to become inward-looking, corporate and to become obsessed with management. They lose their campaigning edge. We are much more agile and we have to be if we are to do our job properly.

*   *   *

The freedom we enjoy was won as a result of either victory in war or prolonged vigorous campaigning against entrenched prejudice. We owe a great deal to those who led these campaigns and those who funded them. As result, we live in a more tolerant and kinder society. Freedom is enshrined in law.

Do we take what we have for granted? Should we be concerned that the world seems to be a more anxious and angry place as elites accumulate more power and wealth and living standards for the majority are either stagnating or in decline? In the US and Europe, populist politicians are attracting more support and human rights are not a priority for them as they play the politics of fear and blame.

We need charities and their donors to continue campaigning in defence of liberty against the power of those who are against rather than for the common good.

CHAPTER 8

INVESTING IN KNOWLEDGE AND INTELLECTUAL CAPITAL

"This is a big and important question for the country: how much do we value our intellectual capital and capacity for research?"
PROFESSOR DOMINIC SHELLARD, VICE-CHANCELLOR, DE MONTFORT UNIVERSITY (DMU), LEICESTER.

*   *   *

In 2014, Working Futures estimated that 45 per cent of occupations in the UK could be classified as filled by 'knowledge workers'. We have a flourishing knowledge economy.

These figures reflect an extraordinary growth in higher education. Before the Second World War, only 3 per cent of the undergraduate age population attended university. The number more than doubled to 7 per cent or 113,000 by 1961. According to Universities UK, British universities were teaching 2.3 million students in 2013–14.

The transition from elite to mass higher education reflects how much Britain has changed. So has the role of philanthropy. Expansion since 1945 has been largely funded by the state but the future of higher education will be determined by the answer to the question: if the state provides less, who will provide more?

Our oldest universities were originally funded by philanthropy. Following the industrial revolution, the newly wealthy merchant middle classes invested in higher education for their own children.

Although some of these colleges were transformed into universities, they remained independent and autonomous. The new redbrick universities established towards the end of the nineteenth and the first part of the twentieth centuries remained independent and were supported by local business families.

Expansion began after the Second World War to accommodate the baby boomer generation. Whilst the redbrick universities were located in the big cities and funded locally, the new universities were the result of state initiative and funding and located in county towns and cathedral cities. Expansion was funded by government. By the 1960s, universities were no longer private institutions and were overwhelmingly dependent upon the public sector. Philanthropy played a relatively minor role although some of Britain's most prominent foundations were established at this time, including the Nuffield, Weston, Linbury and Wolfson Foundations, and they made notable contributions to universities.

All changed with the election of a Conservative government in 1979. At the same time as state funding was cut, universities were subject to even more state control. Rather than encouraging independence from the state, universities were subject to Margaret Thatcher's controlling tendencies, perhaps because she distrusted academics and regarded them as bastions of self-interest at public expense. There was a significant increase in public regulation of universities and a change in emphasis towards research away from teaching.

The combination of more state control and less public funding encouraged some universities to think about alternative sources of funding, not least because philanthropic funds were free from state control, but fundraising in the higher education sector remained well behind the cultural sector until after the millennium.

In the meantime, further radical changes were introduced. In 1992, thirty polytechnics and thirty former colleges in England and Wales were upgraded to universities. In 1997, the New Labour government's policy was that 50 per cent of young adults should go into higher education. Not much thought seems to have been devoted to how this expansion was to be funded. Shifting the cost to students by charging a fee of £1,000 was insufficient.

One solution to the funding problem was to recruit more students from abroad prepared to pay higher, full cost fees. In terms of both finance and Britain's international reputation, this policy has played well in an age of globalisation and has been an outstanding success. Overseas student numbers were more than 436,000 in 2014–15, according to UK Council for Overseas Student Affairs, 12.6 per cent of the global market for students studying abroad. Universities UK reports that higher education brings in an estimated £10.7 billion of earnings for Britain and the £4.9 billion off-campus spending of overseas students subsidises jobs in every region. Some fear that the political rhetoric surrounding the decision to leave the European Union will make the UK a less attractive proposition for students from overseas.

Britain is justly proud of its universities. Although our population represents only 1 per cent of the world's total, we have four of the world's top ten universities according to QS World University rankings: Cambridge, Oxford, University College London and Imperial College London. The university sector continues to thrive and expand despite reduced public funding.

Tuition fees have been raised to a maximum of £9,000 a year for EU students and there are plans to increase some fees in line with inflation. Universities are again looking to philanthropy, and donations to UK universities are at an all time high, having risen from £513 million in 2006–07 to £860 million in 2013–14, according to the *Financial Times*.

Although the UK has a long way to go to match fundraising in the US, where Harvard has an endowment of more than $35 billion, philanthropic and corporate donations are increasing here. James Dyson donated £12 million to establish the Dyson School of Design Engineering at Imperial College London. Hedge funds are now investing in universities. Man Group has launched a centre for machine learning at Oxford University. Cantab Capital has donated £5 million to Cambridge to open the Institute of Mathematics and

Information. Alan Howard of Brevin Howard has donated £20.1 million to create a Centre for Financial Analysis at Imperial College London.

Higher education in the UK is undergoing rapid evolutionary change. University College London has announced a loan of £280 million to fund the expansion of its campus in central London and for a new site in the Olympic Park in east London. So much change begs questions about the purpose of universities and related institutions, how they will be funded and the contribution they are or could be making to the common good. Accordingly, I talked to Nicola Dandridge, Chief Executive of Universities UK. We spoke in the autumn of 2015:

> This question of the balance between the public and the private is live at the moment in the higher education sector. We have moved from a situation where over 60 per cent of teaching funding came from the state to less than 20 per cent now. Debates around what is public good and what is private good are often clouded by confusion in terms of presentation. The student perception is that they are paying for their tuition. However, the reality is that the state is actually contributing substantially towards the cost of teaching but it just isn't that visible. What most people in the sector would acknowledge is that higher education is a mixture of private and public good. Students gain personally from going to university but there is also a public interest in graduates and postgraduates because of the contribution they make to society.
>
> The state continues to have a significant stake because there is a system of student loans to enable students to pay undergraduate fees of £9,000 a year. These loans are underwritten by the state and are written off if the student doesn't earn enough or get a job that pays above a certain threshold.
>
> The average graduate debt is £27,000 for tuition fees alone (living costs are additional) and the loan is repaid if you earn more than £21,000 when 9 per cent of your income over the threshold is deducted. The loan is effectively a form of graduate tax and the amount

that students pay is linked to their own personal circumstances. That aligns with the political priorities of the government.

There are those who say that the system is unsustainable because the government is effectively paying between 25 per cent and 40 per cent of the cost of tuition fees in England and Wales. This represents the current estimate of the extent that the state underpins those loans that have to be written off and the figure depends on changing estimates of future graduate earnings.

I am frustrated by the confusion in the public discourse about how students are funded. In terms of the cost to the state of writing off loans, our response is that it is good that the state contributes to higher education. The irony is that those who complain about unsustainability and the cost of the state writing off loans are often the same people who want even more state funding.

We do not have a coherent narrative about something as important as sustainable funding for universities and higher education. Part of the problem is the politicisation of higher education funding. At Universities UK, we have always sought that tuition fee funding should not form part of political manifestos, but we seem to fail on this every time there is a general election. The problem then becomes that the politics of elections undermine our ability to have a rational public debate.

Students tell us that living costs are far more of a concern than fees because the need for money for living costs is an immediate everyday challenge. Before the 2015 general election the Labour party promised to reduce undergraduate fees to £6,000. We said that was the wrong battle, and the real issue was living costs.

It is remarkable that the number of students applying to undergraduate courses from disadvantaged backgrounds has gone up not withstanding the introduction of fees. That seems to be counterintuitive but reflects that going to university is good for your future prospects and that you don't have to pay upfront. It also reflects the fact that many universities are now providing substantial financial support for students, to assist them with their costs and tuition fees. This support is often particularly targeted at students from poorer backgrounds.

With regard to philanthropy, there is a particular need to raise funds for postgraduate study. There is a worry that students from poorer families will be put off and feel the need to go into the labour market following graduation rather than continuing with their studies. They graduate with loans to repay and, although there is now a new postgraduate loan system in place, the thought of adding to already substantial loans is not attractive, particularly for those who don't have access to funds from family.

What else are universities raising money for? Principally, they are raising funds to support strategic aims, infrastructure and specific areas such as music or sport. More academic chairs are sponsored or endowed. We are also seeing more student bursaries being supported by philanthropists, often to support students from poorer backgrounds.

I do see universities playing a major role in civil society, particularly in the regions. They have strong regional connections and are very involved with Local Enterprise Partnerships between local authorities and businesses and engagement with emerging devolution deals.

Some universities are taking on the role of anchor institutions and are playing a leading role in the creation of a new kind of regional infrastructure. This is especially the case in the arts where some universities provide funding. For instance, the Middlesbrough Institute of Contemporary Art is run in partnership with Teesside University. The University of Northumbria is close to Sage in Gateshead. Universities have strong regional connections. They understand the regional economy and schools and communities. Manchester and Newcastle Universities are good examples. They see themselves as having a substantial responsibility for and commitment to the community.

We have done work with the Arts Council about the emerging partnerships between universities and arts institutions. Universities welcome this because it enhances their reach into communities.

What we have now may be painful in terms of funding but the new collaborations and partnerships are dynamic and authentic and they have an integrity about them because partners are coming together because they need to and want to. The corollary of reduced public funding is greater freedom from government. The higher education sector cares passionately about its autonomy. Whilst public funding is needed and welcomed, success is also contingent upon independence from government.

*   *   *

Matthew Mellor, Development Director at Pembroke College, Cambridge, agreed that independence from government would be a big gain but told me that the university was some way from achieving that.

Pembroke College is the third oldest of the Cambridge colleges having been founded in 1347 by Marie de St Pol, Countess of Pembroke. Whilst Pembroke is the oldest Cambridge College to survive today on its original site, its pitch to the world, Excellence in Diversity, is entirely contemporary. Matthew Mellor told me:

> Pembroke's corporate partnership programme is the only one within the colleges of the University of Cambridge. We have fifteen corporate partners and we elect a senior representative of the companies to a William Pitt fellowship, Pitt the Younger having been a student here.
>
> This may have been above all recognition of a financial contribution in the early days, but it has developed into something different. We are offering a 'home' within the College and a network within the University. Cambridge is so difficult to navigate and we offer a helping hand. We engage at all sorts of levels with our corporate partners, on matters of recruitment and branding for example, where academic experience can contribute to strategic planning. Zurich Insurance is interested in the built environment in which they operate. Zurich wants to see how its buildings can be productive – and adapt to future changes in the nature of work – rather than simply a cost, and we have helped them with that.
>
> As members of the College, our partner companies have access to a range of expertise and excellence. The scheme has been brilliant in stimulating wider engagement between the college, community and society.

Mellor echoed concern about postgraduate funding:

> To survive in the long term, we need much more private sector support for student scholarships, particularly at postgraduate level. There is an increasing demand from employers for Masters qualifications. Postgraduate study is a daunting prospect for those who have amassed debt and we must be careful to hold on to British students who may be tempted to go to better-funded institutions overseas, particularly in the US.

*   *   *

Universities are adapting and evolving. The distinction between town and gown is evaporating. I talked to Professor Dominic Shellard, Vice-Chancellor of De Montfort University, Leicester (DMU)

Professor Shellard joined DMU in 2010. He believes that the future success of the university depends upon building creative relationships with partners in industry and in education in the UK and overseas. His focus on driving up quality and improving the student experience is reflected in the university's £136 million campus redevelopment project.

DMU is recognised for its local community engagement programmes. The Square Mile project works with the community to improve local health, education and job prospects and won the Mahatma Gandhi International award in 2013 for making a distinguished contribution to the community.

Projects offer free support to primary and secondary schools including mentoring in maths, English and science, speech therapy, sports and IT training for parents and children. DMU students are running health projects, campaigning to recruit people to the stem cell register, to help those with diabetes to manage their condition, and to administer free hearing tests. DMU's C Word project, in partnership with Macmillan Cancer, is supporting cancer patients and their families in Leicester. DMU is supporting the city's new Young Transgender Centre of Excellence in the Leicester LGBT centre.

I asked Professor Shellard to explain how universities are adapting and changing:

When student fees were introduced and raised to £9,000, I worried that this would be a deterrent, but I have to eat humble pie because we have seen significant growth in numbers. We are now in the top ten of universities in terms of growth.

However, that may change in the longer term if fees go up more. Debt can approach the £40,000 level including living costs and if that rises, there could be a problem. At the moment, the political discourse is focused on reducing tax and individuals shouldering more of the burden but that may change at some point if, for example, the public perceives that the NHS is under too much strain. I believe that public investment via the state can be a very good thing but I don't expect the public discourse to change for a while.

DMU is benefitting from the current policy because student numbers grew by 37 per cent in the six years from 2009, and by 20 per cent in the last year. This is because we are focused on employability. Of our students, 96 per cent go on to graduate-level jobs.

I am forty-nine and universities have changed so much since I was an undergraduate. One change is that undergraduates now attend open days with their parents. That is the last thing that my generation would have wanted. The parents ask very pointed questions about the employability of their children. They also want to know if they will be able to travel and exactly how much contact students will have with lecturers.

There is a market in higher education and we know we are in a competitive market place. It is very clear that parents and prospective students want to know what they are getting for £27,000.

Whilst there are positives about this radical change in funding, we need to be vigilant that higher education does not become simply a commercial transaction. We must offer students value for money but we must not lose sight of the point that a university education is also about personal development. Our students are intellectually curious, they are concerned about the environment, sustainability,

the welfare and well-being of others and we must nurture that. Our
university has a very strong commitment to the pursuit of knowledge and the exploration of ideas that may contribute to the public
good. We actively encourage our students to volunteer and they are
keen to do this. We have a very strong commitment to the local
community.

I share the concern of those who are worried that the cost of
postgraduate study will deter those who have amassed a lot of debt.
The new loans for postgraduate study recently announced by the
government will help a bit but a commitment to postgraduate study
is a huge financial investment. We feel students need an incentive
to move onto an MA or MSc. We have a new scheme that offers
a discount of up to 50 per cent on some full-time and part-time
postgraduate courses.

This is currently funded by the university but we do need more
funding. This is a big and important question for the country: how
much do we value investment in our intellectual capital and capacity
for research?

There is a role for philanthropy in helping fund postgraduate
study and research in particular, but donors are traditionally attracted to buildings and to capital projects that bear their name.
Also, expectations of alumni donations need to be realistic bearing
in mind that some students may never earn enough to pay off their
tuition debt and that those earning enough will be burdened with
other debts such as mortgages as well as paying off the debt on their
tuition fees and living costs whilst at university.

*   *   *

The Rt Hon. Shaun Woodward was a Member of Parliament from
1997 to 2015 and served as Secretary of State for Northern Ireland
in 2007–10. I spoke to him in December 2015 in his capacity as
Chairman-elect of the London Academy of Music and Dramatic
Art (LAMDA). I asked Woodward for his perspective on a state
that will provide less:

It seems to me that there are two dilemmas. The first is the one that arises from saying that as the state will give less, individuals will have to give or pay more or those enterprises that have relied on the state hitherto will shrink, wither or disappear. Or they must look elsewhere for funding.

The second dilemma that has emerged on my radar as I campaign to rebuild LAMDA is a different issue. We need to raise £28 million. We have raised £25 million. Of that £25 million, less than £500,000 has come from the state.

We don't qualify for Arts Council England (ACE) money unlike the Royal Academy of Dramatic Art (RADA) which had a £7 million grant from the ACE in the early 2000s.

LAMDA is more sought after than any other drama school in Britain. As we did not have our own theatre, we had to rebuild or die. Although we had no great prospects of public funding, we would have lost LAMDA if we did not do this project. Raising £25 million mostly from the private sector is a remarkable achievement but there is a problem in that a number of institutions, like LAMDA, fall between the cracks because of the way the public funding system is structured.

Why does this matter? The creative industries are one of the five main engines of growth of the British economy, accounting for more than 5 per cent of the economy, with twice the growth rate of the overall economy in 2013/14. Both the mainstream political parties recognise the importance of training young people for the future. Some of them are not going to come out of conventional universities. They will come out of institutions devoted to vocational training. Vocational training in the case of LAMDA requires a focus on postgraduates.

Think about Timothy West, David Oyelowo and Benedict Cumberbatch, who are all distinguished LAMDA alumni. Of the actors on stage at the National Theatre tonight, 20 per cent will be graduates of LAMDA. The creative industries would be in trouble without LAMDA.

We are looking at the prospect of young men and women coming

to LAMDA with three or four years of tuition debt plus living allowance debt that has to be borrowed at a commercial rate. They
then study at LAMDA for two years with all the expense of living
in London, and could easily accumulate a total debt of £80,000 or
more and go into a profession where the average person is earning
less than £20,000 a year. LAMDA has an excellent employment
record. Ninety per cent of our students are working regularly fifteen
years after they leave, but many will be earning less than the average.

We are talking about a generation coming on stream with a
colossal debt and where does that leave them?

There is a third dimension to the problem. Institutions struggle to
get their share of the cake, but the young men and women coming out
of them will face such financial difficulty that there is real risk – when
it comes to vocations that require postgraduate training – that this
will become the province of young people from well-off backgrounds.
That seems to me to be a retrograde, regressive way of looking at the
creative industries. We are in danger of not training the new blood we
shall need because the training will be unaffordable.

It won't take long before parents tell their children that they
cannot afford to do this.

We are on the verge of doing something immoral. Young people
could sink under that level of debt. They are certainly unlikely to be
members of a property-owning democracy. The government may
well be prepared to write off undergraduate debt but that does not
apply to living expenses and to postgraduate debt and expenses exceeding £10,000.

This is a new dimension to the problem of a state that provides
less. There is a threat to the professions that are essential for the
success of our creative economy. So in terms of more philanthropy
contributing to sustainability, we will need philanthropic support
for young professionals as well as buildings and institutions. The
question is: in future, will there be a supply of singers for the chorus,
young people to play in an orchestra, and will there be the actors
for film and TV as well as theatres to sustain the creative economy?
There may not be if the vocation becomes unaffordable.

How do we avoid a crisis in one of the engines of economic growth? This may force people to look again at the whole issue of tuition fees in relation to vocational professions.

We have 6,000 applicants for up to 100 places at LAMDA. This is as tough as getting into Oxbridge. We feel a moral obligation not to accept anyone who we doubt will be able to have a successful career. My worry is that those with talent will not be able to afford to come to LAMDA.

The challenge we have to face now is how to find the funds to invest in intellectual capital. We don't have that tradition. The success of the British economy in the twenty-first century is going to depend upon fulfilling the potential for human and intellectual capital. China has a much stronger sense of this. Countries in the Middle East are investing considerable private wealth in sending young people to study overseas.

That is what we are up against. What is the potential for developing Britain as a global centre for intellectual capital? We need the intellectual equivalent of a George Peabody.

It would be a catastrophe for Britain's economy if our vocational professions were only for the upper-middle classes and the very rich.

* * *

My next stop was the Royal College of Music (RCM) in London where these matters were at the forefront of the thinking of those who founded the College in the late nineteenth century.

I talked to Professor Colin Lawson, Director of the RCM, and Kevin Porter, Deputy Director, before the referendum vote to leave the EU. Colin Lawson reminded me that the first conservatoire was founded at a time of extreme if not drastic social mobility:

The start of all this came shortly after the French Revolution with the foundation of the Paris Conservatoire in 1795. This was a state-run Conservatoire that was notably strong on gender equality. The Conservatoire also established all the things to do with institutional life that we know today: formal tuition, timetables, auditions, competitions and prizes. It wasn't long before there were conservatoires across Europe and by 1880, the Prince of Wales believed something similar was required in London.

The RCM was established by royal charter in 1882. From the start, there were fifty scholarships. We always felt that there was a difference between the Royal Academy of Music (RAM), which was founded by and for the aristocracy, and the RCM. We have always been committed to both access and excellence. The then Prince of Wales wanted the RCM to play a role in enabling London to become the world capital of music and that is what it has become.

We are in a similar position to LAMDA. The amount of money students need to invest is huge and, if they are not in receipt of a scholarship, this will be beyond the means of many. Most students will not be earning much if they have a career in music.

Kevin Porter [**KP**] added:

There must be a concern about a willingness to pay if the cap comes off tuition fees. The cost of education here at the RCM is comparable with the cost of a medical education. This is because of our intensive provision, including one-to-one tuition and the need for professional quality performance and practice spaces, with appropriate professional support. If the current stream of public funding were to be reduced or cut completely and we needed to charge the full cost of this education, there must be a point at which parents would be concerned whether investment in an education in music would make a realistic return.

The real cost of educating a student here is over £20,000 rather than the £9,000 we currently charge home students and those who come from the EU. Overseas student fees are over £20,000. Our undergraduate course is also four years rather than the usual three years at university.

CL: There is some evidence that young people are considering applying to American conservatoires because they are much better endowed and can offer more generous scholarships. We are not on a level playing field though 50 per cent of our students already receive financial support and we were able to give scholarships last year worth £2.5 million. In the next five years we aim to increase this provision to support 75 per cent of our students.

In the EU, a conservatoire education is much less expensive and some of our European students find studying on the continent a more attractive proposition. However, the 'London effect' is considerable and we have to ensure that prospective students are aware of the unique opportunities we can provide. We are linked to so many other cultural institutions and our students benefit hugely from such partnerships. The RCM is able to offer more than first-class tuition; we can offer a holistic experience that is hard to find anywhere else. As a result, our graduates enjoy high levels of employment in a wide range of careers including performing, composing, teaching, and work with some of the most prestigious performing groups worldwide.

However, twenty years ago, two-thirds of our income came from the state; now it is about a quarter. There is no specific grant for capital campaigns and, in order to meet the challenges of space and fulfil our modernising agenda, fundraising has become a priority.

KP: Although the contribution the state makes is now a smaller part of our running costs, it provides some indication that government recognises that what we do includes making a contribution to society. However, we rely on others taking a similar view. We have been successful in making the case to generous individuals and trusts to invest in scholarships to support students but many take the view that it is the role of government to support educational institutions and their running costs.

The competition is increasing in that many more countries now have decent conservatoires. That is why the College must continue to invest as we are doing through our More Music campaign. Like LAMDA, we have to invest in our estate and our resources. We have to raise £40 million in capital to ensure we remain competitive in terms of the quality of the education and the experience we can provide here. We also need to open up the College to the music-loving public, as a place of learning and appreciation.

CL: Part of our success is that we have not whined about public funding and we have been keen to take advantage of opportunities. We do recognise that we are in a market. There have been times in the past when institutions have simply waited for the students to come to them. We don't. We are promoting ourselves both in the UK and overseas.

The fundraising challenge for us is that we are an academic institution and we are not the Royal Opera House. We cannot offer the same attractions and we do not have the same appeal. Adding value to the lives of young people is not as attractive for some as supporting a production at the Royal Opera House. We have to work much harder to raise the money.

We make up for that by having an entrepreneurial spirit across the college. We are also on the front foot in terms of our outreach programmes and the work we do with under-eighteen-year-olds in terms of discovering their potential. They are the people who need the funding. I worry about the potential that is being wasted. The people we want to help the most cost the most. We fund that from our own resources with the help of generous donors. There is no state support for what we are doing with young people in the community.

*　　*　　*

Dominic Shellard asked the question: how much do we value investment in the country's intellectual capital and research? The government will point to the research councils, but that will not be sufficient to meet competition from other countries.

Philanthropy is once again investing in the nation's intellectual and cultural capital, but it will take decades to raise adequate endowments unless the government is prepared to commit more matched funding to increase the value of donations and legacies. In the meantime, voices are calling for the government to reconsider its policy and invest more in the growth of Britain's successful knowledge and creative economy.

CHAPTER 9

CULTURE AND THE NEED TO EXPLAIN

"When I hear the word culture, I reach for my gun."
ATTRIBUTED TO HERMANN GÖRING, HEINRICH
HIMMLER AND JOSEPH GOEBBELS.

*   *   *

The Nazis recognised the power of culture. Poets and writers are amongst the first to be removed by dictators. Artist Ai Weiwei was detained by the police in Beijing for eighty-one days without any contact with family or a lawyer. Stalin effectively banned Shostakovich's opera *Lady Macbeth of Mtsensk* so he never wrote another. Hitler banned what he called degenerative art and used film and the operas of Wagner to serve Nazi ideology. Culture can be a powerful weapon to forge political and social change.

The Second World War destroyed Germany's cities, towns and villages but not the belief of the German people in the power of culture to express what matters to them. A crucial imperative for post-war Germany was to invest in culture, and so priority was given to rebuilding opera houses, emblems of spiritual renewal.

We are also a cultured and creative nation but, unlike Germans, we find it difficult to talk about culture and why it matters. This becomes a financial and a political problem. Why fund what is not seen as a priority?

Art clearly matters, otherwise dictators would ignore it. Benjamin

Britten said that he wanted to be useful as a composer. Are the arts useful and if so, in what way? Why should the arts be funded by the taxpayer, and why do they need additional private sector support?

I put Sir Peter Bazalgette, then Chairman of Arts Council England (ACE), to the test in 2016.

> When I became ACE chairman three years ago and after twenty years of raising money for education and the arts, I made a point of asking politicians, civil servants and arts organisations: why do we put public money into arts and culture? Overall, the answers from people who should know better were almost incoherent.
>
> Too many people in arts and culture have not been that good at articulating the benefits that accrue from what they do.
>
> One answer is that they deliver public good and public benefit. But what does that mean? The ACE grant from government has been cut by 30 per cent since 2010, although the Chancellor has given a more positive 'flat cash' settlement to the arts for the years 2016–20. There is still a real need to articulate what the public benefit is.
>
> That need was not so apparent before the crash when the economy and tax revenues were growing. That was then. We had work to do to establish and to define the public benefit that the arts contribute, to persuade people to sign up to and communicate the benefits and to use what we found politically. That meant we needed evidence.
>
> We came up with four headings: Intrinsic, Social, Educational and Economic. Their order is important.
>
> I was well aware of the economic argument in favour of the arts but I was equally well aware that many in the arts were acutely uncomfortable with that. They thought that argument echoed Oscar Wilde's quip about knowing the price of everything and the value of nothing.

INTRINSIC

> We felt that this was almost a philosophical point and beyond measure, that touched on the ethics and values of a society. Culture

can have a galvanising effect on the quality of life, creating a sense of wonder, enlightenment, identity in terms of the person, community and nation, by illumination and inspiration. We should not be embarrassed to say these things.

The arts also enable us to be empathetic citizens and to understand other people. Our research showed how powerful the arts are. There is evidence that people who have more exposure to arts and culture are more likely to vote. If you are interested in and considering the human condition more empathetically, you are more likely to be engaged in social and political issues.

SOCIAL

We were interested to examine the work done every day by artists in hospitals and the health service. We know that music can help some dementia patients. Anyone who has sung in a choir knows what a liberating and fulfilling experience it can be. You come away from singing Haydn's *Creation* feeling like a million dollars.

We cannot afford our health service as it currently operates, as demand outstrips resources. The emphasis is on curing when we should be spending more on prevention. That saves money. We spend more time and money curing obesity than preventing it. I have been to Dance East in Ipswich where I saw professional dancers working in the community and helping people who are overweight and elderly become fitter in a joyful spirit.

ACE has a joint project with the Baring Foundation in Cornwall that funds professional artists to go into care homes where the very old are isolated and lonely. The Liverpool Museums have a project for those with dementia called 'House of Memories' and English National Ballet has a programme for those with Parkinson's Disease.

The recognition of the role art can play in improving physical and mental health will have significant implications. Look at the work being done in prisons. Why is half the global prison population illiterate? How does that exclude them from society? It is not simply a question of can I read and can I get a job? It is more

serious than that: can I read and can I understand other people and
share their emotions? Can I communicate? Can I read stories about
other people and about myself? Can I tell stories in return? This is
the human condition. This is what art and culture is: the telling of
stories.

EDUCATION

Should the arts and culture have anything to do with education?
Is the Pope a Catholic? There is an issue with education because of
the understandable need to raise standards in state schools. There
is more emphasis upon attainment in a small number of subjects
and this involves considerable box ticking. The emphasis is upon
STEM: science, technology, engineering and mathematics.

We say STEAM, not STEM. Art, music and drama in schools
have suffered in this more instrumental age but we are making
some progress. We are now talking to Ofsted (Office for Standards
in Education, Children's Services and Skills) who used not to be
interested.

They should be because the creative industries are 5 per cent of
the economy and growing. The future talent of the creative economy
is now at school. Creative thinking is needed for a range of skills
and professions. Design and creative thinking are also fundamentally important for those who become engineers.

Universities are ambitious about redefining their role beyond
being scholastic institutions. They are also 'place makers' and investors in their communities. They want their community and local
economy to be vibrant in order to attract students. One of their
measures of success is to ask how many of their graduates will be
living and working in the vicinity in five years' time, helping to improve quality of life as well as contributing to the local economy.

Universities are starting to take over the running of arts institutions, sometimes in partnership with ACE because this is part of
place-making. The University of Northumbria is a partner in Baltic
39, an art gallery in Newcastle where students and recent graduates

can work with professionals. The University of Sunderland has taken over the National Glass Centre, a crucial national resource for glass design. The University of Teesside is a partner with ACE in the Middlesbrough Institute of Modern Art. The University of Derby has opened what was a moribund theatre that is now a resource for the city. The University of Bristol has taken over the top two floors of the Arnolfini Gallery whose financial model was failing. Now they have a rental income and can continue to do great things for the people of Bristol.

These are interesting and dynamic partnerships but they are not a new idea. Both Cambridge and Oxford have had world-class museums for a hundred years and the universities have supported them for many years. It is now time for this example to be rolled out across the country.

ECONOMY

We do not invest public money in culture because we want economic growth but there is an economic benefit and it would be foolish not to publicise and see if we can increase it. We were the first country in the world to say there is such a thing as the creative industries.

The arts are crucial because they incubate the talent for the creative industries. Danny Boyle was a trainee director at the Royal Court Theatre, then made an Oscar-winning movie that earned hundreds of millions of dollars. He went on to create the opening ceremony for the London Olympics, a showcase for Britain seen by billions. The state invested in Steve McQueen by giving him an education at Goldsmiths, the Arts Council supported his early video work, and he won Tate's Turner Prize before winning an Oscar for his film *Twelve Years a Slave*.

Arts and culture continue to contribute to urban regeneration. Look at the Turner Contemporary in Margate, The Lowry in Salford, Baltic and Sage in Gateshead. Forward-thinking towns and cities want arts and culture because the arts encourage clusters of creative businesses.

The arts have enhanced Britain's reputation abroad. The British Council has done research showing that those who are exposed to and experience British culture are more likely to trade with us.

Tourism is also often driven by arts and culture. Of tourists visiting London, 25 per cent come primarily for culture, and cultural tourists spend more.

That is the case for public support for arts and culture and this applies to private sector support by business and philanthropists as well. The case has remained the same for some time but the role of the Arts Council in terms of funding our national portfolio clients has changed. Twenty years ago, the average percentage of our funding was over 50 per cent of clients' total revenues. It will be 26 per cent in 2016. Philanthropy grows at a glacial pace and represents about 12 per cent. Commercial revenues have grown to about 53 per cent. That has compensated for the lower contribution from the state.

I agree that in terms of philanthropy, the arts are now in competition with other charities in a way that they were not some years ago. They have had to widen their appeal to the public. Although the major arts institutions attract significant philanthropic support, the arts overall capture much less charitable giving than other causes. We did some research with YouGov that showed only 8 per cent of the public knew that arts and culture have charitable status. The sector does not naturally wish to describe itself as in need of charitable support. Some might think it demeaning. But this is changing and it needs to.

Local authority funding for the arts has also been cut but not as much as the ACE so far. It was Jennie Lee's vision in the 1960s that local authorities should play a big role. They are investing £1.1 billion in arts and culture, including libraries, but this is down by 17 per cent over the past three years. ACE is spending £700 million currently, from the taxpayer and the Lottery.

One of the reasons that local government arts budgets have been protected is because we have worked with them to articulate a much stronger case for support. They can see that they are supporting something tangible. We leverage our partnership with local government. If we co-fund a museum and the local government wants to cut 100 per cent, we say we may have to get out. And we mean it. We want to be positive and keep the partnership going but that is going to be *the* big challenge over the next few years as local government shrinks further.

The future has to be about partnerships. Look at Bristol Cultural Development Partnership and the Liverpool Arts Regeneration Consortium. These are partnerships between local government, local business and higher education. Look at the Arts Impact Fund that lends to arts organisations wanting to be more enterprising and resilient whilst making a social as well as a cultural impact. The £7 million fund is backed by the ACE, the National Lottery, the Esmée Fairbairn Foundation, Nesta (the innovation foundation), Bank of America Merrill Lynch, and the Calouste Gulbenkian Foundation. Public funding remains a critical corner stone, but we need new models as well. This is the way forward.

*   *   *

We have heard the case for investing public money in arts and culture but what should philanthropists do? I put the question that way because in 2015 I was asked by *Alliance*, an international publication for philanthropy and social investment, to answer the question: why should philanthropists fund the arts?

My job was to address the question of whether philanthropists should support art or the needs of society (as if the two were unrelated!), and to make the case for funding the arts by demonstrating how culture contributes to social change. If the case for supporting the arts is neither compelling nor understood, then that is the fault of the cultural sector. The arts are in a competitive market and, to put it crudely in order to make the point, people can choose whether they wish to support cancer research or culture, or both.

Arts and culture will have to work even harder to hold on to state support, to attract those with deep pockets and persuade them to give and, even more importantly, to secure the loyalty and the commitment of the public.

The point that the arts have failed to make is that they are part of what every human being does: see, hear, breathe, speak, sing, move, think, imagine and feel. We have needed art for at least 40,000 years since the first cave drawings appeared.

Throughout recorded history, art has needed patronage. I talked to some of those who chair, run and support some of our leading arts institutions to understand why art and philanthropy are natural partners and how this marriage benefits millions.

John Studzinski runs Blackstone Advisory Partners and is a senior managing director of the Blackstone Group. His motivation in life as well as in philanthropy is the need to respect and to preserve human dignity. He is an active supporter of The Passage, a charity for the homeless in London, where he volunteers on the front line as well as serving on the board, giving and raising money. As a board member, he has used his international contacts to help Human Rights Watch to expand so that it can draw attention to atrocities across the world, not least in Syria and the Middle East:

> I support human rights and the arts. I created the Genesis Foundation more than ten years ago. We provide funding for young artists but beyond that we actively nurture them. Genesis has supported 900 artists, one of whom, Rufus Norris, is the director of the National Theatre. All the causes I support come back to identity, self-worth and dignity.
>
> The arts are integral to life. What drives me up the wall is the idea that they are about entertainment. Both the arts and philanthropy play a huge role in social change and always have.
>
> The UK has the most open society in the world in terms of democracy, free speech and a highly critical media, and all of that is reflected in the arts. Look at the Royal Court Theatre in London. Writers from all over the world wish to write for it because free speech is one of the most precious things we have. Look at the impact that Jez Butterworth's play *Jerusalem* has made. Unless we

encourage that kind of writing we won't have the insight into contemporary society that we need to navigate our way through social change and to influence it.

John Studzinski is also a benefactor and former trustee of Tate, the UK's national museum of British and international modern and contemporary art. I asked Sir Nicholas Serota, Tate's Director, about the role that philanthropy plays in the arts and its significance for Tate, not least in the building of Tate Modern, the world's most popular museum of modern and contemporary art:

There is an innate ambition in some people to leave the world a better place than they found it. The arts appeal to benefactors because they are an enduring part of society. We know a great deal more about the culture of the Greeks, the Romans and pre-Columbians than we do about their rates of inflation.

Most early philanthropy was about commissioning artists, and there are examples in recent times of that kind of patronage when Robert and Lisa Sainsbury bought Francis Bacon's paintings in the 1950s. The impact of the Sainsburys' philanthropy is felt today.

My aim in building Tate Modern was to encourage people to be less frightened of the art of their time, by creating somewhere they could feel welcome, a place in which they could find solace as well as intellectual stimulation, and in which artists could make work that reflects our time.

None of Tate's expansion or the growth in audiences from 1.75 million to 7.75 million over twenty years would have been possible without a partnership between secure public funding – although that has declined by 30 per cent since 2010 – and philanthropy. One of our first significant donations for Tate Modern came from a man not noted for his enthusiasm for modern art. He was motivated to give because he recognised the need for London to have a museum of international contemporary art and he knew that cultural investment in a relatively poor part of London could transform the area economically and socially.

Philanthropists are attracted to Tate because of our ability to reach young audiences, to provide learning opportunities and to take risks with artists. Through expansion, largely funded by philanthropy, we have been able to build new audiences and create programmes for local young people, and we now have an annual membership that has grown from 30,000 in 2000 to 114,000 in 2015. Tate has huge international appeal, particularly to the young, and attracts 20 million online visitors a year. More people are engaged with and participate in the arts than ever before.

Some regard our national organisations as temples of high art for the elite. Alex Beard, chief executive of The Royal Opera house disagrees:

The concept of high art has no currency whatsoever. What opera does best is to use all the art forms to deal with the most signific-ant forces in life: love, death, rebirth, betrayal, power, the tension between the public and the private. These emotions are central to the human condition and opera enables us to explore them with a power and intensity that other art forms cannot quite match.

Of course opera is expensive but it is nonsense that you have to be rich to come here. For every performance, 40 per cent of the tickets cost £40 or below. Our student standby scheme has 20,000 members.

Access is central to everything we do. Some may not see us as agents of social change but that is what we are. Philanthropy is vital, providing 25 per cent of our annual budget. This helps to subsidise cheaper seats but philanthropists are active in other ways helping us to change the lives of others. For example, our recent production of *The Dialogue of the Carmelites*, Poulenc's opera about religious persecution in revolutionary France, engaged a community ensemble for the crowd scenes made up of the homeless, the long-term unemployed and ex-offenders. The energy they brought to the performance was phenomenal. This is outreach of a new order.

What has been the impact upon those who sang in the chorus

in Poulenc's *Dialogue of the Carmelites*? Participants were asked if there were aspects of theatrical life that interested them. Some were offered work experience. One former prisoner said: 'I never dreamed it would work out like this. A year ago, I was in prison and had never acted in my life. In September, I will start studying at the Royal Academy of Dramatic Art.'

Our new workshop in Thurrock, one of the most deprived areas in the south-east of the UK, is part of a cluster of creative enterprises working together with a combination of public and private funding in which philanthropy has been crucial. This has enabled us to work for the public good by providing employment and skills development where they are needed. As a result, Thurrock Council has asked us to work with twenty-two schools to develop a programme around cultural awareness and entitlement. This should be a model for the future.

We must ensure that we reflect and contribute to society today. Those visionary philanthropists who support this mean that we are now playing to a whole different set of concerns that have changed the focus and character of the Royal Opera House.

Few know more about arts funding than Lord (Chris) Smith, Secretary of State for Culture, Media and Sport in Tony Blair's first government, chairman of the Art Fund and the Wordsworth Trust, chairman of the Advertising Standards Authority and latterly chairman of the Environment Agency and the Donmar Warehouse. He is also Master of Pembroke College, Cambridge, where we reviewed matters cultural, educational and political:

As a practical politician, I could not ask the Chancellor of the Exchequer to increase funding because the arts represent beauty and truth. I had to emphasise their economic and social benefit and the need to improve access. I believed that it was my public duty to help people enjoy the great things in life, and that led to free admissions to museums and has helped to enhance the social and economic impact that the arts are making in our towns and cities.

Free entry for museums and galleries is so important because these are the institutions that helped to make us the nation we are through the great collections we have amassed over the centuries. I don't believe there should be a barrier to their enjoyment linked to ability to pay. Many of these collections were amassed with the help of money that came from the state or the British public. Should the public pay twice to see them?

Moreover, paintings and sculptures are best appreciated and understood by seeing them again and again. Think of someone on an hour's lunch break who can come in to see a small number of paintings. You are not going to return again and again if you have to pay. That is why Sir Denis Mahon gifted his collection of paintings to the nation on condition that the public did not have to pay to see them.

In the UK, our mixed economy for the arts has been crucial in their success in attracting audiences and enhancing our international reputation. The key factor is to ensure the independence of artists and cultural institutions. We have avoided plutocracy where donors influence artistic decisions. As a result, the arts are lively and challenging and this motivates audiences and donors. And the arts are fundamental to our growing creative and knowledge economy.

We are one of the most creative nations in the world. Look at the BBC, our museums and galleries, our orchestras, our opera, dance and theatre companies, as well our leading universities. This is what we are known for. Government support has been absolutely critical. If all these things were not publicly supported, none of them would have been possible. The key thing is that public subsidy provides a degree of stability in an inherently unstable environment.

The arts matter because they are what make us a civilised society, they shape the narrative of who we are as a nation, they define us as citizens and souls, they express our joy, our excitement, our sorrow and give us the insight that helps us to be human. Do we remember the names of each Medici? Hardly. They are overshadowed by Leonardo and Michelangelo and all the great artists of the Renaissance. They are what define the era. Exactly the same will be true of us in 500 years' time.

The really important thing for policy makers, politicians and governments to understand is that the arts define the human condition. They should heed the advice of Emma Goldman, the American radical and feminist who told Lenin: 'If I cannot dance, I won't be part of your revolution.' That centrality is where the arts should be.

Philanthropists in the UK like to be partners. We had to raise 50 per cent of our turnover from the private sector at the Donmar Warehouse in London, but this enabled our small theatre to make an impact and exert an influence way beyond its size and to mount pioneering productions such as our all-female Julius Caesar.

The most senior philanthropists are saying to the government: 'Don't assume that if you reduce or stop funding the arts that we will step in to bridge the gap.' They are saying that their commitment runs in parallel with governments and does not substitute for it. The reason they are prepared to give is because the nation, through government, has decided to support what is in the national interest.

The Art Fund, an independent charity funded by donations and public subscription, has been going for more than a hundred years. It was started to save works of art for the nation that would end up in private, foreign hands and would be lost to the general public.

Since then, our commitment has moved towards helping museums and galleries acquire art because they no longer have government grants to do that. The Art Fund is spending around £5 million a year to help museums and galleries to add to their collection and the Lottery also makes an important contribution. We have a large membership of 117,000. Each member has the National Art Pass that gets them into exhibitions free or at half price. We have also started supporting the development of curatorial skills, touring works of art and commissioning contemporary work.

One of our biggest Art Fund triumphs was saving the Wedgwood Collection for the nation and our other projects have included the successful campaign to save the Van Dyck Self-portrait and the current campaign to save the Armada Portrait of Elizabeth I for the National Maritime Museum.

We have a political philosophy that believes in small government, that wants to reduce public expenditure, that does not see much value in public institutions or desirable goals of national well-being and public excellence so we have to find ways of working with reality. The need for independent institutions such as the Art Fund that can do and say things by criticising constructively, campaigning and lobbying, is greater than ever. Well funded, independent institutions are one of the great things about this country.

However, we do not want to pick up what the public sector cannot do. Government must remember that all philanthropy is a matter of either personal or institutional choice. Donors are not obliged to do what government wants them to do.

Arts education and access programmes used to be a required extra for arts organisations but have now become integral. Look at what Vivien Duffield's Clore Foundation has done for arts education. She has helped to change the way museums and galleries think about the way they relate to the public and to the young in particular, and that is good for everyone. By creating and supporting cultural learning centres for fifty years, Vivien Duffield has changed practice and helped to transform the lives of thousands of young people.

*　　*　　*

Whilst the work of Vivien Duffield and other philanthropists has undoubtedly enriched the lives of those who have had the good fortune to experience the arts through their auspices whilst young, what is the state doing to ensure that schools are encouraging the young to be creative and imaginative? A 2015 report from the Warwick Commission on the future of cultural value, *Enriching Britain: Culture, Creativity and Growth*, makes worrying reading. The report says that culture and the arts are being systematically removed from the education system with dramatic falls in the number of pupils taking GSCEs in design, drama and other arts-related subjects.

Between 2003 and 2013, there was a drop of 50 per cent in the number studying for GCSEs in design and technology, a 25 per cent drop for drama and 25 per cent for other craft-related subjects.

In England, there has been a significant decline in the number of schools offering art subjects taught by specialist teachers.

In 2014, ABRSM, the examination board of the Royal Schools of Music, reported that whilst more young people than ever before are playing a musical instrument (69 per cent), children from lower socio-economic groups continue to be significantly disadvantaged compared with their peers from more affluent backgrounds.

Victoria Robey is chairman of the London Philharmonic Orchestra (LPO), a trustee of the Royal College of Music (RCM) and a founding director of London Music Masters (LMM), a music education charity undertaking pioneering work in inner London with the involvement of the RCM and the LPO. I asked Robey for her view on the role of philanthropy in enabling music and education to contribute to the common good:

> Music is particularly powerful because it touches the lives of so many through a shared language. However, the paucity of high-quality music education throughout the UK means that most poorer children don't have the opportunity to learn how to play an instrument properly and have a limited prospect of developing the skills needed to go to a conservatoire. Even worse, their ability to enjoy music is unnecessarily limited.
>
> We founded LMM to pioneer good practice in music education and to transform the lives of the very young in some of the most disadvantaged parts of London. We are now working with seven primary schools in inner London. Professional musicians teach entire classes how to play the violin from the age of four. Our credo is excellence. We give the children music tuition of the highest standard. Children learn to concentrate, to work together, to achieve and to inspire. This approach enhances academic performance as well as improving social behaviour. The programme pulls the families in and has an authentic effect upon the community as everyone aims higher.
>
> We are mostly privately funded and therefore limited in how many schools we can work with. This is frustrating when there is

proof that the arts are a catalyst for social change. Our government must understand that the arts must be embedded in the education system rather than as a desirable extra. Philanthropy can achieve a lot and be pioneering but by working in partnership with public funding, we could achieve so much more.

The government says it is committed to arts education in schools but money and resources do not match the rhetoric. Government is yet to demonstrate the joined-up thinking that will give the young the tools they need to enable them to be the creative people we will need in future. Governments are failing to invest in the future of the creative economy. Meanwhile, Vivien Duffield, Victoria Robey, John Studzinski and others who are investing in young artists and arts education are shining examples of how philanthropy can be innovative, creative and progressive.

Many of the capital's leading arts institutions have been able to invest and expand as a result of hundreds of millions of pounds in philanthropic funding in the last twenty years. However, some of our leading arts companies based outside London have been conspicuously successful in attracting financial support from the private sector and, crucially, their public.

The Hallé Orchestra was founded in Manchester in 1858 and soon came to national prominence, performing the premiere of Elgar's first symphony in 1908. In the late 1990s, the Hallé was on the point of bankruptcy and launched an appeal which raised £2 million from local people. This saved the orchestra. As a result, the Arts Council gave a grant that enabled the orchestra to pay off its debts and, under the artistic leadership of Sir Mark Elder and chief executive John Summers, the Hallé is flourishing. I asked Summers about the Hallé's current position.

> There is no doubt in my mind that without the support of the ten local authorities of Greater Manchester and the extraordinary loyalty of our donors and sponsors, the Hallé would not exist in its current form today.

The Hallé has a unique relationship with its home city, Manchester, one that helps define what it is and what it does. The Orchestra was born out of private money – funded initially by the German mill owners in Manchester who believed that working people should be able to access great music as easily as the wealthy, and was sustained by the Industrial Concert Series which was a very early form of crowd sourcing – where concerts were effectively paid for by block bookings from different companies – before they were performed. These early philanthropists believed in culture as an engine of change – and these original values still guide us today.

The Hallé continues to enjoy remarkable support from both individuals and businesses and the appeal in 2000 really exposed the depth of their loyalty. We have never underestimated the significance of this support and work hard to build strong relationships and develop partnerships that have a genuine mutual value. Three of our biggest sponsors have sponsored consistently, year on year, for over twenty-seven years.

The crisis in the 1990s also forced the Hallé to re-examine its core values and the arrival of Sir Mark Elder as Music Director helped to reposition the quality of performance and the nurturing of new talent. I am proud of the work Mark and I have done in creating probably the largest offer for talented young people delivered by any UK orchestra. Currently our family of ensembles includes the Youth Orchestra, Youth Choir, Youth Training Choir and the Children's Choir. By working closely with the Greater Manchester music hubs and our partner schools we have structured the ensembles to ensure that they offer a route through to higher education in music to children from the state school sector who cannot readily access the additional tutoring and music education that is on offer to young people in the public school sector. As a consequence, we have to fundraise constantly for this work and rely on our sponsors and donors and our own funds to keep these initiatives growing. We have also developed a community choir based in Ancoats to support the communities within the vicinity of our rehearsal facility – Hallé St Peter's – and our Corporate Choirs programme has achieved national acclaim and helps us deepen our engagement with the business community across the region. Alongside our choral work we deliver an education programme for around 70,000 people – mainly of school age – across the ten districts of Greater Manchester. Our education work is central to both our ethos as an organisation and our fundraising and continues to help blend private and public sector funding in a very productive and effective way.

In recent years we have also been able to focus our fundraising attention on our touring programme. The Hallé is one of the most prolific touring orchestras in the UK and we cover a huge geographic area including the whole of Cumbria and Yorkshire including Humberside, Greater Manchester, north-east England, East Midlands, Staffordshire, Derbyshire, the Trent Valley and Lincolnshire. We have successfully built our support base in all of these areas including a developing pool of private supporters in Sheffield, our 'second home'. Most notable is our work with children's charity SHINE and the hugely significant support we have received from the Monument Trust.

Arts and cultural organisations across the country will need to follow the Hallé's example by engaging more with their public if they are to prosper. This will require the active commitment and involvement of everyone, boards and trustees, dedicated fundraisers and the entire executive. People will not volunteer or give unless they feel they have a relationship with an institution, with those who lead and run it. This ought to be obvious. There is no mystery about raising money. We give to those we know, in whom we believe, to those we trust, and to what moves us.

In 2018, the Royal Academy of Arts (RA) will celebrate having survived 250 years without accepting a penny of public money, excluding the Lottery. The RA is entirely dependent upon philanthropy and the private sector. This achievement is all the more remarkable because one of the principal purposes of the RA is to provide education and training for aspiring artists. The RA's school of art is the oldest in the UK and has the additional distinction of being the only free institution of its kind in Britain.

How has the RA been so successful in maintaining its independence and financial viability? The answer is with some difficulty. When King George III founded the Royal Academy in 1768, he is reputed to have said: 'God save me from disputatious artists.' God has not always obliged. The Academy is an elected membership of artists and architects. Inevitably there have been tempestuous times as I witnessed between 1996 and 2005 as Director of the RA Trust.

The RA has succeeded because of its independence. Without public funding, we had to work hard to persuade people to lend works of art, to sponsor or to join the Friends. In our time, we doubled the Friends membership from 50,000 to more than 100,000.

To understand the significance of the RA as an independent organisation, I talked to Christopher Le Brun, a painter who is also President of the RA. We met in December 2015 in the final days of the Ai Weiwei exhibition. I had been struck by the paradox of the President of China riding down the Mall in a gold coach with the Queen that autumn whilst his country's most well-known dissident artist was exhibiting a model of the prison in which he was incarcerated for eighty-one days. I asked Christopher Le Brun why the RA matters, why it deserves the private funding upon which it depends, and the significance of the Ai Weiwei exhibition:

It is vital that there is somewhere artists can speak directly to the public without the sanction, approval or filter of an official establishment As a painter, when I speak as president of an organisation comprising artists and architects, it seems as if my voice carries a different resonance. Given our practical working insights and a lifetime's dedication as artists, we do have a public role. At the same time, for us, this is personal.

The RA in the mid-'90s somehow resembled a famous football team that had slipped out of the premier league. Anyone thinking seriously about its future could see its potential but the question was whether given some energy and belief it might re-emerge and flourish again. Almost twenty years on and with the membership transformed, we find ourselves in a far better position, culminating in the success and prominence of the current Ai Weiwei exhibition.

This came about because we invited a fellow artist, whose work we admired and who had come under sustained pressure, to enable his work to be seen. The effect has been extraordinary. It has certainly contributed to our growing sense of the Academy's potential.

For the Royal Academicians, art comes first and last. Our cause is that of art and architecture and those who support that aim by visiting and supporting us. Being entirely self-funded, our main source of income is from our patrons, Friends, sponsors and the many thousands who visit our exhibitions. Visitors to the Ai Weiwei exhibition totalled 372,000.

That exhibition was put together at very short notice – as an independent organisation we have a great deal of flexibility – in fact we went to Beijing where Ai Weiwei was effectively imprisoned in his studio, just eleven months before it opened. He greeted the idea with real enthusiasm, although we had no idea of whether he would be able to attend. We had elected him as an Honorary Royal Academician about five years previously.

So far, so good, but how were we going to pay for it? The really substantial sponsorship target was £500,000 and the potential risks to any business of compromising a relationship with China made it virtually impossible to find that in the corporate sector. However, the news of our plans was generating excitement, the message was so strong and the artist has such a genius for communication, that some were brave enough to come forward, including David Morris, the Bond Street jeweller, for their first sponsorship. Crowd funding via Kickstarter not only raised £120,000 very quickly but also generated thousands of new individual supporters.

Once Weiwei had understood our funding dilemma, he collaborated willingly to provide items for sale, including book jackets and porcelain flowers. This was the only way we were able to reach our target. Anselm Kiefer had responded to our need with equal generosity for his exhibition in 2014.

Both of these exhibitions by two of the greatest artists of our time would never have been seen by the public if we hadn't created the right environment and the close working relationships between the artists, the Academicians and our staff. I believe that they were moved by this artists' organisation and the risks we were taking on their behalf. At a private lunch we held for the Academicians to welcome him and his family, Ai Weiwei stood up and responded to my opening remarks with: 'Here you say what you think!'

In his case, we realised that we had to negotiate a news phenomenon with all its political implications via art and art alone. Our principal point was that despite his fame, very few had been able to see his work. Also, it is important to note two things: that for five years he had been unable to visit any of his exhibitions and that our exhibition was the first out of one hundred that he had actually seen in person. These facts highlight his situation vividly.

Artists are concerned with truth. Their values speak through their work. Ai Weiwei brings his eye and ear to reflect upon shocking events, and in remembering those who died in the Sichuan earthquake, he creates a form in which we can gather our thoughts. Ninety-seven tons of straightened metal rods, taken partly from schools destroyed in the earthquake damage, sit on the floor of our largest nineteenth century gallery accompanied by the names of 5,000 child victims.

There are fundamental human questions shared by us all that artists of every kind ask endlessly. Who will remember me? What have I achieved? This is a natural and inescapable anxiety. Artists who think about how their work and reputation may survive are not alone in dwelling on this. Everyone does.

My experience shows me that philanthropy and giving at every level is deeply personal and is a serious matter involving intuition, sympathy and empathy, good will and trust. Is this why artists and benefactors so often understand each other? Moreover, the best fundraisers understand the more profound questions and strongly feel the emotional context in which they work. I am not embarrassed to say that emotion is almost always the point of connection.

I returned to a former politician for a response diametrically opposed to those who would reach for their gun when contemplating culture. Lord Smith told me:

Art and society should be inextricably linked in liberal democracies as art is the ultimate expression of freedom. We must feed the hungry, give shelter to the homeless and care for the sick but if we fail to nourish the soul and stimulate the intellect, we are lost.

CHAPTER 10

HEALTH: A PUBLIC SERVICE IN CRISIS

"The key issue for me is the threat to academic medicine. The healthcare system is good at it because it is supported by a strong and excellent academic infrastructure. Academic medicine would be in a terrible state without philanthropic and charitable funding."

PROFESSOR LORD WINSTON.

*   *   *

How healthy is the National Health Service, with a budget of £116.4 billion in 2015–16 and employing 1.2 million people, the fifth-largest employer in the world? Given the scale of the NHS, surely philanthropy's contribution must be marginal?

The NHS seems to be in a state of perpetual crisis and although its budget is supposed to be ring fenced, the government is seeking savings of £22 billion as demand continues to grow.

In 2015 I spoke to the chairman of an NHS trust who wished to be anonymous:

The most important point about the NHS is how intensely political it is. Every single decision taken by the Secretary of State is political. The proposals for seven-day working were announced so that the Secretary of State could say that it was his government and his party that had introduced it. Now seven-day working may be a positive development but whether or not it is the right thing to do and can be introduced is not the point.

I agree with Sir Leonard Fenwick who has been a CEO of NHS hospitals for thirty-eight years when he said recently that the burdens of regulation, monitoring and measurement have become intolerable. This control from the centre makes it very difficult for boards to operate.

The whole principle of an independent board, bringing in external expertise, is not working. Much of the best advice given by our non-executives has to be ignored because of Whitehall control and rules. Ours is a political job and we are not really in control. But we are held responsible, our reputations can be shredded and we worry that we are going to have to answer to the media about the next Mid Staffs crisis. In practical terms, it is impossible to know what is going on in every ward twenty-four hours a day. We have to trust the systems and those who run them. The reputational risk is such that these non-executive jobs are not for people who worry too much about their reputation.

The real problem is not so much the governance structure but the model, the service that we are committed to delivering. It will be very difficult to continue with the current model that is free at the point of delivery and offers everything that is medically and scientifically possible. We are already witnessing controversial decisions about what drugs may be afforded by the NHS and problems around what amounts to a postcode lottery.

The fundamentals about health in the UK are so challenging it is doubtful that we will be able to continue the service as it has been for the last fifty years. If you think about the NHS that was established sixty-six years ago, it provided a service of last resort. If you were ill, you saw your family doctor who knew you and unless you had a broken leg, were seriously ill or needed an operation, you didn't go to hospital but stayed at home and took an aspirin.

Medicine and society have been transformed and this has transformed the NHS. There is increasing emphasis upon prevention and wellness as well as illness. Look at what is happening to life expectancy that has advanced by fifteen years except for the poorest. But when people get into their eighties, they start to present a number of conditions rather than one. They come into hospital and we keep them there. In 1948, a hospital would have been full of people of all ages with broken limbs, with life threatening or chronic illnesses or if they needed surgery. Now inpatients will be mainly elderly with a predominance of respiratory problems.

In order to continue providing a service, the NHS reduces cost by employing younger and cheaper people. This is done by regrading jobs and paying less. This has happened to someone you and I know who works in child and adolescent mental health. She is a highly qualified child psychologist who had to reapply for her job and was reappointed but at a lower grade and with a lower salary. Moreover, the NHS used to provide a one on one service to support damaged and vulnerable children over a period of time. Now, they see most children only once and work from a series of routine questions on a screen, which are used to establish whether a child is in danger. The young get nothing like the level of personal attention they used to, and the impact on the morale of highly qualified and motivated staff is considerable.

Is this really saving money? There is a crisis around child mental health.

The most challenging part of the service is primary care, the family doctor. GPs are now no more than gatekeepers. Where I live, we have big GP practices merging with new buildings, with X-ray and ultrasound machines etc. They can provide a much more comprehensive and effective service but what the public experiences is a postcode lottery. If you are unlucky, if you have an elderly doctor working above a shop, you may get a worse service.

The UK spends less per head on health than almost anywhere else in Europe. (According to OECD, the UK spent 8.5 per cent of GDP on public and private health care in 2013, placing the UK thirteenth out the original fifteen countries of the European Union.) There are lots of alternative models but the politics makes change almost impossible, except perhaps at the margins. Most of us pay for the dentist or for physiotherapy, chiropody and plastic surgery. We part-pay for prescription drugs. There is a debate going on about charging or at least informing patients how much their stay in hospital and their treatment has cost, or putting the cost of your drugs on your prescription, for information rather than as a charge. Government is considering this.

This leads on to the debate about what are sometimes called lifestyle illnesses and the cost of treating them; type-2 diabetes, for example. These are almost entirely caused by the choices we make, about what we eat and how we choose to live. Diabetes is very expensive to treat, £11.7 billion, more than 10 per cent of the entire NHS budget. As funding comes under even more pressure, people will be asking why they should pay for that smoker or obese person who sits in an armchair all day because they are depressed. This is very tricky morally.

There is a big crisis coming this year [2015/16]. The combined deficit is likely to be several billion [a record deficit of £2.45 billion was confirmed by NHS]. The government is trying to put a sticking plaster over a gaping wound. The bottom line is that we do not have enough money to maintain the standards the government demands and the public expects. Without politicians acknowledging that the NHS needs radically increased resources and are prepared to will the means, then the task is herculean and probably impossible.

No one knows where the money will come from. Costs of drugs and treatments will continue to rise. The cost of employing more agency doctors and nurses will rise because we do not have qualified people to fill vacant posts and increasing demands will require more doctors and nurses. And demand will increase inexorably as we live longer and there are more of us.

No one will admit that this is impossible without more money.

The four trusts in my part of the world are going to run out of money and there will not be enough money to pay people by the end of the year. No government can afford to have a notice on the door of hospitals saying they are closed because they cannot afford to pay the staff so that will not happen.

The NHS is bust.

*   *   *

Britain has another serious health problem that politicians would rather ignore and hope that we will not notice: health inequality.

Sir Michael Marmot is Professor of Epidemiology and Public Health at University College London and Director of the UCL Institute of Health Equity. In 2010, he chaired a Review of Health Inequalities in England and his book *The Health Gap: The Challenge of an Unequal World* was published in 2015.

Professor Marmot points out that if you catch the Jubilee line, for each stop east from Parliament, life expectancy drops by one year. Twenty years also separates the life expectancy of the richest from the poorest in Glasgow.

Here are some of the findings published in Marmot's review and his book:

- People living in the poorest neighbourhoods in England will on average die seven years earlier than those living in the richest neighbourhoods.
- People in poorer areas not only die sooner but spend more of their lives with disability, an average total difference of seventeen years.
- The average citizen can expect eight fewer years of healthy life than the richest.
- Health inequalities arise from a complex interaction of many factors: housing, income, education, social isolation and disability, all of which are affected by economic and social status.
- There would be 202,000 fewer premature deaths each year amongst those aged thirty and over if everyone in Britain had the low level of mortality of those with a university education, a difference of 500 deaths a day.
- Health inequalities are largely preventable and the annual cost to the nation is estimated to be up to £40 billion through lost tax, welfare payments and the direct cost to the NHS.

The problem is, of course, poverty. There are those who will say there is no poverty in 21st-century Britain, certainly not compared with that experienced in Africa and parts of Asia. Having lived and worked in Bangladesh, I have witnessed extreme poverty. But poverty is relative. There is poverty in our country. The facts published by Professor Marmot speak for themselves.

Marmot's findings have implications for all of us, not just the poorest. One of the difficulties of getting to grips with an issue of such fundamental importance is that it is not part of public discourse because neither politicians nor the mass media wish to draw our attention to the quality of life of some of our fellow citizens. If there is a concept of the common good, the poor are not part of it. The focus is on 'hard-working families who do the right thing' rather than those who apparently do the wrong thing and are therefore undeserving. And yet the allegedly feckless poor are costing us all a great deal of money.

Professor Marmot says the key to addressing health inequalities is to create the conditions for people to take control of their own lives and this will require action across the social determinants of health that are beyond the reach of the NHS and will need the involvement of national and local government, and the private and voluntary sectors. In other words, we need joined up thinking and action to support a concept of the common good that embraces the needs of all of us.

So what is philanthropy doing to address health inequality and to promote and protect the interests of the many?

As so often, the answer can be found in our history. In 1711, the South Sea Company was a joint-stock company, an early example of a public–private partnership, designed to reduce the national debt. One canny investor was a Mr Thomas Guy, who sold his shares before the company crashed spectacularly in 1720, as the South Sea Bubble burst. Thomas Guy became very rich and when he died in 1724, he bequeathed a third of his wealth for the creation of a new hospital for 'the incurably ill and hopelessly insane' and thus Guy's Hospital was built in London.

What has happened to Thomas Guy's legacy and how is it being spent? I talked to Peter Hewitt, chief executive of Guy's and St Thomas' Charity, shortly before his retirement:

> As a result of Thomas Guy's bequest and others, the charity now has an endowment of £600 million. The capital could be spent entirely on healthcare but the trustees have decided it should be protected in the interests of providing health support in perpetuity. We have a rule that in any five-year period, we must cover the cost of inflation and then disburse 4 per cent above inflation. That gives us about £100 million to spend on health over five years. In the last five years, we have focused on cancer, effecting lasting change and the local population.
>
> We sit alongside the Guy's and St Thomas' Foundation Trust and the other principal NHS providers and although we are entirely independent of all of them, we work very closely together. We see our role as a catalyst to try and engender a better way for our local partners to deliver healthcare. We support new ideas to tackle major health and care challenges in the London boroughs of Lambeth and Southwark. Partnership is important.
>
> One of our greatest successes has been a new £160 million Cancer Centre at Guy's Hospital that will bring together most of the cancer services and research at Guy's and St Thomas' NHS Trust under one roof. We have contributed with £26.7 million, including funding for a programme of performing and visual arts embedded in the building. There has also been a public fundraising appeal to raise £25 million.
>
> Southwark is amongst the 10 per cent most deprived local authority areas in the country. Many children in the borough face social problems. We have funded a Citizens UK project, Parents and Communities Together, that aims to improve the health and development of babies in Southwark by bringing together parents, carers, community and faith groups, education organisations, children's centres and maternity services in order to tackle social isolation and improve access to health centres.
>
> Regarding diabetes, we identified that the pathway through diagnosis and treatment is too often disjointed. We invested £4.5 million

into creating a unit that worked with all the various clinical and community partners in order to improve connectivity. We were able to combine preventative medicine and acute care. The Diabetes Modernisation Project has improved care and outcomes for people living with and at risk of developing diabetes in Southwark and Lambeth, through better detection, better control of blood sugar levels and provision of care in the right place. It is estimated that almost 10,000 people have benefitted in three years.

Lambeth and Southwark are two areas with the highest incidence of sexually transmitted diseases (STIs) in Europe. We have given a grant of just over £3 million to SH:24 online sexual health service, a partnership between Lambeth and Southwark Councils, sexual health clinics at both Guy's and St Thomas' and King's College Trusts, King's College London and the Design Council. This project has brought together public health experts, doctors and other healthcare professionals, designers and software developers.

SH:24 focuses on smart use of digital technology as a means of communicating with those who have concerns about their sexual health. There is a problem about stigma and persuading people to go to clinics. Someone who suspects that they are infected can go online, receive materials from a clinic, conduct their own test, send the test back, receive the results by text or email and the treatment is relayed digitally. People only have to go to a clinic if there are complications.

Our funding helped to establish SH:24, and the charity endorsed its set up as community interest company (CIC) as the best model to deliver its ambitious programme that aims to increase the total number of people tested for STIs in Lambeth and Southwark by 15 per cent at no cost to the NHS.

These are just four examples of what we are able to do. Our philanthropic funding is establishing best new practice. We have chosen to focus on Lambeth and Southwark because the gifts we have received over the centuries came from there via Guy's and St Thomas'. We can make a real impact upon a population of 600,000. Our work can be and is being replicated elsewhere.

We have also supported work around end of life care, and came up with a set of proposals that became the Amber Care Bundle. This is a simple approach used in hospitals when clinicians are uncertain whether a patient may recover and are concerned that they may have only a few months left to live. It encourages staff, patients and families to continue with treatment in the hope of a recovery, while talking openly about people's wishes and putting plans in place should the worst happen. The Amber Care Bundle approach has been adopted in the UK and overseas and is widely used.

We supported a project in Lambeth and Southwark that addressed the deficiencies in stroke services locally that then contributed to a national review which has transformed stroke services throughout the country. This has led to the establishment of fewer more specialised stroke units that patients are taken to for immediate treatment after the stroke has occurred. This has dramatically improved outcomes for stroke victims.

Who is responsible for sustainable change in health? There are up to 250 NHS charities. Some are connected to hospitals and some are completely independent like us. A lot of the NHS charities are fundraising for their local hospitals. What we are doing is above and beyond that. I believe that charities of our kind are catalysts for change and improvement. We have a critical role to play, given all the pressures on the NHS.

We have been around for hundreds of years and we will be here in perpetuity. We have a record of helping to pioneer improved healthcare. We are very privileged because of our endowment. It is interesting that funds donated hundreds of years ago are enabling advances in medicine today.

The charitable and voluntary sector will become increasingly involved in alternative forms of health provision. We need to work out how the charitable sector can help to create sustainable change that others can take on. We need to create new charitable entities that are about stimulating change rather than simply providing better services. Many organisations, charities, and parts of the NHS support useful initiatives but these often have only a short-term impact.

We like to invest in projects with the potential for initiating deep-seated, long-term change. The role of catalyst for change needs to be more manifest, and philanthropy could enable that to happen. We need more of this.

*   *   *

I hope that those who are new to charitable endeavour are beginning to understand the significance and centrality of the voluntary sector despite its relatively small size compared with the public and private sectors. Charitable giving, whether large or small, when well directed can bring about progressive change that can be of immeasurable benefit to millions. Philanthropy and social investment can create social value and make an impact far beyond the amounts of money involved. That is certainly the case regarding the work of my next interviewee.

The Rt Hon. the Lord Winston is a professor, medical doctor, scientist, television presenter and politician. Robert Winston is best known by the public as the presenter of several BBC TV series, mostly about medicine and science, many of them focused on children. We talked in November 2015 in his office at Imperial College, London, where he is Professor of Science and Society and Emeritus Professor of Fertility Studies. I asked Professor Winston about the Institute of Reproductive and Developmental Biology at Hammersmith:

The IRDB is part of Imperial College's Faculty of Medicine at Hammersmith Hospital. The idea was to get scientists and clinicians to collaborate in order to conduct international research. There was no institute like it in Europe in our field of medicine when we opened in 2001. So the establishment of IRDB was transformational.

I decided to approach people I knew who had been touched by women's reproductive problems, ranging from cancer to miscarriage. But the two key donors were the Wolfson Foundation and the late Garry Weston and the Weston Foundation who were extraordinarily generous [see Chapter 13]. I didn't know Garry well but he agreed to see me, and the whole family was there. They left us for about fifteen minutes and came back with a cheque for £2.5 million, including an extra half million for a new scanner in the neo-natal unit.

We started our appeal for £15 million with £5 million in hand. I then put in a quarter of a million which was my entire private income from private practice. A colleague did exactly the same. I had used my income from private practice to fund research before. This is quite common. Some of my colleagues refuse to see private patients and I am very querulous about it. I think private practice can kill academic medicine. I was besieged by huge numbers of patients from overseas and I am deeply grateful to them as their fees were hugely valuable for our research.

Putting in half a million of our own money did impress the donors and helped to raise the capital we needed. This was a very private campaign and we did not rattle tins. The Wellcome Foundation gave just over £3 million and there were a number of personal donations of a million or slightly less. We raised £15 million for the building before it was established, and around £80 million has been raised since for the Genesis Research Trust which we set up.

The IRDB is not a monument to anyone. It is a working building. The Institute has led on ovarian cancer, made important contributions to stem cell biology, many of the improvements in in vitro fertilisation, with which I am associated, happened in IRDB. We have more understanding about miscarriage, and we have massively changed the epidemiology of brain damage in children, so we have new techniques we can use in Third World countries. The work we have done in ovarian epidemiology is probably as good as anywhere.

We have trained a large number of people who are now working all over the world. We give medical students the opportunity to do a research project during their medical degree so that they can also do a Masters as well as their MBBS. The IRDB is also a haven for ideas. There is room for 120 scientists on five floors of laboratories.

None of this could have happened without philanthropy. There was no prospect of getting funding from government or Imperial College. There was considerable doubt amongst my colleagues whether we could raise the money.

The NHS is in a disastrous state because it is massively under-funded. At least 70 per cent of trusts have huge deficits. The Health Service is currently led by a Secretary of State, Jeremy Hunt, who does not understand it. The confrontation with junior doctors is madness. Both sides will lose out. The 2012 Health and Social Care Act was a disaster and I don't see a way out.

The key issue for me is the threat to academic medicine. This is profoundly important because the health service is as good as it is because it is supported by a strong and excellent academic structure. The quality of academic research in the UK is second to none.

Academic medicine would be in a terrible state without philan-thropic and charitable funding. About £600 million is contributed by the Wellcome Foundation, with £400 million from Cancer Research, £300 million from the British Heart Foundation and many other smaller trusts and foundations are contributing towards a total of up to £3 billion of charitable funds each year, the majority of which is for research. Much of this money is coming from the general public and their legacies make a significant contribution.

The Research Councils, funded by government with about £2 billion, support science research in the UK.

How do we create a climate where people give instinctively? Only by example. Maybe we don't do enough in schools. We don't teach ethics and we should. We do live in a very selfish society.

We call ourselves a generous nation. Are we? The way we subscribe to Comic Relief and initiatives such as Band Aid is admirable. How-ever, I thought it was very interesting when Ebola hit west Africa that our anxiety was almost all about our vulnerability and the possibility of our catching it. The entire media conversation was about the risk to us. I don't believe our concern was primarily about the devastating effect the disease was having upon people in west Africa.

*   *   *

My next investigation was of a research project designed to alleviate everyone's secret fear, dementia. The fulfilment of this project depends upon an imaginative and creative collaboration between a charitable foundation, a university and a hospital.

My first call was upon Lori Houlihan, Vice-Provost (Development) at University College London (UCL):

I joined UCL in 2011 around the time that the Wolfson Foundation wanted to make a memorial gift for Leonard Wolfson amounting to £20 million. We had to bid for funds.

Professor Nick Fox was put in charge of the academic process which was complicated because we had to bring together a lot of people with very different ideas. We did not have anything fully formed on the shelf but we knew we should be focusing on our strengths, namely transformational medicine. We had to consult our hospital partners: University College London Hospital (UCLH, including the National Hospital for Neurology and Neurosurgery at Queen Square), Great Ormond Street, the Royal Free and Moorfields.

Our partnership of hospitals has access to more than six million people, or around one in every ten NHS patients in the UK, and they are the national referral hospitals for their major conditions, meaning we get patients from all over the country sent to our hospitals and our UCL research institutes. That was a natural focus for our bid and we were successful. We are creating a new institute for dementia research by developing the facilities at Queen Square.

The original Wolfson Foundation gift was for the Leonard Wolfson Experimental Neurology Centre. At the time of writing, we are conducting more than fifty clinical trials and half of these are with commercial partners. This has given us the confidence to go on to build a new Dementia Institute.

The £20 million from the Wolfson Foundation is a huge amount of money but very small in the context of overall spending on health and research. However, the Wolfson gift has created something for which we would not have been able to find funding from anywhere else. Government and the Research Councils tend to give to silos.

Philanthropic gifts tend to be much more focused and when they meet a real need, they can leverage much more money.

Nick Fox is Director of the Dementia Research Centre and Professor of Clinical Neurology at the Institute of Neurology, UCL. I asked him about the significance of the Wolfson award:

There are only a few things that transform and permeate society, that enter our daily discourse and our behaviour, and are reflected in art and literature. The internal combustion engine, mobile phones, IT and the internet, the industrial revolution – these are some. Some illnesses change how we think and behave, such as the plague and HIV.

Dementia is now doing that and is about to have a major impact on society. It is amongst the most feared illnesses. In this respect, it has overtaken cancer. We are getting better at treating cancer and it does not always need to be a death sentence. Charitable giving has helped that progress. Dementia is a disease that reflects the fact that we are getting older.

Dementia comes with many years of loss of independence. One third of us can expect to spend the last part of our lives with impaired cognitive faculties or dementia. One in two of us will care for a close friend or relative. About half the people attending casualty any night will have some element of cognitive impairment.

The cost of dementia in the UK is estimated to be £26 billion a year, more than the combined cost of cancer and heart disease. There are already 750,000 people with dementia in the UK. This is the only major illness where mortality is increasing rather than decreasing. For every £10 that dementia costs the economy, we are only spending 6p on research. We should make fighting dementia related illnesses a priority now for the sake of future generations. We don't want to condemn large numbers of our descendants to spending the last years of their lives mute and bedbound.

Dementia will change social attitudes, our view of end of life care and our view of the nuclear and extended family.

The Wolfson award has been transformational. At that point, dementia research was undergoing a paradigm shift from treating people after a clinical diagnosis, usually some years after they had shown the first symptoms, and the recognition that there can be a long pre-symptomatic period which can now be picked up by new scanning techniques and new biomarkers. These diseases can be growing in our brains for a decade or two before a clinical diagnosis. This is the area we need to study.

My colleagues and I decided that we should try to understand more about the pre-symptomatic phase of dementia so that people could be treated sooner and to make it easier for academics and clinicians to play their part in finding new therapies. This meant we would need a physical centre that would minimise risk for patients and clinicians.

Too often the different degenerative diseases, whether they be Alzheimer's or Parkinson's, had been researched in silos. The new centre would not only offer economies of scale but also lead to cross-fertilisation of ideas, learning and experience.

We now have an amazing spinal fluid research lab. We have been able to generate new biomarkers and we are supplying these around the world. Ours is now the leading centre in the UK. The clinical facility has enabled us to run trials in pre-symptomatic genetic Alzheimer's disease, to run the first trials on fluid close to the brain for Huntingdon's disease, and the first pre-symptomatic trials of gene therapy in familial Alzheimer's.

The most important thing we have been able to do is to undertake treatment trials. We are now treating people. We have cohorts of patients and we are harnessing clinical expertise. These studies are now happening in a facility that makes that possible. We are fully resourced, able to operate in the most comprehensive way possible and we are right next to intensive care should we need it. We are in the right place to be working on potentially dangerous therapies.

Our aim is to find a cure or a moderating therapy that slows the onset of the disease. If we were able to delay the onset of Alzheimer's for five years, that would halve its prevalence.

None of this would be possible without the grant from Wolfson Foundation, which has attracted other funding. There has been £8.5 million leveraging funding from the Medical Research Council, from the Wellcome Trust, from another foundation and from industry.

The Wolfson Foundation has also generated, indirectly, an extraordinary new source of philanthropy and charitable giving. Through a personal connection, I saw someone in my cognitive clinic. He wanted to see me privately but I don't have private patients. I saw him on the NHS. He said the diagnosis would hit the family and under the circumstances he wanted to give something back. He asked what I needed most and I told him that early onset dementia was being neglected. He said he would raise a million for us.

My patient was Malcolm Walker, chief executive of Iceland Foods. He said there was to be a levy on plastic shopping bags and businesses had to decide which good causes should benefit. Malcolm persuaded Asda, WHSmith, Morrison's and others to donate four pence from the levy on each plastic bag they sell. We hope to receive millions to enable even more research.

The NHS is under acute pressure and the inevitable consequence is that the main emphasis of the service will be to provide urgently needed care. There is a really important role for philanthropy to support trials and research programmes. This kind of work is often preventative and particularly valuable because it can leverage more funding.

You could say that the roof is leaking and we are spending all our time and money on mopping up when we should be mending the roof. Medicine has taught us that the things that were thought to be incurable, such as certain cancers and HIV, if you direct resources there, you can make a difference.

It seems to me that there has been a shift in assets from the young to the old. The older generation represents the greatest challenge to health, social and care services, because of the cost of dementia. The next generation will have to pay for this. Surely, there is an obligation for older people to contribute more?

*   *   *

Professor Fox's plea for older generations to be more generous chimes with the work done by David Willetts to demonstrate that intergenerational inequality is real and much to the disadvantage of the young. If those of my generation cannot afford to contribute more whilst we are alive, then we must give when we die. Legacies are a particularly attractive option for those liable for inheritance tax as this is payable at 36 per cent rather than 40 per cent if 10 per cent of the value of the estate is left to a registered charity.

One disadvantage of writing about £20 million gifts is that this re-inforces a view that philanthropy and charitable giving is for the rich and not for the rest of us. That is not so. Many of us can leave a legacy.

Although the use of plastic bags is in decline, they will still be needed. The Wolfson fortune came from retail via Great Universal Stores and I know that Leonard Wolfson, wherever he may be, will be delighted that the many will be giving millions when they spend five pence on a plastic bag.

CHAPTER 11

WHO SHOULD PAY FOR DOING GOOD?

"'What was your greatest disappointment in government?' Back shot Mrs Thatcher: 'I cut taxes because I thought we would get a giving society, and we haven't.'"
THE RT HON. FRANK FIELD MP, LECTURE GIVEN TO THE CHARITY COMMISSION, 2015.

"We really want to try and keep charities out of the realm of politics ... the important thing that charities should be doing is sticking to their knitting and doing the best they can to promote their agenda, which should be about helping others."
BROOKS NEWMARK MP,
MINISTER FOR CIVIL SOCIETY, 2014.

* * *

Brooks Newmark's remarks demonstrated breathtaking ignorance about the role of charity before he vanished from government after exposing himself on social media.

I trust he is haunted by the ghost of Joseph Rowntree, wealth creator, philanthropist and campaigner. The Rowntree family became rich by making chocolate. They were campaigners for a better world. Their legacy became clear when they established a number of trusts and foundations in 1904, to inspire social change, to correct imbalances of power and to address the root causes of conflict and injustice.

Joseph Rowntree understood that campaigning and lobbying are what independent charities and foundations are supposed to do.

Margaret Thatcher was no less provocative but whereas Newmark was wrong, Thatcher was right. She was pointing her finger at the new super rich in particular, those who benefited the most from lower taxation and the majority of whom are not philanthropic. Margaret Thatcher was a radical and expected the rich to change and behave like our philanthropic American cousins. With some notable exceptions, they have not.

Both Newmark's and Thatcher's remarks raise questions about the meaning and role of charity in the twenty-first century.

According to the Charities Aid Foundation (CAF), charitable giving has not grown in real terms or as a percentage of GDP despite a colossal increase in personal wealth in Britain. CAF estimates that the total donated to charity by adults in 2013–14 was £10.6 billion, a figure which has remained more or less static for decades. However, adjusted for inflation, the total was £13.2 billion in 2005, suggesting that personal giving may have declined in real terms. (The National Council for Voluntary Organisations reports that charitable giving may be increasing but we need more evidence over time to be sure.)

Creating an Age of Giving, conclusions from a Growing Giving Parliamentary Inquiry, was published by CAF in 2014. The information below comes from that report and from CAF's *UK Giving 2014* report, published in 2015:

- There has been a long-term decline in the proportion of households contributing to charity. The participation rate fell from 32 per cent in 1978 to 27 per cent in 2010.
- Charities increasingly obtain their support from a 'civic core' – the 9 per cent of the population responsible for two-thirds of all charitable activity.
- 44 per cent of people give to a charity in a typical month.

- 14 per cent volunteered for a charity in the twelve months prior to interview.
- The share of donations received from the under thirties has fallen from 8 per cent in 1980 to 3 per cent in 2010.
- The total of typical donations made monthly in 2014 was £14 and has not changed much over ten years.

Meanwhile, personal wealth has increased as follows:

- According to an Office for National Statistics (ONS) report from 2010, household *net* worth more than doubled in real terms between 1987 and 2009 from £56,000 to £117,000 per household at 2008/09 prices.
- Measuring aggregate *total* wealth, ONS reported an increase from £9.5 trillion in 2010–12 to £11 trillion in 2013–14.
- Median household aggregate total wealth increased from £216,500 to £225,100 in the same period, an increase of 4 per cent.
- The wealthiest 10 per cent of households owned 45 per cent of total aggregate wealth in 2014, an increase of 21 per cent since 2010–12.

Very little of the increase in wealth reported by ONS appears to have been given to the voluntary sector via charitable giving.

The *Sunday Times* Rich List should be treated with caution and at best regarded as an indication of the wealth of the 1,000 richest people who live or are at least based in the UK to some extent. The figures are based on personal assessment or upon information that is public, which is almost certainly incomplete. However, the findings of the 2016 report suggest that the collective wealth of the one thousand wealthiest people in the UK (whose wealth is worth £100 million or more) has doubled in ten years. Their combined wealth is estimated to be £547 billion. In the 1980s, there were estimated to be five billionaires living or based in the UK compared with 120 billionaires in 2015. The collective wealth of today's billionaires is estimated to be £344 billion.

Estimates of the philanthropy of those who feature in the *Sunday Times* Rich List should also be treated with caution as some include pledges that are legacies. These pledges may or may not be fulfilled.

What should we deduce from these statistics?

The colossal increase in wealth amongst the very richest confirms that asset inequality in the UK continues to grow. There are no precise figures for how many of the wealthy give and how much, but a 2013 survey by New Philanthropy Capital of donors earning £150,000 or more, 44 per cent said those earning enough to pay the top rate of income tax should not feel obliged to give to charitable causes.

It is true that some billionaires are exceptionally generous, giving donations of up to £75 million or more. Not all these donations are in the public domain. However, there is a consensus amongst those who give and the charitable causes they support that a majority of the most wealthy is not philanthropic.

Excluding the top 1 per cent, there are some mitigating circumstances for a lack of growth in charitable giving. Britain has suffered a recession and economic decline that was the most severe for generations. The young were the most badly affected. We have to pay more for housing, for higher education and for care for the elderly. This is likely to be acting as a brake on charitable giving and is just one reason why politicians should not expect giving to compensate for lower public spending or less provision by the state.

There are, however, glimmers of good news. The Coutts annual survey of million-pound gifts reported 298 gifts of a million pounds or more in 2014 compared with 189 in 2007/8. UK Community Foundations (see Chapter 18) are also reporting more gifts to their growing endowments.

On the basis of the information that charitable giving is stagnating, there is nothing to encourage us to believe that the voluntary sector can take on more on its own. The sector is much smaller than the public and private sectors.

According to National Council for Voluntary Organisation's (NCVO) Almanac for 2016, there are 162,000 registered charities with a combined turnover of £43.8 billion. Almost half have a turnover of less than £10,000 and the turnover of 83 per cent of these charities was less than £100,000.

- Donations from individuals represent 44 per cent of the income of charities.
- State grants and contracts provide 33 per cent of the sector's income from government, which fell from £15.2 billion to £13.3 billion between 2009 and 2013.
- Government funding has moved from grants to contracts. Grant funding is one third less than ten years ago.
- 78 per cent of charities operate locally, 13 per cent nationally.

There have been laudable initiatives to encourage more giving, amongst them The Giving Campaign of 2001–2004, the Philanthropy Review of 2011 and the Give More campaign of 2012–14. Through no fault of those who led these campaigns, giving has not increased. Why?

Putting recession to one side, it seems that not enough people were listening, partly because our culture of giving has been diminished, a lack of political and moral leadership, insufficient leadership by example and peer group pressure, an indifferent and sometimes hostile media that denigrates the poor and sniffs at the rich, and a failure of the voluntary sector as a whole to make a case for support that resonates with the very rich as well as society at large.

I hesitate to criticise the voluntary sector in such terms because some charities have been outstandingly successful in capturing the imagination of the public. The sector, however, does have its problems and these have been well aired in the media. These reports must undermine public confidence in charities. According to a YouGov survey in 2016, only 38 per cent feel charities are trustworthy, compared with 54 per cent in 2013.

These problems are matters of public interest. The failure of governance at Kids Company dominated headlines. Kids Company received £46 million of public money with little if any oversight or evaluation. There is a public interest in good governance because taxpayers are contributing billions annually through gift aid and other tax incentives totalling £3.4 billion in 2013/14 according to HM Revenue and Customs. In addition, the state paid charities £15 billion for the provision of public services in 2013/14 (81 per cent of which was for contracts and fees) according to NCVO.

Some charities appear to have lost the plot. Their aggressive marketing has caused a backlash and the sector has been forced to change how it relates to the public. Meanwhile, 'chugging' continues. Charities employ young people and put them on the street to harass the public into making instant charitable commitments. Thus, most sales resulting from this questionable practice are merely transactions and are less likely to be renewed.

In 2016, the media reported that Age UK's commercial operation was in direct contradiction of its mission when it made money from the people it was supposed to be supporting. Apparently, Age UK was selling energy plans on behalf of Eon, the energy supplier, for which the charity received £6.3 million. Age UK came under fire for selling an Eon two-year fixed tariff that was pro-rata more expensive than a one-year fixed tariff. It was subsequently reported that Age UK had made tens of millions in recent years by selling funeral plans to older people.

Age UK is at least transparent in separating Age UK Enterprises from the main charity. There is less transparency amongst some charities that accept national or local government contracts to deliver services. Only the larger charities are in a position to compete for multi-million pound contracts and in order to secure them, charities under-bid and fail to receive compensation that accords with the real cost of delivering a public service. In these circumstances, charities will fundraise, smudging the lines between what is public and what is private and putting donors into a situation where they are, unknowingly, subsidising public expenditure.

This confusion goes to the heart of a contemporary problem: who is responsible for the common good, who should be responsible for doing good, how should it be paid for and by whom?

One way to solve this dilemma is more transparency. Charities taking on the delivery of public services should either form a distinct body that trades as a social enterprise (in which profits are reinvested or transferred to the parent charity) or become a business. That was the decision taken by Lord Adebowale when he became chief executive of Turning Point, a national health and care provider supporting those with problems around substance abuse, mental health, learning disabilities, the criminal justice system and employment. Turning Point was founded as a charity in 1964 and whilst it has retained its charitable status it now operates as a social enterprise. I asked Victor Adebowale why:

> When I got to Turning Point, I found that for every pound we raised, we were spending about one pound and two pence. Most of our service agreements were with local authorities. They would offer a grant of £50,000 towards something that would cost £200,000 and they would expect us to fundraise for the remainder. Meanwhile, private sector companies that are doing exactly the same would be fully funded and entitled to make a 15 per cent return on their investment. They have a right to earn a profit from being funded by the taxpayer.
>
> That is wrong. Turning Point runs a substance misuse service. We run a needle exchange programme in Westminster. If we closed it on Monday, you would notice the difference by Wednesday afternoon. Should that be funded by money put in a tin? I don't think so. This is a public service and should be publicly funded. If you have a life or death issue, you don't go to a charity. We are effectively a business that is providing a public service.
>
> Our turnover is £130 million. We have up to 80,000 clients and a further 30,000 use our phone services.
>
> We transferred Turning Point into a social enterprise when I arrived in 2001. We had a lot of external flak and there was anger internally. The policy was regarded as a betrayal and much of the criticism came from the left. All I had done was say that from now on Turning Point would get full cost recovery and we are not going to bid for things that do not cover their cost.

I know of charities that raise hundreds of millions and have massive reserves and they go out there and subsidise their contracts in order to win business. If you are giving money to a charity, you need to know what your money is going to.

Being a social enterprise has not affected our ability to campaign and to lobby. People thought we would go bust being reliant on public contracts. This has not happened. If the public sector cuts when you have a contract, you have an argument. If you have a grant, you cannot and you don't.

Charities that are competing for local authority government contracts should either form a business or a social enterprise but most of them won't and that is dishonest.

By bidding for public contracts, charities run the risk of losing the independence that is supposed to be the hallmark of the voluntary sector. The Baring Foundation, a long established and highly respected grant-making charity, works to improve the quality of life of people experiencing disadvantage and discrimination. The Foundation is also committed to strengthening the voluntary sector and ensuring its independence. It initiated and funded a report, *An Independent Mission: The Voluntary Sector*, in 2015.

In the foreword of the report, Sir Roger Singleton, Chair of the Panel on the Independence of the Voluntary Sector, wrote:

This last report by the panel says that unless we act now, the future of an independent voluntary sector is at risk.

There is so much lost when independence is threatened. Our country needs a thriving and independent voluntary sector – speaking up on behalf of often vulnerable and relatively powerless groups, helping to design better public services, and providing trusted support for countless communities and individuals across the country.

Charities' knowledge of what happens on the ground can help governments meet needs more effectively. Yet the Trussell Trust, which runs hundreds of food banks across the country, told us how they were threatened with closure when they raised issues with government that could have led to fewer people going hungry. Women's Aid informed us that 'gagging clauses' in contracts for public services, self-censorship because of fear of loss of vital public funding and active threats by some local authorities to those that do speak out are having a damaging effect on the services victims of domestic abuse receive. Gagging clauses are being used more widely, the new Lobbying Act has had a silencing effect on many charities and further restrictions have been placed on the ability of NGOs (Non-Governmental Organisations) to support individuals challenging government decisions in court. The proportion of government consultations that are cut short has also doubled.

The causes and effects of this are of deep concern. Under successive governments, the voluntary sector has increasingly been seen as a contractual arm of the state, without an independent mission or voice, interchangeable with the private sector. We are also starting to see a defensive attitude towards the campaigning voice of charities from some politicians, perhaps because more people are turning towards the voluntary sector to express their views, as engagement with traditional politics declines.

This won't be reversed without strong and inclusive leadership from the voluntary sector that stands up for its independence and communicates why it is important. Just as vital, the Government must work with the sector to establish a 'new settlement'. It is very welcome that the Baring Foundation is now fundraising to establish a Commission on the future of the voluntary sector. There are many fundamental issues for it to consider, including a new model for working with the public sector.

I believe that much of the problem in the relationship between the public and voluntary sector, and with politicians in particular, is due to a lack of understanding about charities and unrealistic expectations about what they can do.

Given an expectation that the sector will do more if the state does less, an examination of the role of charities and of their potential is required. This is to be found in an illuminating book called *The*

Logic of Charity: Great Expectations in Hard Times by John Mohan and Beth Breeze (Palgrave Pivot, 2015). Professor John Mohan is Director, Third Sector Research Centre, University of Birmingham, UK, and Dr Beth Breeze, Director, Centre for Philanthropy, University of Kent, UK.

Mohan and Breeze are keen to counter expectations that charities can and should do what politicians wish. They say that there is a 'logic of charity' that is at odds with the perspective of politicians on both the left and the right. The authors question whether expectations that the voluntary sector can plug gaps left by a retreating state are realistic:

> We contend that the nature of the logic that guides charity action – especially that related to donor decision making and the consequent distribution of charitable resources – is not well understood, acknowledged or taken into account by politicians who seek to encourage charity, and to harness it in support of their political programmes.

Mohan and Breeze point out that whilst some may assume that the purpose of charity is to alleviate deprivation and support the disadvantaged, there is no legal requirement for this and only a minority of charities are relieving poverty. Those charities that are committed to mental health, social and community development and related causes receive less than 1 per cent of funds donated by individuals whereas those causes that attract the most from private donors are medical research, emergency relief and animal welfare.

What of those causes that attract very little philanthropic funding? Mental health, economic, social and community development, employment and training, and law and legal services are all fields of activity that receive less than 1 per cent of funds donated by individuals. A majority of charities in the mental health, social services, law and legal services, employment and training are receiving at least 70 per cent of their income from government or the public sector.

Only 9 per cent of neighbourhood charities are committed to

health and well-being and a further 9 per cent regard community development as their primary purpose.

This calls into question the capacity as well as the ability of the voluntary sector to fulfil expectations that it may replace or supplement publicly funded programmes in deprived communities, not least because of the distribution of charities. Mohan and Breeze point out that:

> Evidence shows that neighbourhood charities are concentrated in the most prosperous parts of the country where they are much more likely to be entirely voluntary in character and to regard voluntary sources of income as being of greatest importance to them. In contrast we find that poorer areas have a lower proportion of neighbourhood charities per head of population and are located in such areas that are more likely to be reliant on statutory income.

Mohan and Breeze remind us that giving a donation is a private decision and a voluntary act. Inevitably, this and an unequal distribution of wealth leads to areas of 'philanthropic insufficiency' and the unequal distribution of charitable resources. There have been government initiatives to redress imbalances in funding and resources, including matched funding opportunities designed to encourage donors to support local causes and projects via their local community foundations. Whilst matched funding programmes have been successful, funds raised have yet to match need:

> Finding private donors to match government funding is likely to prove more difficult in areas of disadvantage. Thus far, the resources generated by community foundations are typically £4 to £5 per head of population, contrasting with the c.£250 per head that will be withdrawn from some communities in anticipated public funding cuts. While these foundations are certainly focused on community needs, this indicates the scale of the challenge ahead.

Mohan and Breeze conclude:

For the most part, private giving occurs without any reference to a government agenda. Supporters of charity will take heart from the historian Frank Prochaska (2014) who pointed to the continuing reliance on charities with the resonant phrase 'we are always with the poor'. Maybe we can rephrase this in the light of the present reality. Charity is always with us, but not always in the places and causes where it is most needed. The logic of charity cannot result in a proportionate matching of needs and resources, regardless of the hopes of politicians. And that situation is not likely to change, given the inherently individualistic nature of the processes whereby individuals give financial support to charities.

I agree with Mohan and Breeze but, whilst they are correct to point out that the logic of charity mitigates against donors being persuaded to support public policy, we should remember that the great philanthropists of the nineteenth century, such as George Peabody, pioneered new policies that were subsequently deemed to be in the public interest. In addition to providing homes for the poor, Peabody's aim was to encourage new thinking about housing. Is it possible that the philanthropists and social entrepreneurs of today could formulate policy and establish good practice that could be adopted by the public sector or delivered in partnership with it?

The Centre for Social Justice (CSJ) was established by Iain Duncan Smith, former leader of the Conservative Party and a former Secretary of State for Work and Pensions, in 2004. The CSJ describes itself as an independent think tank campaigning for social justice. I met Baroness (Philippa) Stroud, CSJ's former Director, in December 2015:

The CSJ was set up to put social justice at the heart of British politics. We want to identify Britain's major social challenges, identify what are driving those at a profound level and to find solutions. We are convinced that someone, somewhere, is solving these problems and we can find the solutions in embryonic form. We are most likely to find them in the charities which are working 'at the coal face', then we can bring the best of what we find on the front line into Westminster. We want government to take that thinking, pilot it and replicate it if it can be shown to be effective.

I pushed Philippa Stroud on the question of political independence and she gave me a robust reply:

We reach out to anybody who wants to address these issues and who has something to contribute and these can be people in any political party. We have been supporting David Lammy (Labour MP, Tottenham) this week. He has launched an all-party parliamentary group on fatherhood. We have also worked with Labour politicians such as David Blunkett, Frank Field, and others. We have also worked with other think tanks such as IFS and Policy in Practice.

In the recent spending review [November 2015], I publicly called for the abolition of cuts to tax credits despite being a Conservative special advisor until two months ago and as a Conservative member of the House of Lords.

I don't mind who I work with if we share a mission to address poverty and to find effective solutions. At the moment, there is political controversy about how you define poverty and how you measure it. I am trying to build a left/right coalition of significant people and organisations who will come together and form a commission that will recommend what appropriate action should be taken.

We moved on to discuss the future of the voluntary sector:

I think there is something transformational happening. Charities that are surviving are becoming much more business-minded and outcome-focused. They are asking themselves how they can become sustainable. Resco, a social impact business aiming to break the cycle of long-term unemployment, works with a café in Hammersmith called Kettle+Crust that provides work experience for those wanting to develop a career in the catering and hospitality industry. Ten years ago, Resco would have been a charity raising money to support mentoring for offenders; it has now created a business model that provides jobs for offenders.

How helpful is it for charities to secure three years' funding that then comes to an end? Those kinds of grants will always be needed and are useful but in the interests of long-term sustainability, charities should be looking for alternative forms of funding.

I questioned the lack of transparency in some cases where charities, usually the larger ones, are delivering public services without donors realising that they are subsidising public expenditure.

Philanthropic giving should always represent the added value to a project. Charities are inclined to go the extra mile to ensure the most positive outcome and if there was more transparency by charities about what they are doing and what they need in terms of delivering services, this could be attractive to donors if presented in a way that asks them to be active partners with the charity and the local authority and that their donation can be seen to be adding value.

Something that would help is the mapping of need. We have noted 'charity deserts' and 'cold spots'. The challenge is to align charities with need. CSJ has an alliance of poverty fighters so if someone comes to us to ask us to recommend the top ten charities working in a particular field, we can recommend them.

There is a cultural problem in that we are unlike the US where there is a social obligation to give. Also, we seem to have no framework for regular giving, certainly not in terms of tithing. The young may be different; look at this emerging generation which seems to have a social conscience. We are throwing away an opportunity if employers are not encouraging or challenging their new young employees to act on their social conscience and to be philanthropic when they receive their first pay cheque.

CSJ charts five pathways to poverty: family breakdown, economic dependency and worklessness, educational failure, drug and alcohol addiction and serious personal debt.

I would add the difficulty in finding somewhere to live and expressed surprise that this was missing:

> Peabody and Cadbury were big investors in social housing. We are doing a piece of work at the moment on business and charities. Both are changing. Parts of business are becoming more socially aware and charitable and some charities are becoming more business-orientated.
>
> It was in Cadbury's interest to build Bournville. Is business waking up to this dynamic? Take a businessman contemplating a million-pound donation. My point would be that they might consider a million pound loss by setting up a business in a community that is desperate for employment. That might be more worthwhile than giving a million to charity. My message to business people is to keep their business hat on when they are thinking about charity and philanthropy. They should think more in terms of social investment.

CSJ has commissioned a number of reports investigating various aspects of social injustice in different parts of the UK, including *Turning the Tide: Social Injustice in Five Seaside Towns.* (See my observations on Blackpool in Chapter 16.) These reports are compiled by working groups representing the voluntary sector and those with specialist knowledge.

John Mohan and Beth Breeze challenged CSJ's 'charity desert' concept in *The Logic of Charity* and in an article in *New Statesman,* January 2016:

> Our research highlights the uneven distribution of charitable resources across both geography and causes – though with more complex origins and drivers than advanced in the 'charity desert' thesis beloved of the Centre for Social Justice. A reliance on charity to fill gaps left by public spending cuts would likely result in the aggravation of disadvantage in communities of both place and purpose. The supply of

charity is not a matter of simply switching a tap on and off as the state advances or retreats. Indeed, in some places and for some less popular needs, the tank is already dry – not because (as CSJ would argue) of a lack of voluntary effort in poorer communities, where informal and mutual aid has always been plentiful, but because the knowledge, time and resources required to run registered charitable organisations are in short supply.

In 2015, CSJ published its report *Social Solutions: Enabling Grass-Roots Charities to Tackle Poverty*. In an executive summary, the CSJ working group sets out the challenge:

> We must act if we are to unlock the unique powers of the social [i.e. voluntary sector] to tackle poverty. A government in 2015 will face the huge challenge of providing services with less money available. Local authorities will face a £14.4 billion deficit in funding. Tackling this challenge means unleashing the capacity of the social sector to find new and innovative ways of working, to reach communities and build relationships that save lives.

The report recommends:

- Increase the role of the social sector in providing public services.
- Rebalance the distribution of charities and charitable resources throughout the country.
- Extend the vital role the public and businesses have in resourcing the sector and ensuring that the smallest organisations are able to make the most of these opportunities.

These are ambitious aims but they will be hard to achieve because they require fundamental cultural change for the voluntary/social sector, government and local authorities and ourselves as citizens. Everyone will have to think again about their purpose, their responsibilities and, crucially, their relationships with each other. 'Sovereignty' must be pooled, there must be mutual respect between sectors and people must be prepared to work together in new ways. Top down may have to change to bottom up. There are few if any examples of pop-up charities in 'desert hot spots', to echo the point made by Mohan and Breeze, and both time and more money will be needed to create sustainable new local charities and social enterprises.

In addition to calling for a reformation in the commissioning of services to enable smaller charities to participate in delivering public services, the CSJ recommends that the Big Lottery Fund 'incorporates the task of building the social sector in cold spots into its long-term strategy' and calls for the strengthening of community foundations.

Community foundations are based on a US model that provides a link between social need and donors within communities and regions. They do excellent work and have the potential to do more, but resources are limited (see Mohan and Breeze). The CSJ Social Solutions report calls for the government to recommission The Endowment Matched Challenge that helped community foundations to build endowments in the most deprived areas. Between 2012 and 2013, community foundations increased endowments by 13 per cent with the help of a fifty pence match to donations from government.

The government has failed to take the advice of CSJ and there will be no further matched funding initiative to help community foundations build their endowments so that they may meet more social need and also build the capacity of the voluntary sector. Ministers have made a strategic error and their decision casts doubt on how serious government is about solving the problems in the most disadvantaged parts of the country. Deeds are not matching words.

I applaud the ambition of CSJ, but their proposals call for radical changes that need widespread support if they are to be implemented. CSJ's proposals to increase personal giving and social investment are unlikely to be any more successful than those that have been proposed before by others until we re-create a culture of giving. That is a big deal.

Very little progress will be made without more money. As CSJ has proposed that the Big Lottery Fund should play a significant role in supporting communities, I talked to Dawn Austwick, Chief Executive, and asked for her view of the challenges and the opportunities ahead:

The tectonic plates are shifting and the relationship between citizen, state and society is being reshaped. Clearly, there is less money but I don't think change is just about that and I'm not sure we've quite reached a critical mass of people who have either intellectually or emotionally got this.

As a result, what we're tending to see is business as usual with less money as opposed to transforming the way that society works along with the systems that underpin it.

The mission of the Big Lottery Fund is to help communities and people most in need. We distribute 40 per cent of the good causes cash raised by National Lottery players across the UK, around £650 million a year, with a broad mandate embracing health, education, environment and charitable purposes. That mandate comes from the people who buy lottery tickets and that guides the approach we take to supporting communities.

We operate nationally but are able to reach into neighbourhoods across the UK: our average grant is about £10,000 and that makes up 90 per cent of the grants we make. People and communities use these grants to run small but vital projects in their local areas. Those grantholders are an incredible source of insight and information on what communities are experiencing. It is too easy to sit in an office in London and think we know what that grass-roots picture really looks like. Citizens have to invest in their community and build their social capital. Our job is to foster and facilitate that, working with the grain to help people to realise their aspirations.

The resources we have give us an opportunity to think, to explore and to be innovative in how we support civil society to thrive. On top of that core business of making small grants, we have the ability to make much larger strategic investments. That blend of approaches brings us into contact with a hugely diverse range of actors seeking to make change happen in their communities.

Look at what is happening in local authorities. Doncaster is not alone in the severity of local government cuts, and between 2010 and 2015 saw its funding cut from £270 million to £148 million. With cuts on this scale, local authorities are having to radically re-consider their role.

Sheffield has had a similar scale of cuts to Doncaster. The council had to decide what to do about libraries and said that it would con-tinue to fund some but not all of them. The council is now running thirty-four, or 60 per cent, of libraries. The other 40 per cent are either co-managed (council and voluntary/community), run by a voluntary sector or a community organisation, or by volunteers.

This is all starting to challenge the idea that public sector finance initiates, leads and ultimately pays for the things that make com-munities work. That doesn't seem sustainable any more – but did it ever really work? That challenge is coming not just because money is tight, but also because the systems it creates don't really work for people. The way we try to support those with complex needs is a case in point – multiple interactions with different agencies who all seek to address a facet of the problem and not the core. The Big Lottery Fund is testing out new approaches through its Fulfilling Lives programme, investing £112 million over eight years to support people with multiple and complex needs. These long-term grants are administered by cross-sector, multi-agency partnerships, led by the voluntary, community and social enterprise sectors, bringing together services for needs such as housing, reoffending, substance misuse and mental ill-health. In that way, the person is supported to change their life, to break patterns of behaviours and avoid cycles of need that put pressure on services.

There's a simple underlying philosophical shift here. The idea that those who are disadvantaged should have things done to them in order to 'fix' their problems is outdated. It must be healthier for people and communities to determine what they want and then seek ways to make that happen – and for those with power and money to work in response to that. Instead of asking people 'what is the matter with you?' we are increasingly asking: 'what matters to you?' That opens up new opportunities for rethinking how we do things, such as shifting resources toward preventing problems from developing rather than simply addressing the resulting symptoms. For example, we're working with Esmée Fairbairn Foundation and Comic Relief on the Early Action Neighbourhood Fund to invest £5.25 million in three innovative projects. These seek to support people to be able to cope better with challenges and explore opportunities, thereby reducing demand on public services. One of those, the Ignite project, is led by the Coventry Law Centre and seeks to build knowledge, confidence and skills in people so they can deal with everyday law-related issues. The goal is to ensure fewer people ever reach crisis point, relieving pressure on a whole host of statutory services.

So there are plenty of pockets of great practice but, as yet, we haven't seen this translate into a really unified movement. That's perhaps understandable when you think about the scale and complexity of the challenges facing society – from demographics to inequality and the advancement of technology. Here at the Fund, we're trying to create an opportunity for people to come together in new ways to respond to these challenges, through our work on 'the future of doing good'. This is exploring questions like 'who sets the agenda?', 'what's stopping us from collaborating more?', 'what can different sectors bring to bear on the task of doing good?' That debate is so much broader than just money and who provides it.

Our aim is to stimulate the market to come up with the answers. We need new thinking.

There is a danger that the charitable sector might miss an opportunity to determine its own destiny. We need to change that so that younger people who want to change the world continue to believe that the social sector can be a credible vehicle to achieve that. For that to happen, we do need to sort out the fundamentals, such as how does a charity that delivers public services differ from the public sector? We need clarity, direction and focus if the sector is to attract creative thinkers to work for it.

There are some terrific people doing extraordinary, innovative work and we need more of it. For example, Blackpool is an area of immense need and a priority area for us as a funder [see Chapter 16]. In the face of serious challenges, people are coming up with bold and inventive solutions.

Andy Rhodes is Deputy Chief Constable of Lancashire Constabulary and a brilliant advocate for rethinking traditional responses to demand. He's an advocate of 'preventative policing' as a long-term solution to reduced budgets. Their approach is about recognising the core drivers for demand on their services. So for example they've identified the most frequent users of their service through call volume and 999 call analysis, realised how complicated their needs are, and are working in partnership with other agencies like health and social care, to prevent them reaching crisis point; that is built on learning from a very similar investigation of demand on paramedic services in the same area.

Lancashire Police have also recognised that repeat offending is a major problem in their area. They've come up with a remarkable model of a social enterprise, Jobs, Friends & Houses, that buys properties and turns them into hostels. Working with offenders prior to leaving prison, they then offer a wrap-around service providing accommodation, volunteering and apprenticeship opportunities renovating those same properties that will eventually accommodate released offenders.

This all started in Blackpool and is run by a couple of senior policemen and a former offender. When I visited, I was met by one of the policemen who said they'd had an incident that morning. The manager of a hotel opposite their building had run into the street appealing for help as one of the guests was murdering another. The only people to respond were the ex-offenders who piled into the hotel, disarmed the would-be murderer and held onto him, tending to the injured party until the police arrived, and then submitted evidence. The fascinating element in this for the police is that they were assisted by people they would previously have been locking up. This is a very successful social enterprise – it is absolutely remarkable!

It is now time to examine the moral and practical steps being taken to support the common good.

PART TWO

TOWARDS A
NEW WORLD OF
RESPONSIBILITY
AND
ENLIGHTENMENT?

CHAPTER 12

DEFINING AND ACHIEVING
THE COMMON GOOD

"We realised that we were lacking a coherent and convincing story
of national change that was hopeful. There was silence from the
political parties. Without a sense of hopefulness, things get worse
and we think the worst of each other and of our institutions."
STEVE WYLER, *A CALL TO ACTION FOR THE COMMON GOOD*.

"A sense of belonging is at the core of what it is to be a human being.
How do you deal with social isolation? You build a community."
CORMAC RUSSELL, MANAGING DIRECTOR,
NURTURE DEVELOPMENT.

*   *   *

We know the answer to the question 'if the state provides less,
who will provide more?' We will provide, whether by paying
more tax, by being charged for what was once free, by paying even
more than we do now or by volunteering and giving to the voluntary sector as it takes on more on society's behalf. One way and
another, the state will devolve more responsibility to us and our
country will change.

If we are to sustain and renew civil society and thereby to protect
liberal democracy, we need visionary and inspirational leadership
with the determination to deliver change that is wanted and needed.

Political and moral leadership, however, is conspicuous by its absence. Politicians seem to follow public opinion rather than lead.

I wrote the first half of this book in the midst of the campaigns for the referendum on Britain's membership of the European Union in the summer of 2016. I cannot be alone in thinking that our political discourse has sunk to new depths of negativity, dishonesty and ineptitude. A tide of populism seems to be gathering pace. Our politicians lie to us so shamelessly that their mendacity will soon seem unremarkable. This is dangerous. Does the future lie with demagogues? If so, the prospects for civil society and a tolerant liberal democracy are not promising.

For optimism and positivity, we should look to those working in our voluntary sector. Remarkable people are dedicating themselves to working for the common good. The second half of my book is devoted to interviews and conversations with very different people who are united by a commitment to serve their fellow citizens. The public, private and voluntary sectors are all represented. Some are rich, others are working for very little, or volunteering. These are the people who are effecting positive change and making a difference.

*   *   *

Dan Corry is the Chief Executive of New Philanthropy Capital (NPC), a charity think tank and consultancy. NPC describes itself as being at the nexus of charities and funders. Corry was formerly Head of the Number 10 Policy Unit and senior advisor to the Prime Minister on the economy in 2007–10. I asked him for his view of the state of the voluntary sector and how it may prosper and contribute to current and future need:

> The premise of your book is correct. The charity sector does feel vulnerable, nagged by worries about funding, independence, and criticism over marketing and pay. However, I see a resilient sector. There will always be need and causes. The sector never gives up because it is supported and sustained by people with a sense of mission. The

real question that should be asked of charities is: are they having any effect? And are some charities working better than others? That is NPC's agenda.

The state is retreating partly because of austerity and partly because the way it was operating was crowding out some voluntary activities. The state is not going to come rushing back. This is not just about size but also about function.

The voluntary sector is being asked to do more, there is more need and needs are becoming more complicated. Troubled families are not easy things to sort out even if the state had all the money it needs. The voluntary sector is often better suited and equipped to do this work but finds the way the public sector tries to get it involved is a challenge.

The public sector says it doesn't want to be a provider but then invites bids for contracts that are not appropriate for much of the voluntary sector through things like payment by results, and therefore also payment in arrears, and that is just too much of a risk for charities. Most of the public money coming into the sector is now via contracts rather than grants, and this is also a problem for many charities.

We have to accept that the voluntary sector at its most effective cannot provide comprehensive nation-wide services. So what is the role of the sector? Is it about innovation, so that charities can say to the state: here is something that works, why not replicate what we are doing and apply it elsewhere?

The sector does not have a very good track record in replicating success in one place in another. Nor do successful local projects expand because sufficient capital is rarely available. The solution must be for various players in a locality to get together, to decide what the issues are and how they might work together. That's often not straightforward as there is often a lack of understanding between them.

Despite the difficulties, I am optimistic, particularly about the move towards city regions. That should encourage more local collaboration and there must be a role for community foundations here. A local focus should make it more clear who deserves funding.

NPC has been doing some work on how the voluntary sector could play into plans for a Northern Powerhouse and the Manchester city-region as this could be a model for what happens elsewhere. But progress is not encouraging as yet.

The voluntary sector, more philanthropy and social enterprises must have more of a role in determining how to build or rebuild social capital. The key point for NPC is to encourage more philanthropists to support programmes with good and proven social outcomes.

I am on the advisory council of Impetus-PEF. The Foundation is the charitable arm of the private equity industry. Impetus works with UK charities and social enterprises that have a successful track record in helping 16- to 24-year-olds succeed in education, find and keep jobs and achieve their potential.

This is a form of venture philanthropy. They find a charity, invest in strengthening its staff and resources and enable the charity to scale up. This is very challenging, particularly for those who have founded a charity. However, it can be done. [See Andy Cook, Chapter 19.]

The good thing about venture philanthropy is that it has attracted those working in private equity and venture capital to the social sector. Social investment will attract a particular kind of philanthropist who is interested in sustainable projects that make an impact and contribute to social change.

Our concern at NPC is that the social impact may not be being measured adequately and so may not be achieving much. And this kind of social investment model is not relevant for the majority of charities, as they don't have enough revenue streams to offer financial returns.

*   *   *

Dan Corry has set out the challenges facing the voluntary sector and the opportunities for the sector to be innovative and creative, pioneering ways of creating social capital and attracting the support of philanthropists and social investors looking for ways of making a social impact. Cormac Russell has a complementary approach that focuses on the needs of communities and ways of empowering their members to create social capital that is based upon their innate strengths or assets. The emphasis is upon communities rather than programmes, about enabling people to do things for themselves rather than having things done for them.

Russell is an advocate of asset-based community development. He is the managing director of Nurture Development and director of the Asset-Based Community Development Institute (ABCD) Europe. I asked Russell how he had come to the conclusion that a new approach is needed:

My background is in psychology. I am Irish and was working for the Irish Health Board in the early 1990s. The issue at the time was how we could move away from ossified institutional forms of care for young people run by religious orders into what we then called community care.

I discovered this was not straightforward. One of the kids in the homes said to me: 'The judge has taken me away from my mother, taken me away from the community where I live, put me in a place where people are paid to look after me, in a community that doesn't want me, in a house that is far from the kind of house I will ever live in or have come from. And you call this care.'

That cut me to the bone. This was typical of the time. People were taken out of their indigenous families and we put them in a middle-class construct of what was good for them. I realised that the notion of community care was questionable. We had conflated two words together, community and care, and we had failed to involve community in the process.

I came to realise that psychology had inadvertently taken things that were social and political and had made them medical and personal. We try to solve problems by turning them into programmes. This also happens with some philanthropy. Programmes and projects are appealing because you can measure things. And this is attractive to philanthropists.

A sense of belonging is at the core of what it is to be a human being. Those being helped told us that they recognised the difference between care being provided by paid professionals and by real neighbours who are not being paid.

Traditional community development starts with what is wrong and then brings in external forces to offer palliative treatment. Human history and behaviour shows us that the way to solve problems and overcome challenges is to start the other way around by acknowledging strengths rather than weaknesses.

One of the things that threatens to blight our work is the fantasy that you can take a really good idea and scale it up across the country. The key question to ask is this: how do you support community inventiveness in a local way, neighbourhood by neighbourhood? We try to work with relatively small communities by identifying 'change makers' without any idea of scaling up what they do. We should only attempt to draw conclusions from those things that were common to all projects.

My team and I were called into Croydon after the riots of 2011 because we had a relationship with the council and local voluntary sector before the riots. I said that we have to understand that gang problems are not the result of the failure of the young people but the failure of the older generation to create 'villages' for younger people. They don't feel they belong. Don't think about this as a programme to solve the problems of gang violence. Let us get to the root of the problem and understand what caused what.

This kind of approach can be very attractive to some philanthropists. If I was a philanthropist and I was investing money that was not dealing with the root cause, I would be very cross. I was fortunate to work with the CEO of Croydon council who really understood this. We assume that services and programmes will solve all problems. How do you deal with social isolation? You build a community.

There is a new movement in Europe that supports investing in community engagement at neighbourhood level with no formal agenda. We have been too orientated in targeting needy people and have failed to recognise that so called deprived indigenous communities, such as Blackpool, also have assets and resources and have a capacity to build a community and economy. The best approach is not always to look at what is wrong. Get people to take responsibility for themselves and for those within the community who are excluded and who need their help.

All this is deeply political. If we live in a government-centred democracy, then the centre is unlikely to be interested in or concerned about what happens at neighbourhood level. This will become even worse if we become more plutocratic.

I like to tease both the left and the right. I tell them the one thing they can agree on is that the poorest cannot determine or influence their own futures. The right thinks it is because they are lazy and the left thinks they have not had sufficient state support. Both are wrong. The right versus left model is politically bankrupt because it has created a schism between government and people. And if the schism is big enough, politics are broken.

We need to give more credence to the idea of smallness and not get drawn into the narrative of the big state, small state. This is a cognitive trap. If Monsanto comes into this country on the scale that it has in Canada and the US, then our rural communities will be decimated. I want a state that is beefy enough to beat them down. There is an argument that says let's make the state small, without articulating what it is going to do about globalism gone rampant, without addressing damage to the environment, or levels of consumption. The narrative of the small state is masking the issue of big institutions over which there is no control.

The core point is that corporate issues are dictating and regulating social interests and policy. Our view of social life is interpreted through the lens of individualism and consumerism. The voluntary sector could help to change this – but only if the sector is not beholden to a government that is beholden to global consumer interests that are not interested in indigenous living.

This could be a significant opportunity for community and philanthropic foundations that are not dependent upon government. And there are some corporates which really care about the importance of sustaining civil society and are interested in social investment.

This is a real dilemma: the need for the state to be both big and small at different times. We need government to be big in relation to Monsanto and small in relation to local issues. We do not want a government that says you cannot do that because of health and safety. Absolutism about whether we have a big or small state is nonsense.

What is the message for philanthropists? Philanthropists need to be hosts rather than heroes. The Jacobs Family Foundation in California is exemplary. The Foundation's mission states: 'The Foundation was founded on the premise that philanthropy must not demean people, make them dependent, or fail to challenge them in problem solving. Instead, it is the inherent dignity of people and the affirmation of people's ability to apply their talents, and hard work that truly makes community change last.'

The Jacobs Family Foundation is hosting conversations with people in which they invite them to say what they want to do and then reply: 'Show us your invention and then we will invest in it'.

Philanthropists should be asking themselves: How can I do no harm and do real good? This is a very different proposition for philanthropy.

*   *   *

'As I look to the future of the voluntary sector, I ask myself a simple question. To what extent will it contribute to the common good?'

These are the opening words of an article sent to me by a philanthropist and I resolved to ask the same question of its author, Steve Wyler.

Wyler has been working in the voluntary sector for thirty years. For half of that time, he ran Locality, formerly the Development Trusts Association, a national network of community-led organisations working together to help neighbourhoods thrive. He is now a member of the steering group for 'A Call to Action for the

Common Good', an initiative established by a group of civil society organisations, supported by the Carnegie UK Trust and CCLA, managing £6 billion of assets for charities and the public sector. I asked him why the Common Good initiative had been set up and what it hoped to achieve:

> This came about on the initiative of Lucy de Groot who runs a charity called Volunteering Matters. She brought together a diverse group to talk about the future of civil society at a time of austerity.
>
> We realised that we were lacking a coherent and convincing story of national change that was hopeful. There was a silence from the political parties. There was nothing from the think tanks.
>
> We reminded ourselves of what happened in the aftermath of the Second World War. Circumstances are different but at a time of huge financial challenge for the country and having gone through a period of adversity, it must be possible to generate a national mood and contribute towards a national story that is more hopeful.
>
> We seek to illuminate good practice so that people can understand what is possible so that practising what supports the common good becomes the norm rather than the exception.
>
> We soon realised that others were working in parallel. An organisation in the faith sector called 'Together for the Common Good' has built a big following. For them, common good thinking is not new, coming from a rich tradition that they would trace back from Aquinas and Augustine and beyond that to the classical age of Cicero and Aristotle.
>
> Our group was not from a religious background and some of us were wary but we did find that there was great affinity between what we both valued, despite a difference of language. We agree that the common good is dependent upon the commitments people make to each other. Most organisations and institutions do not operate in this way.
>
> Much of our interaction between people is reduced to transactions. This also applies to our public services. The fact that we have public services is an aspiration to achieve the common good but

the way they are delivered often misses the point by failing to help people change their lives for the better on their terms.

There is a different way of doing things, by working from the bottom up. If all authority and responsibility rests with those in charge, things will appear to be done but may not change. Asset-Based Community Development is an idea whose time has come.

It is natural for institutions and those who lead and work for them to protect their own interests and to carve out territory they want to hold on to. This also applies to charities. The problem is that this can lead them away from their mission. Protection becomes the driving force. The way to overcome this is to develop a strong conviction in favour of the common good.

We have found allies in the business world and this has been a revelation. A Blueprint for Better Business is a charity backed by the chairman of Unilever and senior executives from JP Morgan, Vodafone and the *Financial Times*. The charity recommends companies should have a deeper commitment to social purpose.

For a business to survive in the long term, they need to think about what a great company could be in relation to its position in society. Look at ICI, a company that was very successful for most of the twentieth century. The company invested in research and development which took years, often without a short-term pay off, but in the long term the return on investment was considerable. In the 1990s, ICI was taken over by people for whom the prime motive was profit with a focus that was much narrower and short term. ICI was soon a shadow of its former self. Similar has happened in banking. Look what happened to Royal Bank of Scotland.

The behaviour of charities and social enterprises is as subject to vested interests as any institution.

When we ran a seminar about the future of charities in relation to the common good, the strongest insight was that the more the charities work with the resourcefulness of the people they are supporting, the more will be achieved for the common good and the less likely they are to be driven by the need for organisational self-preservation.

The Carnegie UK Trust has examined the changing relationship between the state and charity. This is not about the abdication of government responsibility but finding a new role and a new way of behaving: the enabling state.

The enabling state is about statutory bodies enabling others to flourish. This requires a fresh approach from both the public sector and those working in the voluntary sector.

What would happen if we were to apply the lens of the common good to the big challenges which society faces; the widening poverty gap, the ageing population, the decline in democratic engagement, the threat of climate change for example? In all these cases, if it is true that common good can only be produced by relationships and commitments between people, then we will need to build and to practise new forms of association, which embrace many more people, many more interest groups, from neighbourhood level to national level, in politics, in business, in public services, and indeed in the voluntary sector.

*   *   *

From now on, we will witness the common good in action, driven by people who are, in diverse ways, changing the world for the better.

CHAPTER 13

HOW CAN GREAT WEALTH RESPOND TO SOCIAL NEED? INDEPENDENT FOUNDATIONS AND THEIR CONTRIBUTION TO THE COMMON GOOD

"I want to promote debate and argument so that it is embraced and understood by the entire political class. Resolution aims to encourage all parties and governments to adopt policies to ensure more shared growth."
SIR CLIVE COWDERY, FOUNDER, RESOLUTION FOUNDATION.

"We are placing emphasis on youth, welfare and community as these sectors have been the hardest hit. Youth services have been decimated across the country and yet we know if society fails to engage with young people, the results come at a great cost."
PHILIPPA CHARLES, DIRECTOR, GARFIELD WESTON FOUNDATION.

*   *   *

Charity and philanthropy cannot replace government but they can change how things are done. In the past, philanthropists and charities have been pioneers of new ideas and best practice. In a developed and wealthy society, we should expect thoughtful people who are financially independent to invest in the common good by establishing charitable foundations.

I talked to one founder and two chief executives of three of Britain's most influential foundations. Their work and the causes they support have an impact upon all of us.

When I met Sir Clive Cowdery in the summer of 2015, he was celebrating the announcement that eight million low-paid workers over the age of twenty-five would be entitled to a new national living wage from April 2016. The national minimum wage of £6.70 an hour in March 2015 could become a national living wage of £9 an hour or more by 2020. Cowdery has been campaigning for ten years.

He established the Resolution Foundation in 2005 as an independent, non-partisan research and policy organisation working to improve the living standards of those in Britain on low to middle incomes. In 2015, it was announced that he had donated £50 million to establish the Resolution Trust, probably one of the largest endowments for public policy research in Britain. The Foundation will continue to focus upon topical research, including intergenerational inequality (see Chapter 3), whilst the Trust will tackle questions about long-term trends in the economy that are unlikely to be addressed in the shorter term horizon of most politicians.

The Foundation's commitment to independent analysis is manifested by the appointment of David Willetts, a former Conservative government minister, as executive chairman, and Torsten Bell, a former director of policy for the Labour Party, as director of the Resolution Foundation.

Clive Cowdery made his fortune in insurance in the UK and the US and I asked him what had persuaded him to be philanthropic and why he had decided to focus on improving incomes for the low paid:

Some people give in a hands-on way. I cannot imagine doing that. They have taken in foster children, they have no wealth and yet they share their bread, or are involved in helping those with mental health problems. These people are giving much more than I am. My realisation that I cannot keep all that I have, and the fact that

I am not selfless enough to give of myself, means that my response is to look at the key levers of change and decide what I can do through intellectual enquiry and campaigning. My philanthropy is in keeping with who I am. The greatest thing in life is to find where the needs of the individual and the needs of the collective can meet.

There is a need to change systematically how wealth distribution and opportunity are shared in this country. So I would rather spend my time and money addressing this huge topic. The wage share and capital share of wealth needs to change. Capital is often unproductive, relying on the sweat of others to pay dividends. The very rich and the very poor are living off other people's work. We need to find a way where wealth is being put to work and having a more positive impact on increasing income levels across the board. As shareholders, the value of our dividends from Tesco, for example, is based on the fact that Tesco is not paying its workers enough.

I want to promote debate and argument so that it is embraced and understood by the entire political class. Resolution aims to encourage all parties and all governments to adopt policies designed to ensure more shared growth. This will take decades.

The Resolution Foundation decided not to be grant-giving but to campaign to shift pay for eight million people. It took the UK ten years to get a national living wage but we got there. I have chosen to try to achieve the macro effect and to hunt a few big elephants so that public policy can be adjusted in favour of poor people. That is my purpose. Rented accommodation; the national living wage and the way tax and benefits operate so that people do not fall into gaps; pay policy; the relationship between younger people trying to enter the workforce and older people: these are the questions regarding fairer distribution that we are addressing.

The left has never been good at achieving growth. The right does not do sharing very well. There needs to be polarisation around what a sustainable thirty- or forty-year model could be in a post-industrial environment. Pay is important but dividends are key. We need a new meaning for the word 'share'. If the momentum is towards more assets rather than income, then we need to start sharing the assets.

The great thing about Thomas Piketty (author of *Capital in the Twenty-First Century*) is that he started this debate. The wealth tax he has proposed won't happen for ages, if ever; the important thing is to make a start with thinking. Look at the revolutions in Europe in 1848. People asked for radical change. They did not get all they wanted but they did get the vote. Thomas Piketty is calling for a wealth tax but I would be happy to start with profit-related pay and move on from there.

It is time for a more collective settlement. The Thatcher/Reagan model enhanced the role of the individual versus the collective. The collective was important and needed but it went too far. The collectivism of the post-war years had clashed with the aspirational middle classes. The pendulum needed to swing again but it went too far the other way so that people demanded lower taxes and thereby undermined the common good.

People were thrown to the mercy of the markets. We will never get back to the post-war sense of collectivism but we do need to understand that a more collective approach is the only way to address the big challenges we face. The only way to challenge poverty, environmental, social and infrastructure issues is for an enabling state or for the collective to organise on our behalf.

I asked Cowdery how he had come to his worldview and to this point in his life where he has donated a significant share of his wealth in order to improve the quality of life for millions:

My childhood was worse than that of most of the people I am most concerned about, low- to medium-earners. There are ten deciles of earnings and Resolution is focusing on deciles two to five, beneath median earnings but not those on welfare. I grew up on welfare. When I saw the parents of the children I was at school with, I would look at them with hero worship. These were the men who washed the grease off their hands before they ate their tea. These were people who were holding everything together.

My family was largely ignorant of the needs of working people. Not a pound of earned income came into our house. I knew instinctively that when it became possible for me to do something that I would do what I could to improve the lives of these working people.

Dependants and the very rich will always be with us. They both have needs but they are both morally equivalent. They are the two most economically useless classes. We are only surviving because of the people in the middle who are doing the work. They are the people who have the game rigged against them because wealth creation is flowing towards assets. That is the system that needs unpicking and so I have decided to focus on a piece of work that may last twenty years, not to give money to individuals but to try to change the nature of the rigged game.

Personal charitable giving in Britain is about £11 billion a year with a further £2.5 billion of grants from charitable foundations. These are not large figures in relation to the cost of running the country, which is around £740 billion. Even by spending £740 billion of public money, we are not addressing every social need. If that £13.5 billion is considered alongside national income, it is a generous contribution but if it is considered in relation to total aggregated wealth of £11 trillion, it is too modest a figure. There is a huge sum owned by a relatively small number of wealthy people and much of that money is unproductive. This is wealth that has temporarily stuck to private fingers and is doing little if any social good.

Some of us will win the lottery and that may not need a great deal of skill. I don't feel much guilt about this and enjoy the lack of fear that wealth brings. Then, at the end of our lives, we do not get asked to hand it back. I find this almost unbelievable. The natural moment of handing wealth back to society seems to be at death. I am a huge fan of inheritance tax. During your life, you should be able to enjoy it, spend it, invest it, give it away as you wish without guilt or fear. That is morally fine as long as it is in the context of a generational reset. At my death, I should give my wealth back to the country. I have six children. The thought that I can give 60 per cent of my wealth to only six of the five-and-a half million children in the country and I get to name them – this strikes me as bizarre.

Libertarians can argue that tax is theft. Almost any action you take can be described as an injustice to the individual. It is only in the context of the greater injustice it is remedying that tax can be justified. There is not enough respect shown to people who pay tax.

The generational reset whereby we give back at death is crucial but we also need to consider what we do with our wealth in our lifetimes. If we were allowed to give a relatively modest amount of our wealth to our children, say 20 per cent, giving money away to charitable causes in your lifetime would feel completely different.

This ought to be a debate but it isn't. And I do not think my gift of £50 million to the Resolution Trust is that big in this context.

We need to be hard-headed about the nature of human beings and recognise that everyone is motivated by enlightened self-interest. Consider Maslow's hierarchy of needs. Start at the bottom with the need for food and shelter, then love and affection and then at the top of the pyramid, we reach self-actualisation.

What is the picture of myself and do I like what I see? When people have truly disposable wealth, meaning so much that if they gave some of it away it would not make any difference to their own well-being, then unless they are so fatuous that they must have a boat that is bigger than anyone else's, the picture most sensible people should want is that they do not appear greedy.

I am not comfortable with the idea that philanthropy should be considered an alternative to a continuing, redistributive focus in public finance. I was concerned when the Conservative concept of the Big Society was first mooted that it provided a fig leaf whilst the state was rolled back. I think it is important to have a debate about how government spends public money. Should the government be in the business of providing or enabling? The latter sounds more interesting.

I am not blaming the Conservatives for being conservative. I am worried though that we are moving towards a new sense of normality, being that government retreats over decades from a high water mark of social inclusion and care and thereby provides space to be filled by philanthropy and charitable giving. We have a problem in deciding how best to spend less public money on the most vulnerable people in society. The only way we can do that is by reordering priorities. That is tough because it means choosing between groups of poor people. What constitutes a fair outcome? We need to find ways of recycling from rich to poor. That means reconsidering how profit is shared and more tax. Philanthropy will make some contribution but cannot be *the* answer.

We must save the concept of the collective before it is eclipsed. This is where we should focus our hope. The big problem is that people are not prepared to fund collective need. The policies and ideology of the 1980s have inflicted great damage on our sense of the collective and, by implication, on liberal democracy.

In seeking to cut out special interests, like unions, the Thatcher government nearly killed the patient. When you cut out a sense of the common good, you end up facing a dystopian future. If we are moving towards a state where citizens are expected to do more as the government does less, then we need an initiative that encourages more citizens to participate.

My second subject is the Wolfson Foundation. Clive Cowdery and Lord (Leonard) Wolfson would almost certainly have disagreed about Margaret Thatcher, but I suspect they had more in common than their politics might suggest, namely a conviction that those who have surplus wealth have an obligation to use it to bring about a more just society.

In 2015, the Wolfson Foundation celebrated its sixtieth anniversary. With assets of more than £800 million, the Foundation has made 10,000 grants over sixty years with a cumulative value in real terms of £1.685 billion. During that period, the Foundation has been active and influential at the very centre of science, medical research, higher education and culture.

I talked to Paul Ramsbottom, chief executive of the Wolfson Foundation:

I agree that we are seeing a paradigm shift in the way the state relates to various social activities and to civil society. We should regard the amount of public money that went into the voluntary sector in the 1990s and the first part of this century as quite extraordinary and exceptional rather than the norm.

The amount of philanthropy from all sources is remaining stubbornly consistent. There is no new golden age of philanthropy despite the creation of so much wealth in recent times. I am particularly concerned that there are not enough new foundations being set up on the scale of those that were established in the fifties and sixties. This was a golden age with the establishment of, among others, the Weston Foundation, the Esmée Fairbairn Foundation and the Sainsbury trusts in addition to the Wolfson Foundation. Those who were creating great wealth were able to invest part of it in a tax-efficient manner and thereby create social wealth.

I see a well-run endowed foundation being one of the highest forms of philanthropy, being able to invest for the long term, to give grants strategically to fulfil clearly defined objectives based on collective decision-making following the finest professional advice. Cultures of giving are critical in persuading people to set up foundations. Faith-based societies tend to be more generous because they have cultures of giving. This is something we lack in Britain.

We need to use the education system to get young people to think about voluntary action and how best to use resources to strengthen society. The portrayal of philanthropy in the media is also a serious problem. There is as a general rule a very cynical view of the wealthy and successful in the UK. It is not helped that political donors are often equated with philanthropists in some way, for example when philanthropy is used as a cover for an essentially political honour.

One of the problems is a traditional British reticence that discourages philanthropists from speaking out. There are few if any people in Britain willing to stand up like Bill Gates and say: 'This is what I believe in and this is what I am doing and you should be thinking about doing something similar'. There may well be an option for a well-established institutional foundation to put out subtle messages but no more than that.

This cultural reticence is understandable but unfortunate because it means that a key part of our social history is hidden from all but the most inquisitive and cannot easily be used to stimulate and motivate others to follow the example of some particularly generous and public-spirited people. However, Paul Ramsbottom has written a history of the Wolfson Foundation's work from 1955 to 2015, an account of what an extraordinary family has contributed to the nation over sixty years.

This is the story of an immigrant. Solomon Wolfson, a cabinetmaker from what was then Russian Poland, settled in Victorian Glasgow. His son Isaac was born in 1897 in the Gorbals, a notorious slum with some of the worst housing conditions in Europe, riddled with the diseases that plague the poor: tuberculosis, rickets and scarlet fever. These beginnings enabled Isaac Wolfson to understand the importance of health, education and culture. After he became rich via the success of Great Universal Stores (a group of eighty companies of which he became the largest shareholder) he created a foundation in order to address a fundamental issue: how can great wealth respond to poverty and deprivation? Isaac Wolfson knew what deprivation meant. His task was to improve the health of people, to enable them to access education and to fulfil their intellectual potential. Accordingly, the Wolfson Foundation's priorities are: health, medical, scientific and university research, history and the arts.

Sir Isaac Wolfson, who was made a baronet in 1962, was a devout orthodox Jew and is quoted as saying 'No man should have more than £100,000. The rest should go to charity.' He was chairman of the Wolfson Foundation from 1962 until 1972 when he handed over to his son, Leonard, who remained chairman until his death in 2010.

The long list of projects supported by the Foundation in Ramsbottom's illuminating essay is impressive, not simply because of their number but because of their significance and their geographical distribution. These are just a very few examples:

- Providing halls of residence and founding colleges for women in the Universities of Oxford and Cambridge.
- Establishment of the Wolfson Brain Imaging Centre at Addenbrooke's Hospital, Cambridge.
- Creation of the Wolfson Research Centre, Institute for Ageing and Health, University of Newcastle; the Wolfson Institute of Biomedical Research, University College London; and the Wolfson Medical School, Glasgow.
- £44 million to health and disability projects, including a project on Uist, Outer Hebrides.
- Grants to 130 hospices and further funding to look at palliative care research, including the Cicely Saunders Institute of Palliative Care, King's College London.
- During the 1990s, in partnership with government, 282 awards to 200 museums, mainly for refurbishment. For every £1 from Wolfson and government, a further £7 was raised. A total of £140 million went to museums across the country.

Unsurprisingly, these kinds of projects do not register on the national consciousness but one did, not least because it featured in the 1963 Bond film, *Dr No*.

In 1961, the Duke of Leeds sold Goya's portrait of the Duke of Wellington to an American couple for £140,000 by auction. There was a public outcry so the buyer agreed that if £140,000 could be raised, he would be happy for the Goya to remain in London's National Gallery. The Wolfson Foundation agreed to buy the picture for £100,000 on behalf of the nation on condition that the government also contributed. Working in partnership with government has been a feature of the Foundation's philanthropy. Harold Macmillan, then Prime Minister, declined to give support, claiming the country could not afford to contribute £40,000. The Wolfson Foundation trustees refused to proceed without the government, which gave in; so a total of £140,000 was pledged.

At this point, the National Gallery displayed the picture on a freestanding screen in the front vestibule. Eighteen days later, it was stolen.

The thief, a Newcastle lorry driver, had climbed into the gallery through an open lavatory window and simply lifted it off the screen. He wrote to the National Gallery trustees saying that if the government would spend £40,000 on providing free TV licences for pensioners, he would return the painting.

Not much happened for a while except that in 1963, *Dr No* showed his fabulous collection of stolen art to James Bond who remarked: 'So that is where it is.'

By 1965, the thief decided he had had enough, put the Duke of Wellington in a bag, stored him in left luggage at Birmingham railway station, and sent the ticket to the press.

At the trial, the judge decided that as the lorry driver had always made it clear that he would return the picture if the government would provide free TV licences for pensioners, he should not be charged with theft but he must be sent to prison for three months for losing the picture's frame.

The unintended consequence of the Wolfson Foundation's £100,000 'gift' was that museum security was transformed across the country. The other benefit of this surreal episode was that the Foundation's insistence that government should be its funding partner set a precedent that operates to this day.

The £20 million donation in memory of Lord Wolfson is described in Chapter 10. I asked Paul Ramsbottom to tell me more about the dementia research project and partnership with government:

We had become increasingly aware about the potential time bomb of an ageing population and the impact of degenerative neurological conditions on British and other western societies. We asked the question: what would twenty million do to advance research into neurology?

We brought together a team of international experts and went through a rigorous process that led to our trustees putting twenty million into the National Hospital for Neurology and Neurosurgery in London and created a facility with University College London as the academic partner.

We do like to look for partnerships, including with public funding. We can help leverage government funding. We have a creative
partnership with the Department for Culture, Media & Sport. We
sat down with the civil servants and said we will put two million a
year into the unglamorous end of things such as refurbishing gallery
space – will you match it pound for pound? This is an intelligent way
for the philanthropic and public sectors to work and plan together.

*   *   *

Distributing almost £60 million a year, the Garfield Weston
Foundation is one of the wealthiest family-founded and family-run
charitable foundations in the UK and amongst the most admired
and respected. This is due to the patriarchal figure of the late Garry
Weston and his children and wider family who are trustees of the
Foundation and who share a concern for the common good.

Although Garry Weston (1927–2002) was an outstandingly
successful businessman and a billionaire, he was notably modest,
almost shy and retiring. He travelled to work by tube. He is reported to have said: 'Money only attracts envy and weird people.' His
father created Associated British Foods (ABF), an empire which
includes Kingsmill, Ryvita, Twinings, Silver Spoon and Primark.
The Weston family also owns Fortnum & Mason in London. The
Garfield Weston Foundation was established and endowed with
shares in the family business in 1958 by Garry's father, and the
Foundation is on course to donate its billionth pound to charity in
its diamond anniversary year in 2017/18.

Garry Weston was exceptional because he understood and valued
people and causes that were far removed from his personal taste and
opinions. He backed people he believed in. He ensured that the
Weston Foundation made the first donation to the campaign for
the building of Tate Modern because he understood why it was
necessary for London to have a museum of modern and contemporary art. He is not known to have liked contemporary art but that
was not the point.

There are many examples of Garry Weston's legendary generosity, including a gift of £20 million to the British Museum, as well as countless acts of personal kindness. This concern for others and also for the most disadvantaged continues in the Foundation today. According to its website:

> Mindful of the challenging economic climate, the Foundation has continued to grow its donations to nearly £60 million a year and the trustees are especially keen to see applications for core and project costs for charities delivering services directly to beneficiaries, especially in the welfare, youth and community fields and also in regions of economic disadvantage.

In recent years the Foundation has been unable to rely only on applicants to bring forward great projects; following the recession there was a drop or stagnation in applications from certain regions of the country, even though significant need existed, and this was most acutely seen in the north-east.

I talked to Philippa Charles, Director of the Weston Foundation, in October 2015. She explained to me that the trustees, all of whom are descended from the founder, are motivated to try and answer the question: how can we do more and do it better?

> We commissioned Professor Cathy Pharoah [Professor of Charity Funding and Co-Director of the Centre for Charitable Giving and Philanthropy at Cass Business School, City University, London] to conduct an enquiry into three main areas: youth, welfare and community. We were particularly interested in those kinds of smaller charities working at community level and doing preventative work. These types of charities have been especially vulnerable to cutbacks in public funding and yet their work can have such a positive impact and can represent real savings to the public purse such as social services and the NHS.
>
> The report, *An Insight into the future of charity funding in the North East*, was delivered to us in 2014 and was widely shared with other

funders, many of which were reporting a similar trend in applications. This commissioned research demonstrated that charities
in the north-east with a turnover of less than half a million were
hanging on by their fingernails, but only just. They had reduced their
costs, including fundraising staff, and over two thirds of charities
had lost statutory and local government funding but also lacked
confidence with funders who did not know them and were reluctant
to invest scarce resources in uncertain applications.

As a result, the foundation launched a series of interconnected
and proactive initiatives across the north-east region designed not
just to provide funding but also to strengthen the sector and help
charities build skill and resilience. We have supported the Tyne &
Wear and Northumberland Community Foundation jointly with
the Esmée Fairbairn Foundation by funding a member of staff to
advise smaller charities.

Informal and practical partnerships have become increasingly important to help to build the capacity of the voluntary sector. A good
example is our partnership with the Clore Duffield Foundation's
social leadership programme. The programme supports emerging
leaders in the charitable sector because charities rarely have the resources to develop managers in the way that the private sector does.

We are placing emphasis on youth, welfare and community as
these have been the hardest hit. Youth services have been decimated
across the country and yet we know if society fails to engage with
young people, the results come at a great cost.

OnSide Youth Zones are fulfilling a mighty need. This is a charity with one aim, to give young people a high-quality, safe and affordable place to go in their leisure time [see Chapter 23]. What
we like about the Youth Zones' preventative work is that it has
attracted serious and significant local financial support. We have
just announced a grant of £500,000 to set up a Youth Zone in the
Wirral. Before the grant, we needed to be reassured that OnSide
could obtain support from local authorities. It is not always about
how much money they contribute but also how much effort they are
prepared to put in.

Our work in the north-east is only the beginning. We have learned that smart partnerships mean that we can do more and we need to be connected to people who know their locations better than we do. This is why we have asked the Institute for Public Policy Research (IPPR) to conduct a survey of civil society and the voluntary sector in the north of England, its prospects and its needs for the future.

The Institute for Public Policy Research seeks to promote social justice, democratic participation, and economic and environmental sustainability in government policy. Ed Cox is Director of IPPR North and I visited him in Manchester. He explained to me that 'The Future of Civil Society in the North' will be a three-year programme funded by the Weston Foundation.

We have told the Weston Foundation that we will deliver twelve reports exploring what is happening to the voluntary sector. Is it growing or is it shrinking? How much is being given, how much is being received, from where and from whom? We shall also be examining the role of the voluntary sector in the provision of public services and considering the role of other independent organisations, local political parties such as Yorkshire First and special interest groups united by social media. We have additional funding from the Lloyds Bank Foundation to study the current state of the voluntary and community sector.

Whilst we are concerned with the north of England, I don't doubt that our findings will be relevant to other parts of the country, excluding London.

*   *   *

The Resolution, Wolfson and Garfield Weston Foundations, along with those they partner, are investing in the nation's social, intellectual and cultural capital and contributing to the well-being of millions. They are making a national impact and we must hope that what they are achieving will encourage other wealthy individuals and families as well as corporate bodies to follow their example by endowing their own charitable foundations. The work of the Resolution, Wolfson and Weston Foundations illustrates the importance of having well-resourced independent bodies whose sole purpose is to support and enhance the common good.

CHAPTER 14

THE WOMAN AND THE DRESS: INEQUALITY IN SURREY AND ZAMBIA

"If we are raising people to the bottom rung of life, there are still too many below the bottom rung. If these people are left behind by those who are ascending the ladder, then they sink lower. And this concerns me greatly. We decided that the poorest of the poor have to be a community responsibility."

PATRICIA NAPIER, FOUNDER, BAYNARDS ZAMBIA TRUST.

* * *

Surrey's appearance as a wealthy county is deceptive. Throughout there are tight pockets of deprivation, enclosed within housing estates or even within a few streets, with high levels of child poverty, low income, poor mental health and other significant problems. Often they are adjacent to affluent areas that camouflage the extent of need, driving down statistics and diverting funds to areas of more widespread poverty in other parts of the country.

The quotation comes from a report, *Hidden Surrey: Why Local Giving Is Needed to Strengthen Our Communities*, written by Dr Helen Bowcock in 2009. Because Surrey is perceived to be a wealthy county, the local authority receives significantly less funding per person for essential services than the national average. The *Hidden Surrey* report continues:

It is clear that the government is neither able nor willing to provide the resources necessary to address many local needs ... government at local and national levels needs to be honest about the limits of what they are willing and able to do so that we can clearly delineate the role and scope of local giving.

As well as being a sociologist, Helen Bowcock is a philanthropist and former High Sheriff of Surrey, Chair of the Kent, Surrey & Sussex Air Ambulance Trust, and a member of the Council of the University of Surrey. She and her husband Matthew established the Hazelhurst Trust in 2001 to support local causes, particularly groups in communities that want to be more self-reliant and sustainable.

Before I visited Surrey to witness some of the community work being funded by the Hazelhurst Trust, Bowcock and I talked about the need to revive or reinvent philanthropy for the twenty-first century and the challenges to be overcome:

I am concerned that philanthropy has become characterised by extreme wealth but it can be for everybody. I chair the Kent, Surrey & Sussex Air Ambulance Trust. We raise over £7 million a year, mostly from small donations.

Air Ambulances are run by independent charitable trusts, and provide an extraordinary service to society. For example, when there is a serious accident on the motorway time is crucial to whether the patient lives or dies. In our region there are up to 2,500 helicopter missions a year and many of those people would have died. Young people are disproportionately represented in the number of casualties in road accidents.

The role of volunteers is essential in supporting this, for example, in delivering blood from hospital to the helicopter on a daily basis.

It also delivers considerable value to the NHS, immersing doctors in intense, highly specific on-site training and experience. The site of an incident can be far more demanding than an A&E department. Doctors then return to the NHS much more highly skilled than they would be otherwise.

Air Ambulance charities are a very good example of the willingness to give right across the board when people understand what they are funding.

Dr Bowcock invited me to Surrey to visit a housing estate on the outskirts of prosperous Farnham which was featured in her *Hidden Surrey* report. The housing estate ranks as an area of high deprivation. Many of the residents have been trapped because of poor transport links, unable to obtain employment through lack of skills and education. A high proportion of the residents are single parents who have not completed their education. Helen Bowcock wanted to show me Opportunities, a project supporting lone parents to build brighter futures and change lives, and the crucial role that philanthropy is playing in the absence of any other significant funding:

Before 2004, statistics were collected at ward level in Surrey and deprivation was largely invisible. In 2004, the entire population was divided into subsets of 1,000 or 1,500 people, which are known as super output areas. This enables you to see a very different picture. There are three super output areas in the electoral ward we are visiting. In two of them, few people earn below average income but in one of them, the area we are visiting, many, particularly single women, are below it.

Some years ago the local Housing Association decided to employ a tutor to teach the women how to use IT, acquire some skills and gain National Vocational Qualifications (NVQs). Carol McFarlane was recruited in 2002. She knows the area and cares deeply about it. She soon realised that other things needed to be addressed. She spent time with each of the women and revealed stories of emotional and physical abuse and significant personal problems. Social isolation was one of the most debilitating problems of all.

So Carol created a community around the project and decided she could enrich their lives by bringing in other activities. One of the biggest hurdles she has to overcome is persuading people to attend, as often there is a lack of self-confidence.

Carol is paid for the teaching that leads to NVQs, but she probably gives as much time again. There is no regular local authority funding. Matthew and I were introduced to Carol through Surrey Community Foundation whilst I was writing the *Hidden Surrey* report and we agreed to give a grant.

Helen Bowcock and I visited the Bungalow on the Sandy Hill estate, HQ of the Opportunities project, and met McFarlane. She told me how the project has developed and what difference it has made, and introduced me to Dawn, Karen and Sal:

Opportunities has changed the lives of so many of our students. We started off with IT skills but it soon became obvious that we needed to provide additional classes in English and maths in order to help them move forward and to support their children in their school work. We had funding from Surrey County Council for a year to fund tuition but the money ran out. We are now almost fully funded by the Hazelhurst Trust and have expanded our work into other parts of Surrey.

We are currently working with about sixty girls. The numbers are going up because the Job Centre is pushing people in our direction because of changes in benefits. One of the biggest challenges facing lone parents on benefits is that they must find some form of further education or training once their child is two, which for many is hard. This is a government requirement to ensure that people are trained and ready to take up a work placement when their child is five. Childcare is a big issue for lone parents during school holidays when they are required to work. If unemployed people on benefits do not conform to this requirement, they are sanctioned and benefits are reduced.

We are providing a social service. The saving to the state must be enormous. We have to address the student's problems before they can move on to learning and training, but the system does not recognise this. The stresses for our students are huge. They can suffer appalling crises involving violent and abusive relationships.

Karen confirmed this, telling me what the Opportunities programme had meant to her:

> I was a student working with Carol and this programme brought
> me out of isolation. A lot of women like me are having to deal with
> a load of problems.
>
> Coming together with girls of a similar background and exper-
> ience is a great emotional support. I was unemployed and dealing
> with the Job Centre was very intimidating. I didn't have a computer
> and I wasn't on the phone because I could not afford it. So the Job
> Centre put me in touch with Carol.
>
> I now have a part-time job doing youth work which I enjoy, but
> my finances are a challenge and so is dealing with the Job Centre. If
> they find us work, we have to stop studying.
>
> Ideally, having got my degree, I would like to go on and do a mas-
> ter's degree in criminology. Unfortunately, you cannot get student
> finance for postgraduate studies and you have to fund it yourself. I
> cannot reach my full potential at the moment. I will need to get a
> full-time and better-paid job and wait until I can fund myself but I
> need to be there for my twelve-year-old daughter who has problems.
>
> I have worked really hard to get to where I am but it is also hard
> to make the most of it. What is really important is that I don't slip
> back to where I was.

The government has announced loans for postgraduate study since
I met Karen but she might not want to take on debt. Carol said,
'This is a big problem because the rules are stopping people from
furthering themselves. You have to be really strong to overcome
these challenges. Those who are less strong are not going to make it.
The system does not encourage people to want to achieve.'

Next, Sal confirmed the value of the Opportunities programme:

> This has given us a much greater sense of self-worth and confidence.
> With encouragement from Carol, I realised I could do more than
> IT. I am a hands-on person and I love people so reflexology and

aromatherapy have turned out perfect for me. We all continue to
support each other and the project so it is good to give back. I am
both employed and self-employed with my work as a therapist. I
also work as a volunteer at a local hospice.

Carol told me that she was always thinking about what more could
be done:

> We have come to realise that the answers are on our doorstep in the
> community. People we know may have what we need. So we have
> set up a networking group. We link with the local churches which
> can give us space. The students are producing great artwork so we
> invite the community in to see it. We have formed a network for
> lone parents who have autistic children.
>
> Someone said to me recently that they feel a new sense of com-
> munity in the village.
>
> It is hard to prevent family breakdown because the girls are being
> forced back to work. If they don't, they won't have any money. One
> woman had a big problem because her mother was ill and she was
> her carer. Her benefits were docked and she was without money
> because she did not fill in the correct form because she could not
> read it. We are having to help women in their fifties with reading,
> and some have undiagnosed dyslexia.

Carol McFarlane is one of those indefatigable people who seem
able to overcome almost any challenge but as the Bowcocks are
providing a significant proportion of the funding for Opportunities,
what are the prospects for its sustainability? Helen Bowcock and I
discussed this and other aspects of philanthropic giving on our way
to the Watts Gallery, which is also supporting Opportunities:

> We do need to think about diversifying income in the interests of
> sustainability. Establishing a community social enterprise may be
> one way forward. Carol has ensured that the Opportunities project
> is developing links within the local community, setting up courses

which are open to the members of the village, thus integrating students into the community.

George Frederic Watts was one of the most popular and some say one of the greatest Victorian painters and sculptors. He and his wife Mary created the Watts Gallery in Compton, near Guildford. Carol McFarlane told me that her students now visit the gallery regularly and that for some it is a kind of therapy, helping them to relax and find time for themselves, at the same time helping them to discover new activities and achieve new skills. She is aiming to set up a social enterprise in craft with the skills that have been learned.

Helen Bowcock and I talked to the director of the Watts Gallery, Perdita Hunt:

Watts believed that art could transform lives. He participated in the Toynbee project in the East End of London that took his work to impoverished communities and that led to the founding of the Whitechapel Gallery. His wife, Mary, taught terracotta modelling to the 'shoe blacks' who polished shoes on the streets of east London.

When the Watts moved to Surrey, they believed they should continue that offer to the rural community. Mary Watts started evening terracotta modelling classes and that led to the building of the cemetery chapel at Compton with seventy local people, from the squire to the milkman.

They founded a pottery business, an early example of social enterprise, which was successful for fifty years, and they finally established the gallery with a hostel for apprentice potters. They had this high aesthetic ideal that practical learning skills lead to opportunities for social transformation. When we set about trying to revive not only the building here that was seriously at risk, but also the collection, we had to ask ourselves, how do we try to fulfil what the Watts were trying to achieve in the context of the twenty-first century?

We quickly came to a view, helped by Helen Bowcock's report *Hidden Surrey*, that there are real pockets of deprivation. We have one of the largest populations of women prisoners just up the road at HMP Send. We decided to take replicas of the collection into the prison with an artist to talk about the work and what lies behind it. Watts painted some stark images of London in the 1840s, including prostitution, death by homelessness and exploitation of labour that resonate today. With financial help from the Hazelhurst Trust, we have provided materials so that the prisoners can paint and model clay. We have been able to show and to sell this work and the participants get the money. This is now being replicated in two other prisons and at Feltham youth offenders' centres.

Some of the women who have visited for the Opportunities project had never travelled beyond Farnham, so coming to the gallery was a real journey, and to see them with their children making art was extraordinary. One of the youngest said, when you work with clay, it does not matter if you make a mistake, you can start again. As someone once said, if you are able to put a mark on paper, that is the beginning of self-expression and finding some value inside yourself.

The Watts' legacy is extraordinary. There is no other artists' village in Britain as you see here. It was Watts' money that built the chapel, the pottery and the gallery. He was an extraordinary philanthropist and supported thirty-four charities. He was a great supporter of women and believed in women's suffrage. He was president of the anti-tight-lacing society which championed the cause of women who did not want to wear tight corsets, and his paintings depicted women in looser dresses. Watts was a social activist as well as an artist.

Some neighbours comment how busy it is here now and I say that this is what it was like 100 years ago when there were special trains bringing visitors from London. This is what real heritage should be, to recreate the energy and the power of the time. This is what Jonathan Ruffer is doing in Bishop Auckland [see Chapter 15]. The reason why ours is a genuine revival is that it comes from a real heritage bequeathed by the Watts.

The Bowcocks have played a leading role in supporting the restoration and revival of the Watts gallery. Their Hazelhurst Trust continues to support the creation of much needed social and cultural capital in Surrey in order to address hidden inequality in one of the wealthiest parts of the country. They are also supporting an initiative in Africa and our next stop is Zambia. The link between Surrey and Zambia is the role of community.

*   *   *

Patricia Napier and I are almost exact contemporaries. We met by chance and I sensed someone extraordinary with a story to tell:

> I was brought up to be philanthropic in a non-conformist family in Southport, Lancashire. Giving was part of our everyday culture. My father was treasurer at our local Congregational church. This was the church that founded the London Missionary Society. Every year, when missionaries came back on furlough, they had six months' leave which included duties visiting churches. These were known as Deputation Weekends so that is how I grew up — knowing a lot about what was happening in Zambia and other parts of Africa. At Sunday school, we had London Missionary Society Collecting boxes that were in the shape of a thatched hut.
>
> I trained to be a nurse and midwife and applied to Voluntary Services Overseas (VSO). I had always wanted to do VSO. And I wanted to go to Africa. It was in my soul.
>
> I was sent to Zambia in 1970. I had been qualified as a midwife for four weeks! I went to a United Church of Zambia support mission in southern Zambia, forty miles from the nearest town. I ran a rural health centre with forty beds in a number of scattered buildings in a field, and I was there for two years. I was twenty-three. There was no electricity or running water, no communication, no doctor. I didn't see a doctor the entire time I was there.
>
> I didn't think I was being very brave. I had been sensitised for so many years that I regarded it as perfectly normal. And I did want to do it. I loved it despite the hard work and frustration and being ill a lot. It was tremendously fulfilling.
>
> I came home after two years and crashed. I was an only child and

had elderly parents so I just had to grit my teeth and get on with it. Because I knew I could not do it again, that I could never repeat that experience in Zambia.

Through VSO, I was then invited to become part of a group that was supporting work in Zambia. This led to the founding the Baynards Zambia Trust (BZT) in 1996.

By founding BZT, we were providing a new source of funding to the charity in Zambia we had been supporting for some time. The funds would go direct to support work in the field and we decided to run our charity in a way that meant the trustees took on all the responsibility and that we would have no paid staff and we would absorb all the costs in the UK. This was to avoid empire building. We started very small. We were asked to build a mothers' shelter that cost £5,000 at an Anglican Mission Hospital. We had no idea how we were going to raise that but we did.

The field office that we had been supporting decided to become a Zambian non-governmental organisation (NGO) called Hodi, a generic Zambian word meaning: 'Can I help you?'

We were very focused on filling funding gaps for Hodi. Hodi got bigger and after some time challenged us to take on an entire programme. We were initially quite nervous but we rose to the challenge and instead of sending £5,000 to £10,000 per annum, suddenly we were responsible for £50,000 and more. This was about eight years ago. Now it is £200,000.

The Hodi trustees got to the point where they realised that some of the projects we had been supporting were ready to be spawned off. The field officer of our main project, Brandy Mungaila, realised that they could become an NGO, so BZT became their partners and funders. Brandy and I are the current owners of the Zambia Rainbow Development Foundation (ZRDF).

We are supporting ZRDF so that in time they have sufficient funding from others as well as from us to stand on their own feet. They act as facilitators and provide technical support. Starting with education, BZT believes that community capacity-building, im-proving access to primary education, raising income levels, and HIV and Aids awareness raising and treatment are mutually supportive, justifying each component in what is an holistic approach for the long term.

ZRDF, with the help of BZT, is offering communities the possibility of providing education. The government cannot afford to build primary schools. If a community can provide a sustainable school building to a government specification and provide a teacher's house (absolutely critical) the government will provide a trained teacher.

Brandy's job is to support the communities. The first thing everyone has to understand is the importance of working together. But these communities are scattered. So they make the bricks in one place and then they have to think how to get the bricks to the site. Brandy and colleagues don't tell them how to do it but tease out of them how they are going to solve their own problems but the key point is that these are Zambians helping other Zambians to sort out Zambian problems.

We are now beginning to think about the quality of education in these schools. Most teachers want to go to urban areas. To go to a rural area, where it may be a week's walk to get to the nearest town, is a real challenge. In order to recruit the teachers, we need to support them.

We are now working with 50,000 people in 2,500 square miles. There are now ten ZRDF schools.

Farmers grow only maize to feed themselves. We encourage them to diversify and grow something of higher value. We encourage farmers to come together to clear land where there is year-round ground water so they may grow bananas. This has been very successful. Where there isn't ground water, they now grow soya, a rain-fed crop. Both are nutritious and of high value. They grow in groups and come together to sell. This has also been successful. They are given loans to start that are then paid back and then they are on their own.

We do a lot of work around HIV and Aids in Zambia and you cannot undertake anything meaningful without engaging with it. The Mkuohi district of Zambia, where we work, has a 14 per cent incidence of HIV. The key is clearly prevention. Many adults are illiterate. Radios are beyond the means of most. So information is through word of mouth. Sensitisation is done through the training of peer educators and supporting the dedicated HIV teacher in each school. Secondly, community volunteers are trained as care givers to families managing a sick relative and thirdly and importantly, some senior well respected members of the community are trained to counsel those who wish to be tested or those who are unwell.

If we are raising people to the bottom rung of life, there are too many people below the bottom rung. If these people are left behind by those ascending the ladder, they sink lower. And they concern me hugely.

So on this last visit, I insisted I had time to visit the poorest of the poor. I visited a woman who was seventy-three, living on her own and looking after five grandchildren. She earned money to buy maize by weeding people's maize plots and she had to weed five seventy-metre rows to get enough money to buy a five-kilo bag of maize and then she would have to weed another two rows to get enough money for it to be ground. So the children sometimes had food and sometimes not. She did not have a best dress and did not come to the meetings and was therefore losing out.

The dress is about self-exclusion. This is a socio-economic problem for poor people everywhere. People like to dress up for meetings. They work very hard, walking a mile or more to get water. They are pounding maize, washing clothes in the river, they are pregnant, they are ill, they have drunk husbands, there is no money so an afternoon out is a treat. People who don't have a dress don't go to meetings.

We decided that the poorest of the poor have to be a community responsibility. We talked to them about how the most vulnerable can be identified and what response and contribution they could make. One suggestion was that those relatives of the poorest who farm soya in groups could have a larger plot to produce more food so that the most vulnerable are fed as part of a plan.

Because of our holistic approach, what ZRDF is doing is unique in Zambia. This could be a model for other local Zambian organisations and ZRDT's work needs to be documented. As trust-ees, we meet all costs and run the charity from two computers and a kitchen table.

* * *

As the Bowcocks are supporting the work of the Baynards Zambia Trust, I asked Matthew to comment on what lessons might be learned from Zambia and whether there are any parallels with the UK.

Patricia Napier's account of the woman who could not afford a dress and did not attend a women's finance cooperative meeting in Zambia shows that economic investment in that village was creat-ing inequality. We are helping to create more and more 'haves' and leaving behind a number of 'have-nots'.

What lessons can we learn? Can we transplant that into com-munities in the UK? How do we apply that same philosophy to a local problem, such as to dealing in drugs behind the supermarket?

The Opportunities project Helen and I are supporting in Farnham costs £25,000 a year. Local authorities spend many times more on trying to solve problems like that and are getting nowhere. The problem is when public or external agencies say that they know how to fix other people's problems. I believe that people know the answer to their own problems. What matters is accessing the solutions.

One of the problems communities face is a sense of disempower-ment and a lack of ownership. How do we get people to change the way they think?

In our town, local kids burnt down a bus shelter for fun. People said the police or the council should do something. Maybe they should but the most effective way to deal with anti-social behaviour is to support the local youth charity that is trying to keep the kids off the street. This is about owning your own life within a local com-munity. Policy and action needs to be bottom up.

In 1948, polls reported that the vast majority of those surveyed thought there would be no further need for any charities. A generation of baby boomers expected care from cradle to grave. We paid high tax in exchange and expected social problems to be solved.

Now, our generation realises that many social problems have not been solved, but do not believe that these problems are ours. One answer, of course, is to put more money in. But the economy is suffering and people do not seem to be prepared to put more money in through increased taxation. So our generation is perplexed and lacking in ideology.

There is no new revolutionary thinking coming out of teenagers but there does seem to be a greater social awareness amongst the young. We do need to be aware that with the baby boomer cohort moving into retirement, though the younger generation may be more empathetic, it will be saddled with student debt, the cost of raising families and looking after their parents and we might see a fall in charitable giving.

With the retreat or redefinition of the state, there is a great opportunity for private wealth to recreate a philanthropic culture. In order to change the culture, government, the private sector and civil society must be independent of each other and there needs to be robust investment by civil society in civil society. I don't want the government to get in the way.

The true role of philanthropy is to invest where neither business nor government will go. We do have a serious problem in that the majority of very wealthy people do not feel a sense of obligation to society. Philanthropy is not just about giving money: it is a commitment to other people and to society. Philanthropy is time, talent and treasure.

I agree with Matthew but with one exception. His wish for the government to keep out of the way is understandable given the record of politicians whose ignorance and prejudice about philanthropy has caused so much grief to donors, to charities and to campaigners like him. The voluntary sector must maintain its independence. However, government has a stake in charitable giving via tax reliefs and can help to generate more private giving by matching personal donations. We must not give up on persuading politicians to understand how philanthropy works and how the state could work with the voluntary sector in an enabling role.

I agree that we need to foster a greater sense of community and community responsibility, but this will be a challenge given that our present cultural focus is upon aspirational individuals and hard-working families. There are ways of engendering a sense of community and commitment and I will investigate how to do this on a grand scale in the next chapter.

CHAPTER 15

RENAISSANCE: A TALE OF TWO MEN AND TWO TOWNS

"I firmly believe that there is a strong connection between community spirit and commercial success. We generated enormous goodwill in the local area."

SIR ROGER DE HAAN, FORMER CHAIRMAN OF SAGA,

FOLKESTONE.

* * *

A town in north-east England of which you may never have heard is to become an internationally recognised destination for lovers of Spanish Art and is mounting the biggest live event in Britain since the 2012 Olympics, all because one man has dug deep into his pockets and found the £75 million to pay for it. Unlikely as it may be, this is true and in July 2016, the vision of one man was made manifest in County Durham, with the premiere of *Kynren*, a pageant, with a cast of 1,000 local volunteers, telling the story of Britain from the Romans to victory at the end of the Second World War, seen through the eyes of a boy from the north-east, performed in the shadow of Bishop Auckland castle.

Jonathan Ruffer, the benefactor of Bishop Auckland, is determined that this part of Durham will have a very much brighter future than its recent past following the collapse of coal mining. Ruffer has a plan but denies having a vision:

I come from this part of the world and I want to see Bishop Auckland a wonderful place socially, economically, morally, spiritually. What I want to see is a change in the way people are.

I am doing what I am because I feel called to do it. One of the things I find nonplussing is people who ask me about my vision. I haven't really got one. I have been called on a journey, like Abraham was.

I always knew that I wanted to do something that combatted deprivation. After the coal mining went, this area somehow lost its personality and sense of being so I thought it a good place to tackle.

Jonathan Ruffer's company manages other people's money and is well known in financial circles for calling the 2008–09 recession correctly. His clients made money when other people were losing it. Ruffer is also an art collector and particularly keen on Spanish old master paintings. When he heard that the Church Commissioners were planning to sell twelve seventeenth-century paintings by Zurbarán that had hung in the Bishop Auckland castle's long dining room for 250 years, he bought them and established the Auckland Castle Trust to preserve the castle and its contents with a donation of £15 million.

He has spent a further £18 million on redeveloping the castle, which has one of the grandest medieval halls in England, restoring a vast walled garden that will be open to the public for the first time, and creating a Museum of Religion that will tell the story of religion in the British Isles from pre-history to the present day. The Trust has spent a further £5.5 million on converting a former bank in Bishop Auckland's market place into a gallery, and an adjacent school will be a centre for the study of Spanish art and its history. There are also plans for a new hotel in the town centre. The plan is to make Bishop Auckland an internationally recognised centre for Spanish art history and thereby restore the fortunes of a community where unemployment is twice the national average.

Another draw for tourists will be *Kynren*, a series of fourteen epic after-dark performances below the illuminated castle for a nightly audience of 8,000 between July and September. There are

1,000 volunteer performers from the local community who have been trained by professionals, masterminded by Steve Boyd who has been responsible for the mass performances and parades at the Olympics since 1992.

Kynren, in which Ruffer has invested over £30 million, is intended to run for decades:

> The idea is to create a force that helps people find a purpose without coercing them, to give them something that encourages them to come together and do things they did not think they could do – it is not simply about spending a vast amount of money.

I talked to Jonathan Ruffer in his London office nine months before the premiere of *Kynren*. I wanted to know what had motivated him to make such a huge commitment in order to revitalise a community:

> I was not brought up to be philanthropic. I am utterly uninterested in money. I find it a very dull thing. People find that strange when I am in investment but I reply: 'Would you appoint a drunk to run a bar?' Being uninterested in money is a great help. It is much better to be able to view it from a distance, and cynically on occasion.
>
> I dwell in the realm of ideas. I am not a practical person. I became interested in urban deprivation. I could see how people had to be so resourceful with money. The trouble with money and those in need is not the dependency culture which most people speak about, but the unfairness of it. It sets a society on edge if a rich man comes around bran-tubbing the locals. It can be very unfair and hard on those who are left out, and that is why I have gone down the route I have at Bishop Auckland which is to try transform life for everyone to some degree.
>
> Giving is as personal as falling in love. There are no rules. I have never been very interested in funding excellence – for instance, the person who lives in a slum but who might be the next Shakespeare – I have more of a heart for the people who cannot help themselves and where the hidden extras can transform a life.

This is not a virtue but simply the way I am made. I have always treated everybody the same. This is not an intellectual thing. It wouldn't matter if you were Princess Margaret or unemployed from Nuneaton, I would not have a different sense of engagement.

I am supporting the Durham Community Foundation. I give as much as I can directly into deprivation and I am extremely gratified that there are different ways of doing that. The Community Foundation is one way. The important thing is not to use that kind of giving as a comfort food.

One of the tensions about Bishop Auckland is that although I believe that I am doing this to bring about an opportunity to see the region regenerated, there is a parrot sitting on each shoulder and one says: scrubbing up a palace seems a fairly odd way of doing that. I am pretty 'God-ey' and I do find myself saying to God: 'I do really know better than you, God, about how to use this money.'

I was brought up as an evangelical Christian and evangelicals would have me planting churches and doing gospel work. And there is a bit of me that is saying, Jonathan, you are not doing enough gospel work.

Then there are the heavy-duty people who are used to working with deprivation. They see what I am doing as a cop-out. They say I am pretending to do it for the good of Auckland but really I just like scrubbing up castles.

I feel called to this. It is not a pleasurable calling because I don't really know what it is. Abraham was told to go off on a journey and never knew where he was off to. And I feel that is happening to me.

I agree we lack moral leadership. I am not a proselytiser, but one of the things that makes me really angry is how almost none of us who have earned such an extraordinary sum of money through the city behave properly in the use of their money. These are people who twenty years ago had nothing and now have an amount that even if they kept 5 per cent they would still be amongst the richest people in the country.

I don't regard myself as being in a selfless position because I have an income that is likely to continue. I still have the business. That is why I remain in the Rich List. I see myself as having no savings and giving away almost everything that is coming in.

People who give have to have the right attitude of mind and they need to be brave. If a burglar breaks in, curiosity is not going to solve your problem whereas a rugby tackle might. The donor has to select the right emotion and the right virtue to be effective in response. Many people think in terms of sacrifice when they contemplate giving. If you do that, then fine. You will give away a little. But money is a bully so be careful. It is a bit like having a casual affair. If you get a taste for this it will louse you up.

I start on the basis that I am frightened of money. I see how it shackles people. The people who hang on to their money are un-spoiled in the sense that they are exactly what they were before: greedy shits. I have seen a lot of people who started out nuanced, interesting, fun and self-deprecating, and when they get a lot of money, they are no longer like that. It is like getting old. Some people get fat and have double chins or a bad back. Age coarsens the body and money seems to coarsen the mind. Think about food. It has to go through you but if it gets stuck it will do you harm. Money is no different from that.

Giving should be seen as common sense but then what you give it to can be a nightmare. But you have to work at it.

Investment is exactly how I see the Bishop Auckland project. My original intention was to become the patron saint of the soup ladle in Sunderland. But some fierce lady asked me: 'What qualities do you bring to ladling out soup?' I replied: 'I have a very nice smile.' She gave me a look of utter contempt and said: 'Do you think your smile is going to get people off drugs, do you?' She was absolutely right. Game over on the soup ladle idea.

What I can do is unite people and encourage people. It was at the time that the Church Commissioners were trying to sell the Zurbaráns and it seemed to me to be such a shitty thing to do. They were the last thing of value that were not nailed down in the county. I thought I would do what Peter Cook called a futile gesture. I am going to buy these pictures and give them to the people of the north-east. The soup lady would no doubt have been withering about that helping everyone feel better. I would have said to her of course not. But my gift was a way of saying that someone is coming into the community who wants to be part of it and wants to help.

Neil McGregor (former Director of the British Museum) persuaded me that to save the pictures but do nothing about the castle was to unlock a door and not to open it. I could not decide if helping to open the doors of the castle would prove to be a cul-de-sac and give a reality to the gesture I had made. Neil was absolutely firm that to 'save' the castle would be an act of reinforcement. I needed something external to help me to decide.

The act of trust is that this will act as a catalyst for the region. How that will happen is only gradually becoming clear. It took time for me to understand that what I was doing was about Bishop Auckland itself, a small town of 27,000 people. That was a revelation.

There is the most beautiful piece of land there that is surrounded by the River Wear. In the eighteenth century, it was believed to be a Roman forum. They used to celebrate the Olympiad there every June. It has always been a place of entertainment. We are going into a joint venture with a French organisation, Puy du Fou, an entertainment company in the Vendée, which is the armpit of France. It was a place of oppression because they were monarchists and they rebelled against the French Revolution. The place was razed to the ground and 300,000 people were killed. It is a dark part of France where the people are inward-looking. Puy du Fou puts on a huge light show there that involves locals. Everything is done by volunteers and it is as grand as the Olympic opening ceremony, winning Oscars for being the best theme park in the world and attracting two million people per year. This has completely transformed the area and the people because so many are involved in a world-class show and this is what we are going to do in Bishop Auckland.

We will create, or re-create, a community and bring people together. The key thing is that within so-called ordinary people there are many excellences. This kind of experience helps people to feel that they are somebody. We have someone working with us who will be training up to 1,000 people in Bishop Auckland and he has been involved with every Olympics since 1992. He is a kind of people whisperer.

My total personal investment in Bishop Auckland will probably be about £75 million with an additional grant of £10 million from the Heritage Lottery Fund.

Am I pleased? I have spent the last three years operating almost exclusively within an emotion of fear. I feel completely vulnerable, like a gentoo penguin. I am like the king in chess, and I can see that, but the pawn can move so much faster than I can. I don't share the triumphalism that people feel for this project.

I am also endowing curators at the Art Fund and it has been a marvellous success. I feel that a continuum of knowledge is so important for us to know who we are. When you consider what is happening with museums closing down or scaling back, the natural thing is to cut back on curators, and that means you can so easily break the thread. It is vital to keep that thread with the past.

One of the things I find very chilling about the ranks of evangelical Christians is that they are miles away from anything good or worthwhile or lovely. People think they have no faith and what they have found may be nameless but it is there. Prepositions matter. If you bring a blessing *to* somebody you are a menace but if you do something *for* somebody it is better but still directionally wrong. But if you work *with* people, if you have money and they need money then you must try to give in a spirit of equality.

*   *   *

Jonathan Ruffer does not want anyone to think that he is remarkable and I guess Sir Roger De Haan would feel the same. De Haan is the former chairman of Saga, the insurance and travel provider for the over-fifties. He sold the company to Charterhouse, the private equity group, for £1.35 billion in cash in 2004. He has donated and invested more than £50 million in charitable and creative projects in Folkestone since the millennium. The town and its prospects have been transformed. Although I spoke briefly to Sir Roger at an event in London and he agreed that we should talk further, his reputation for being a private man was confirmed when he referred me to Nick Ewbank. Ewbank is the founding director of the arts and regeneration charity, the Creative Foundation, and of Nick Ewbank Associates. Ewbank, together with Roger De Haan, steered the project to revitalise Folkestone between 2001 and 2010, a project that continues.

Folkestone had been in decline as a resort since the 1950s, a fate shared with several other coastal towns, including Blackpool, our next port of call. Folkestone was a small fishing village on the Kent coast before the arrival of the railway in the middle of the nineteenth century. Lord Radnor, who also enjoyed the title of Viscount Folkestone, decided that the town should become an upmarket resort, as there was a fashion for holidays by the sea. This was to be Belgravia-on-Sea. Two very grand hotels were built at the turn of the century and aimed at the aristocratic market, including the then Prince of Wales and Alice Keppel, his mistress.

One of these hotels was the Metropole. By the 1950s, the market for that kind of holiday had evaporated and the Metropole was an apartment block, although one with a difference. Gerald Glover, its owner, was a friend of Kenneth Clark, the art historian and owner of nearby Saltwood Castle, who helped the Glover family mount a series of diverse exhibitions in the former hotel's vast reception rooms, of work by Turner, Henry Moore and Yoko Ono. By the 1990s, the art experiment and Folkestone had lost their way.

Meanwhile the De Haan family was prospering. Saga, as it became, had been founded by Roger De Haan's father, Sidney, after the Second World War, initially offering low-cost out-of-season holidays for older people at a single, modest hotel. The De Haan family strongly believed that they should support the community and institutions of Folkestone where the company was based and from where it drew the majority of its workforce. By the time Sidney retired in 1984, the company had become Saga and one of the UK's largest and most successful family-owned companies.

The commitment to the renaissance of Folkestone was made

before Roger De Haan became a billionaire and it is notable that, unlike Jonathan Ruffer in Bishop Auckland, he was not steeped in the arts. I asked Nick Ewbank to take up the story.

The rise of Saga mirrored the decline of the town. The Metropole Arts Centre was in terminal decline. The management went to Roger and asked for help. He agreed to replace the lost Arts Council grant with a pledge of £30,000 a year for three years. Within a month, Roger realised that the centre needed more than financial help and, somewhat reluctantly, he agreed to become chairman. They looked for a new director and that is how I became involved in 2001.

The initial view was that a shiny new arts centre might be the answer. But there was no answer to the question: where was the audience? The old town was dysfunctional and considered a no-go area by many local people because there were so many issues with drugs, alcohol and fear of crime. Educational attainment was low and unemployment was high and this was a problem for Saga in terms of recruitment. Saga was committed to staying in the town but the young unemployed people who applied for jobs often lacked the literary and numeracy skills and the confidence they needed to work in the company's call centre. The local secondary school that served the east end of Folkestone was the fourth worst in the country in terms of GSCE results.

Although Roger was not interested in the arts, he was very interested in architectural design. Saga needed a new HQ and he decided to appoint an architect of exceptional quality. Michael Hopkins – architect of Glyndebourne, the London 2012 Velodrome, Portcullis House and Westminster underground station – was selected. Interestingly, Saga found there were much lower levels of staff sickness and absenteeism in a new, attractive, light-filled building. And staff turnover was lower. So great design led to higher economic efficiency and Roger became a convert to the importance of good design.

We considered how creativity and culture could make Folkestone a better town to live and work in and to visit. We looked at Bilbao.

We decided that tourism was not the way forward because the nature of tourism had changed so much. Roger understood this because Saga had originally been a holiday business. Tourism is poorly paid and seasonal. In any case, the tourist industry in Folkestone was more or less dead by 2000.

In 2002, 800 people turned up for a public meeting to discuss: 'Is Folkestone dying?' We decided to join forces with the organisers, a local action group called 'Go Folkestone'. This helped to alleviate any feeling that what we might propose was coming down from on high.

This is a problem for any kind of philanthropic intervention. Very wealthy people have an understandable tendency to believe that they know best. It is also natural for people to resist change. However, if you are interested in helping communities to help themselves, solutions have to come from the community.

I also learned how an entrepreneur thinks and works. Roger had a lot to learn too. He had not had much experience of working with local authorities; this requires huge reserves of tact and diplomacy if you want to assert your sense of vision and drive. About this time, Roger became chairman of a local authority programme called 'Believing in Folkestone'. By the time he joined, he was shocked to discover that all the money had been allocated without any clear over-arching plan. That was an eye opener.

We agreed we needed a plan and I wrote the brief setting out our aspiration to revitalise the old town by creating artists' studios, letting them out on cheap rents, placing creative education at the heart of a reformed education sector, exploring the possibility of utilising the marine promenade, where Henry Moore had lent work for display, as a sculpture park, and this eventually morphed into the Folkestone Triennial of contemporary art. We examined the feasibility of and potential for the film, video and media sector as employers, and establishing an arts and health research centre. This formed the basis of the plan.

Everything was a struggle at the beginning because we were almost entirely dependent on public funding, but the situation was transformed by the sale of Saga. The family charitable trust had shares in Saga and became cash rich after the sale. This gave us the opportunity to act.

We focused our attention on regenerating the old town. We looked at the way Hoxton, in east London, had been regenerated and decided to invest in property. However, we became aware of the Hoxton effect whereby property prices rise after regeneration. Artists moved out of London to Hastings and Margate. Roger's solution was to buy property and to keep the rents affordable so that creative businesses could remain in situ.

Public and private collaboration is very difficult to achieve. The staff of publicly funded bodies have conflicting demands upon their time and resources. There is a temptation that if you see someone who is passionate and wealthy and doing good, you pat them on the back and say carry on, you are doing a wonderful job and here are a few crumbs. There is an even worse tendency for the local council to ask: 'Who is this person who thinks he can improve our town, how dare he?' This was not said explicitly but there was a definite coolness. It was years before the work of the Creative Foundation was seen to be core to the policy objectives of the local, democratically elected authority. That has now happened. All this took an enormous amount of Roger's time.

Roger also sponsored the Folkestone Academy and another in Ramsgate, and is chair of the board of governors. These were first-wave academies in wonderful buildings. The pupils originally in dilapidated sheds are now in temples of light and enlightenment. The Folkestone Academy has transformed the educational attainment of the community it serves. In 2003, only 8 cent of pupils achieved five good GSCEs; in 2010, 73 per cent reached this benchmark level.

For the art Triennial, we loved the idea of a gallery without walls. We could see that we would need substantial grants from the Arts Council and the County Council and these were unlikely to be forthcoming. So we were persuaded not to create a sculpture park but do something that was more integrated with the town. The result was that we were able to commission cutting-edge contemporary art and a number of the new pieces were left behind afterwards. Folkestone has a legacy of work by artists such as Tracey Emin, Cornelia Parker, Yoko Ono, Richard Wilson and Mark Wallinger. Roger committed £4.5 million to fund the first three Triennials which began in 2008, and has since renewed his support so that further exhibitions can take place.

When I came to Folkestone, I was keen to see what could be done with the arts and health. I knew that Roger De Haan and Saga were interested in the well-being of older people. What I didn't know was that Sidney De Haan, who died in 2002, had dementia. Roger had noticed that attending music concerts had a transformational effect upon his father.

We created an arts and health research centre in Folkestone linked to Canterbury Christ Church University. This focused on the importance of singing for health and physical well-being. The centre has run the world's first randomised controlled trial on community singing and has produced evidence of a significant effect on pulmonary conditions such as emphysema that appear to be as effective as drug treatments.

The Sidney De Haan Research Centre is the only part of the entire project that has taken the family name. My consultancy and the De Haan Centre have done a joint project looking at the impact of engaging with mainstream arts activity on people's health, well-being and social capital. We have now built a wider partnership in order to bid to the Wellcome Trust and the Paul Hamlyn Foundation for funding to investigate the links between cultural engagement and health and well-being.

In my view, there is a paucity of evidence about the public benefit of culture and we need much more robust evidence. Evidence of impact is everything for an entrepreneur.

Roger also bought the harbour for £11 million as well as a neighbouring site on the sea front. The regeneration of this area will also make a significant impact. A mixed use for leisure, residential and retail will enhance Folkestone's appeal even further. Eight miles along the coast, Dover has remained much the same, but Folkestone has really moved on. There are new shops, restaurants, new bars, a new café culture and new music clubs. People feel much more positive about the place. There is a sense of optimism that was not there fifteen years ago.

Jonathan Ruffer and Roger De Haan have chosen to devote a significant proportion of their personal fortunes to benefit their fellow men and women, by investing and in and rebuilding communities and thereby reinforcing the common good.

In this, both men are unusual. They have a sense of obligation to others that is lacking in the majority of their peer group. Imagine what Britain would be like if others were to give on this scale and with such commitment.

CHAPTER 16

THOSE WERE THE DAYS: WHY THE REBIRTH OF A TOWN MATTERS

"There is an ongoing generational cycle of poverty in Blackpool that is very difficult to break."
JOSEPH ROWNTREE FOUNDATION.

"We don't do pessimism."
NEIL JACK, CHIEF EXECUTIVE, BLACKPOOL COUNCIL.

*   *   *

Why do we need to know about Blackpool, the poorest town in Britain according to its chief executive? The town is a microcosm of some of the most challenging problems facing Britain. Fixing these should be a matter of public interest, not least because the cost of welfare and housing benefit is enormous and funded by all taxpayers.

Blackpool's renewal can teach us how to invest in communities whilst public funding is being cut. There is also much to learn from Blackpool's history about what may be achieved by local leadership and commitment to the common good.

In 1889, Sir John Bickerstaffe, Mayor of Blackpool, visited the World Fair and the new Eiffel Tower in Paris. He returned determined to build a tower for Blackpool at a cost of £300,000. Sir John invested £20,000 or almost £2 million in today's money.

Bickerstaffe's optimism, ambition and determination paid off and the Tower was opened in 1894, confirming Blackpool as a British institution, the world's first mass-market seaside resort and with a proud heritage stretching back over 150 years. At its peak, Blackpool was the most popular resort in the world with 20 million annual visitors.

Blackpool became the world capital of fun; its success was due to the foresight and enterprise of local business people in the nineteenth and first part of the twentieth century. Sir John Bickerstaffe was my great-uncle and others who were the original shareholders and directors of the Tower Company included my great-grandfather. These Victorians had been hoteliers and property developers since the 1700s and with the coming of the railway in the 1840s, they were well positioned to exploit opportunities.

Blackpool was run by entrepreneurs. They invested in local businesses, served on the council and supported local charities, and the town prospered.

However, with the advent of cheap travel overseas, Blackpool went into decline and my family sold all their investments in the town in the 1960s and 1970s.

Blackpool's renewal is being driven by the public sector via local government, a reminder that public money must continue to play a key role. Public money, including the Big Lottery Fund, is fundamentally important because Blackpool's voluntary sector and private sector are small. There is no prospect of the kind of philanthropy that is transforming Bishop Auckland and Folkestone.

Blackpool is showing extraordinary resilience in the face of adversity and my conversations with local people were most inspiring. However, we need to look at the bad news first in order to understand the challenges that need to be overcome.

In 2013, the Centre for Social Justice published *Turning the Tide*, a study of five seaside towns, including Blackpool. Here are some excerpts from the report:

> Blackpool is the ninth most deprived local authority district in England, with an increase in overall deprivation of 17 per cent since 2007.

Social problems plague Blackpool: family breakdown, crime, drugs, poor education attainment, low aspiration.

Unemployment in Blackpool is above average and increasing. No industry has taken the place of tourism. Many jobs are seasonal, poorly paid and part-time. Workers in Blackpool earn on average £120.50 a week less than the national weekly wage.

Cheap housing has led to coastal towns becoming dumping grounds for those with problems such as unemployment, social exclusion and substance abuse. Blackpool is no exception and has attracted a vulnerable and transient population.

The transience of the population affects the severity of family breakdown. Thirty per cent of high-risk domestic abuse referrals involve families who have been living in Blackpool for less than three months.

Blackpool has the highest alcohol specific mortality rate for men and the second highest for women in the UK.

Life expectancy for men is the lowest in England. 13,500 young people aged sixteen to eighteen have mental health problems.

Blackpool has the highest rate of children looked after by a local authority in England, 150 per 10,000 population, far exceeding the English average of fifty-nine. One in every sixty-six children is in care, up from one in every 107 in 2008.

Further gloomy statistics come via the Community Foundation of Lancashire:

Thirty per cent of the population is estimated to smoke, the fourth highest level in England. Levels of cancer mortality are well inside the worst 5 per cent nationally.

Blackpool is rated the worst district in Lancashire for levels of obesity and levels of diabetes prevalence and heart disease are well above the national average.

Thirty per cent of children and 27 per cent of people over the age of sixty live below the poverty line.

Blackpool Council has published an ambitious recovery plan for

2015–20. The plan reveals that the council's budget has been cut
by £93 million since 2011, representing 40 per cent of the total reduction expected by 2020. Blackpool is estimated to have lost local
authority spending of £261.52 per head since 2011 compared with a
reduction of 58 pence in Guildford.

In his foreword to the plan, Neil Jack, chief executive, says the
council is on the cusp of fundamental change in how it serves local
people and the time for simply delivering services has gone.

I visited Blackpool for a few days in 2015 and met Neil Jack and
some of his senior team, including Merle Davies, Director for Early
Child Development. Since 2010/11, the council has lost a third of its
workforce and the number of council employees will continue to decline. I asked Neil Jack to set out the challenges facing Blackpool, how
they might be overcome and for his vision of what Blackpool could be
in the future:

> Excluding housing benefit and schools spending, our gross budget
> has been cut from £272 million in 2009/10 to around £219 million
> in 2014/15; this includes growth in spending in both child and adult
> social care. We have more cuts to come. We lose another £25 mil-
> lion next year, around £20 million the following year and probably
> around £15 million for the two years after that. This will result in a
> total cut of over 50 per cent. And we have more responsibilities and
> more demand for services than we had before.
>
> We are the poorest town in England. Our particular problem is
> the transience of our population which is not seen elsewhere on this
> scale. Much of our holiday accommodation was fit for the 1950s but
> not for the twenty-first century. With 17 million visitors last year, we
> remain the most popular resort in the UK but many are weekend or
> day visitors rather than staying a fortnight as before. We no longer
> need the volume of accommodation that we have, and what we do
> need is more of a high quality.
>
> We have 3,500 properties that are houses in multiple occupation.
> They are densely packed together often full of poor quality bedsits
> or small flats. Over 80 per cent of the tenants are on housing benefit.

The private rented market in Blackpool is not one you would recognise anywhere else in the country. Many of the people who live in these properties have multiple problems.

The big challenge is to stabilise communities when accommodation is of rock-bottom quality.

The Big Society idea is completely missing the point: it feels like a Home Counties answer to an inner-city problem. There is an assumption that money and volunteers are as available as they are in the south-east. We don't have wealthy bankers or the WI here. We don't have the big charities here. Our voluntary sector is small and doesn't have the resources of larger charities. We do have a number of Big Lottery Fund programmes, such as Blackpool Better Start and HeadStart, that have brought some of the bigger charities into town, the NSPCC and MIND, but our local voluntary sector is small.

But to suggest that money is the only answer is misleading if not plain wrong. Under the previous Labour government we had centralised decision-making and more money but they didn't understand the nature of the problems. Jobs are the obvious solution, but we cannot improve our local economy without addressing the housing problem. If we were to create 1,000 new jobs, all that would happen is that these people would come into town during the day and then drive away again. We cannot change the economic landscape until we tackle the fundamental problem of the local infrastructure.

The one thing that we think could enable us to bring about real change would be local control of housing benefit. At the moment there is no relationship between the quality of housing and the amount of housing benefit paid to a landlord. All that happens now is that landlords need to meet a minimum legal standard. These standards are barely acceptable. There is no financial incentive for landlords to invest in their properties. In many places, the market may act to drive improvements, but there is no market when over 80 per cent of tenants are on housing benefit. There is an incentive for landlords to cram as many people as possible in cheap to run properties.

We are looking for control of local housing benefit that will allow us to link benefit to standards, including space, amenity and management of properties.

The council has set up a company that aims to buy up substandard properties, both reducing the number of units in them and improving the quality. We will borrow £30 million initially to get this started. I believe that in order to get traction and change the market, we will need the company to own at least 1,000 units. We will need to share the risk over time, we cannot take on all of it. While it is important for us to lead on many of these issues, we are only interventionist to the extent that we need to be; we want to bring better-quality private providers into the market, but we need to show that it can work.

We have made huge investments in the Winter Gardens and the Tower, worth nearly £50 million, and these have been instrumental in starting to turn around the town. These are the town's key assets, and they were being seriously neglected by the previous owners. This is the first time in their history that they have been in public ownership.

There are signs of progress. The numbers of those who are coming to visit and to stay are increasing, the amount of activity in the town is up, the private sector investment in terms of restaurants and hotels is continuing to increase. You only have to look at the transformation of the promenade and the tramway to see how we want the future to look.

The council used to have its staff and offices spread out all over the town but the move to a striking new building, close to the railway station and next to a new Sainsbury's, is making a difference. Now that the council offices are in the centre of town rather than at the end of the motorway, more working people are coming into the town every day. More money is now being spent in the town, creating a different feel and leading to new businesses.

Blackpool is not just about the tourists, and that means that there have to be things that locals want to do and places they want to go. The key thing is to have shops that make money every day of the week and not just at weekends. Moving the council HQ back into the town is part of that strategy.

Another key thing for us is to confront those who come here with a bag of problems. Blackpool is not the best place for them to be. We are working with other authorities and trying to persuade them not to send people here.

Our priority is to persuade people to stay here and put down roots. That means good jobs, somewhere attractive to live, good friends and neighbours and having an environment where you would want to bring up children. We are talking about communities that people want to belong to.

One of the challenges here is that our schools could be better. We have a majority of academics in Blackpool, so a partnership approach with schools and their sponsors is essential. But the key issue is not how the schools are governed, but how they are run. Our primary schools are doing well; secondary level education is work in progress.

In respect of our economy, there has always been a shyness about tourism and how dependent we are upon it. We are very good at tourism, the most popular resort in Britain, with some of the best leisure attractions in the country. We should build on this and become even better.

We have a great deal to offer: theatres, ballrooms and, of course, the Tower. We can make much more of this. The Grand Theatre is linked up to the RSC and the National Theatre, and we have more plans for the Opera House, including some new collaborations with English National Opera, that should bring new visitors to the town. The Arts Council has been really valuable in helping us build on our cultural heritage.

We are reinventing ourselves as a holiday resort and the emphasis is upon higher quality. This includes the need to address the quality of our hotel accommodation which is weak. We are currently working with a number of developers to bring more four-star quality to the town, both branded and boutique.

The Big Lottery Fund is playing a major role. Their support is phenomenal. Resilient communities are one of the Fund's highest priorities, one we share. This is about stabilising communities and encouraging people to feel proud of Blackpool. This is where the

Big Lottery Fund is so important. HeadStart is a programme that works with ten- to sixteen-year-olds at a critical time in their lives. Blackpool Better Start is making a massive difference to the youngest children and families.

The Big Lottery Fund's A Better Start initiative aims to improve life chances by supporting families during pregnancy and for the first three years of a child's life. According to Merle Davies, Director of the Centre for Early Child Development, the support of the Big Lottery Fund will put Blackpool at the forefront of projects designed to transform prospects for disadvantaged children:

> The Big Lottery Fund has brought in £45 million via Blackpool Better Start over ten years. This has enabled us to do some great innovative work. And this should change long-term outcomes for families. We have been able to go to the root of problems and help families through that critical period of pregnancy and birth. If people have a healthy gestation and birth, we can predict a much healthier long-term outcome for the family and the child. This can break some of the intergenerational cycles that we see.
>
> This positive change then impacts upon communities. The effective literacy age for our communities is eleven. We have to teach the adults how to pay rent and manage their money and persuade them not to smoke and not to drink too much. By doing that, over time we can change communities for the better.
>
> From September, we will be the first place in the country to have a universally targeted and evidence-based antenatal programme for all parents.
>
> Blackpool Better Start is changing how we think about some of the big issues. We are shifting the power balance so that more services and support are delivered by the community themselves. They want to do things themselves. Our communities really understand how important it is to support families that are having children. Building resilience in our communities is critical to what we are doing and so this power shift is really important.

Essentially the answer to every problem needs to be work. That means addressing health issues, particularly mental health.

We support people to get ready for work by helping them to alleviate their personal problems. Many are in a forgotten group of people, most of them are 35- to 49-year-olds. The percentage of those in this age group who do not work is up to 10 per cent worse in Blackpool than the average in the north-west. These are the people who are suffering the worst mental health problems. They are unable to contribute.

Our job is to help them become people who can contribute to the community and who thereby live happier and more fulfilling lives.

I said it was refreshing to see what public money is able to do in an era when the prevailing message seems to be that public is bad and private is good.

The key thing is to ensure that public money is being spent in the right place. However, without public money, we would have no chance of turning things round. As well as £10 million from the Big Lottery Fund for HeadStart, we have another £10 million from the Big Lottery Fund through Blackpool Fulfilling Lives to address multiple complex needs around mental health, drug abuse and criminality. We also have the Department of Health's Vanguard programme that aims to avoid unnecessary hospital admission, particularly of the elderly.

These programmes are all about prevention at all the different stages of life. They encourage us to believe that it is possible to turn Blackpool round by addressing all its problems. In addition to all the support we have from the Big Lottery Fund, we are working across the public sector, with the NSPCC, the Police, community groups and health professionals working in partnership with the council.

As our money decreases, the demands upon us are increasing. We have to change perceptions of what the council can do and how we can support the people who live here. We have had to rethink our role and how we can help people help themselves. Many people think that when they get old and needy, that is the state's sole responsibility. That will have to change.

We know that loneliness is one of the biggest problems for the elderly and if we can find ways to overcome that, then the saving to the health service would be immense. So many old people need friends and family, not services. But this problem of social isolation does not only affect the old. Single mothers arrive here who are very isolated and because they are vulnerable, they can make very bad decisions.

I asked if a bigger, even more effective voluntary sector might emerge from the publicly funded initiatives and Merle Davies said: 'We need more "Hello, Loves!" as we call them. These kinds of volunteers could be trained up. The key thing we need is more social capital.'

I reflected that politics can bring out the worst as well as the best in us but the worst seems to have the upper hand. Neil Jack concurred and concluded our meeting:

All the political parties seem to have accepted that there are the deserving and undeserving poor. We believe that this kind of over-simplification demonises people and divides rather than builds stronger communities, something that we believe is essential.

*   *   *

The year 2014 marked a turning point in Blackpool's fortunes. A marketing campaign proclaiming 'Blackpool is back!' appears to have worked. Seventeen million people visited the town and overnight stays increased by 300,000 or 30 per cent. Some £300 million has been invested in a new and stylish promenade, designed to improve flood defences as well as to attract visitors. The number of three-star or higher quality beds has risen from 800 to 3,000 since 2007. The ambition is to raise this number to over 60,000. Several national restaurant chains are planning to open in the town.

In its heyday, the town had a jaunty, sexy swagger that was

irresistible to millions of mill workers from Lancashire and York-shire. Entire towns closed for a week or a fortnight and decamped to Blackpool by train and by coach in their millions. Then Black-pool became a sad place as the number of holiday visitors and the economy declined.

Blackpool now has a buzz about it again. It may need more social capital, but the potential offer for entertainment far exceeds anywhere in Britain outside London. At one time, Blackpool was offering over 30,000 theatre seats a night.

The Winter Gardens is vast. Built in 1878 as an indoor palace of entertainment for the millions of visitors that Blackpool was then attracting, the complex includes the Empress Ballroom, said to be one of the finest in the world, and the Opera House, Britain's largest theatre outside London. Notable performers included Dame Nellie Melba, Caruso, Judy Garland, Marlene Dietrich, Duke Ellington, Nat King Cole, Mae West, Bob Hope and Frank Sinatra. The Beatles performed many times in Blackpool and seeing them at the Opera House in 1964 was a transformative experience for me.

My visit to the Tower was no less inspiring. An estimated 70,000 people entered the Tower buildings on its first day in 1894 to enjoy a menagerie and zoo, an aquarium and restaurants as well as a circus designed by Frank Matcham. Matcham also designed the Tower Ballroom, perhaps best known by addicts of *Strictly Come Dancing* on television. The ballroom is a jewel of jaw-dropping opulence. In addition to the ornate splendour of the ballroom, I was moved not only by the pensioners gliding back and forth between rests for tea and cake, but by whoever amongst my ancestors thought to quote Shakespeare on the gilded proscenium arch: 'Bid me discourse and I will enchant thine ear.'

What really struck and moved me was the confidence and vision of my Victorian forebears, their willingness to take huge risks and to insist on the highest possible standards. No expense was spared in creating palaces of entertainment and art. Blackpool was a work-ing-class resort by the time the Tower was built. The people were entitled to the very best.

In a neo-liberal era, it seems counter-intuitive that Blackpool's cultural heritage should have been 'nationalised' in 2010 when the council bought the Winter Gardens and the Tower for £50 million. This was a shrewd move. No one else was in a position to invest and to borrow on this scale and the council sensibly brought in the private sector, Merlin Entertainments, to manage the Tower and all its attractions which are now open 364 days a year instead of being virtually closed in the winter. The Winter Gardens is also being restored and opened up to the public and will provide the venue for a new museum as Polly Hamilton, Blackpool Council's Head of Culture, told me:

> My brief here is to embed culture into the regeneration of Blackpool. All this is in the context of huge challenges for local government. Despite huge cuts, there has been a net gain for culture with funding from other sources.
>
> When the Tower and the Winter Gardens were bought by the council, there was no clear vision for how the buildings would be used. Merlin was given a contract to run the Tower. There are artistic opportunities that are yet to be realised in the Tower Ballroom and the circus. We are all working to deliver a vision for the Winter Gardens.
>
> We have been interested in new ways of doing things and we have been talking to people in Folkestone. I am interested in their Asset-Based Community Development approach. Blackpool Council has taken on the role of Sir Roger De Haan in Folkestone. One of the big problems we have is the quality of the built environment, particularly shop fronts which are of very poor quality. People make a lot of money during the season but spend it elsewhere. This has contributed to Blackpool's decline and its deteriorating appearance.
>
> We are trying to create a model that will support a sustainable cultural programme through the redevelopment of shops and vacant properties. Working with Left Coast, a local arts venture, and with a range of other supporters including Arts Council England, we have bought a former guesthouse and are turning it into a boutique

bed and breakfast called the Art Bed and Breakfast or A B&B. This follows Folkestone's example of attracting people who work in the arts and, if it works, we have a model that we can replicate and so contribute to a burgeoning creative economy.

Sometimes it feels as if we are sitting on an extraordinary secret in Blackpool. Everything in Blackpool is on display except its fabulous interior architecture. For too long, the town failed to promote this. Access to these palaces of enchantment and entertainment is too often linked to events. Until recently, the Winter Gardens would only open for conventions that are closed to the public.

We need to find new ways of creating access. I am trying to build cultural leadership in the town. The Grand Theatre, with one of the finest examples of a Frank Matcham interior, was going to be knocked down but was saved by a private initiative. Ruth Eastwood, the chief executive has secured Arts Council funding and transformed its programming. She is working with the National Theatre, the RSC and the Royal Exchange Theatre in Manchester.

I have decided to focus on the project to create a museum in the hope that this will stimulate more thinking about the rest of the Winter Gardens. We have created a vision for the museum which is about celebrating British popular culture and the importance of Britain's role, not least in developing what a seaside holiday could be and the development of the creative industries and the arts, including music and dancing, illuminations and variety in all its forms.

The plan is that the museum will open in 2020 at a cost of £26 million. The council has pledged £2 million, understanding that its commitment will leverage more finance. We have received in principle commitment from the HLF of over £13 million, and a further £1.5 million from Growth Deal fund.

We are looking at something that will be game-changing for Blackpool. The project will bring in more investment, contribute to the growth of the local economy, ensure a future for architecturally important buildings that would otherwise be at risk, and will create a new year round day time offer in the Winter Gardens and a new learning programme for schools. We hope that the museum will help young people to have a real sense of place and contribute to addressing issues of social isolation, building a sense of confidence and encouraging the development of new skills.

We will need private sector funding. We are in the process of establishing a fundraising foundation and will need a dynamic leader and a business champion to chair the fundraising campaign and the Foundation.

Despite being impressed by the vision and determination of those I met, I have doubts about a lack of diversity in funding and over-reliance on the public sector. The council's strategy of investing in cultural as well as social and economic regeneration must be correct and continues the Blackpool tradition of being ambitious and taking risks. All involved deserve applause for progress to date. However, the museum project needs private sector funding and that will not be forthcoming without charismatic leadership. There is significant wealth in north-west England amidst great poverty. An exceptional person must be recruited, preferably from the region, to chair a new Foundation and be a champion for Blackpool. Such people are not easy to find, even in London. On the basis of what I have heard so far, the success of the Blackpool Museum depends upon it. The town has done well by public investment in recent years but Blackpool also needs philanthropy and social investment.

*   *   *

My next appointment was with Carmen Conquer, the founding Director of Aspired Futures (AF), 'a local independent charitable organisation offering long-term, bespoke therapeutic support to the most vulnerable children and young people across Blackpool and the neighbouring Fylde who are living in complex, chaotic home environments and who are at risk'. Aspired Futures describes its therapeutic centre as a 'home from home'.

AF HQ is an attractive Victorian house, and the front door opens into an enchanted world. This is more than a home, rather a haven of light, colour, warmth, comfort and, most startling of all, bowls of fresh fruit.

Here is an introduction to some of the children and young people being nurtured by AF and a glimpse of part of Britain in the twenty-first century:

> One of our boys, Chris, struggles to commit consistently to Aspired Futures as he does not relate to his peers. His mum is severely mentally ill. Chris was referred to us by his primary school as they have big concerns for his mental health. He has scar tissue across his upper body where he has set himself alight.

> *'My mum makes healthier meals for me now. I am getting healthier. I have lost three stone. I used to get bullied. I have learned to cope.'* – Adam, aged twelve.

> David came to AF aged eleven. When he was two, he was removed from his biological mother because of severe physical and mental abuse and placed in the care of an aunt. He had been left unattended in his bedroom for days on end with no physical contact or interaction with other family members. He would also be locked in the wardrobe. David has been diagnosed with an attachment disorder and ADHD (attention deficit hyperactivity disorder), is unpredictable, can be aggressive and often offends and upsets others as he doesn't understand how his behaviour upsets others. After four years, David has blossomed and the joint commitment of his aunt, his school and AF has given him a future.

> *'When you come here and you listen to the other kids' stories you cannot believe they look so happy and you feel you should get on with it as well; if they can be happy after what they have been through, then I feel I should try to be happy as well.'* – Mark, aged fifteen.

> *'This place is like Narnia, coming out the other side of the cupboard, it is pretty and nice.'* – Chantelle, aged nine.

I asked Carmen Conquer why she had started Aspired Futures:

> We started Aspired Futures because of what happened to our pre-
> vious charity, Home-Start. Home-Start is a national charity run as
> a franchise. I set up a Home-Start scheme in 1996. I built that up
> over fourteen years across council estates in Blackpool. It was a huge
> journey and I learned how to build up a sustainable charity.
>
> There were fourteen of us in the team. In 2012, our charity was
> dismantled and the council wanted to take us in house. At that
> point, half my team went to work for the council and seven of us
> decided we wanted to stay outside.
>
> Independently, my team came to the conclusion that we no
> longer believed in long-term family support. I believe most of the
> work being done with the most high-risk families is a waste of time
> and money. I am not talking about families where a little bit of
> input will help them get from A to B. I am talking about third
> generation families supported by a range of agencies over fifteen
> years or more where nothing changes and the children get destroyed
> in the process. I felt OK about making that statement having been
> on that journey.
>
> We decided to do something completely different. We had set up
> Aspired Futures some time before and worked on it in our spare time
> at weekends or in the evenings. We decided to focus on children and
> young people in very complex situations. We decided to remove all
> the barriers and take the children out of the home and give them
> positive experiences. We would become their surrogate parents.
>
> We accept children from pre-school to eighteen-plus. The chil-
> dren are referred to us through a variety of channels, including
> schools, social workers, mental health services and the police.
>
> It is crucial that the child decides to engage with us, even from
> the age of four. This has to be their decision and they have to own it.
> We are offering long-term support in the truest sense. If somebody
> comes to us aged four, we will stay with them until they are adults.
>
> The children come to this extraordinary house but they do not
> sleep here. Many youngsters in the UK are living in child protection

but are not removed from their families. These children live in ter-rible circumstances. We are the in-between service. We help these children learn solution-focused positive behaviour. This is all about solutions. We give this message to the children when they are very young. We cannot change what is going on at home. However, here in this house, we are here just for them. Remember, these children live in chaos and they have no one they can trust. Learning to trust takes a long time.

I don't talk about poverty because these children are not starving. Money is not the point. We are dealing with mismanagement and the emotional damage that it causes. We have just over sixty children with us. They are poor in the sense that they are very fragile. Without help, they are destined to be the mentally ill adults of the future.

Some of the children are very bright and education can be a way out for them if they can excel in another area. The children who are the most emotionally damaged and who are not the brightest, these are the ones who struggle the most to get out of a cycle of destruction. Unfortunately, we do have a group of children who are never going to be right again and we are the only place that can hold them.

We have fifty-six volunteers, many of whom are in day jobs and come to us in the evening. When a child comes to us for the first time, there will be three adults looking after him or her for at least six months, then we might move to two adults.

Some of the volunteers are professionals but by no means all. The first thing we require from volunteers is long-term commitment. Reliability and punctuality are essential. Being morally sound is crucial. However, if you are going to be able to help the children, you have to be curious in order to know what is going on in the children's lives.

The key thing is to get to know the child and to discover what their talents are. This can take two or three years.

As the children get older, some of them become helpers and start to give back. After sixteen, some of the young people can go on to the volunteer scheme. Every young person here has to be either in

education, in training or in work. We may take in the most damaged
for a few days if they are in a state of collapse but we must get them
back to school as soon as possible. We are tough!

We have young people who have been with us who are now at
university. Sometimes we see them in the holidays and sometimes
they come back to us as volunteers. We do encourage the young to
build their own lives, this is really important. We are a surrogate
family and aim to be role models.

We work like social pedagogists, believing that bringing up
children is the responsibility of society as well as the parents.
The children come after school and the entire house is turned into
a play centre. There are no limits to play but the children are closely
monitored. We cook a meal for everyone, children and volunteers,
and we eat together. We have our own football club, our own drama
group, in the holidays we go on city trips. We can go to the local
Water Park free of charge and they provide our transport.

I was lucky that when I set up Aspired Futures, I had people
who had worked with me for twenty years. Three of us are the core.
To start the charity, we each had to go on to Jobseekers' Allowance
for six months. We had a £250,000 grant given to us without any
conditions from the local NHS trust in 2012 which is when we went
full-time.

We fund ourselves in lots of different ways. We are so fortunate
to have this extraordinary Victorian house owned by the Kensington Trust. Environment is 80 per cent of what we offer the children.
The Kensington Trust is a local trust based in Lytham, set up by
Kensington builders. They allowed us to move in here and we don't
pay rent. That is a significant donation. We could not afford to pay
rent for this building. We have raised a lot of capital to invest in the
house.

The gift of this house is also very useful as matched funding when
I put in bids to grant-making trusts. The Big Lottery Fund's Reaching Communities programme has been very important to us. That
was the first big bid we put in and we needed the Health Fund's
£250,000 to give us credibility.

My running costs are quite high because the children are transported to everything they do otherwise they would never get here. My food costs are £150 a week. Our annual costs are about £250,000. This is a seven-day a week operation.

Our sponsorship money brings in about £300 a month and includes donations from local companies and individual donations ranging from £10 to £100 a month. For example, a local dentist is donating a £100 a month and has been doing so for the last two years.

I have found ourselves being compared to Kids Co. It had a very chaotic form of leadership which is exactly the opposite of what young people need. I am devastated that this has happened because it has sowed seeds of doubt. We are completely transparent. Anyone can turn up without an appointment and go through our finances. People were bewitched by Camila Batmanghelidjh.

We cannot take all the children who need what we offer. We know exactly how much money we need to look after up to seventy children and that number becomes the cutting off point. We are not like Kids Co. who seemingly never turned any young person away on cost grounds.

I spend all my time chasing money. I know there is someone out there who could fund all this but finding them is an issue. I don't move in those kinds of circles and I am also a front line worker.

We are saving the state a lot of money and much of what we are doing is experimental. We have some who are interested in replicating what we do. Whilst a few kids are destined to be dysfunctional, we do seem to be able to turn many of them around. It is very powerful when you see children who really want to change their behaviour.

How do we get people to pay attention and to understand the value of what we do? It is as if we are living on an island in Blackpool. I meet people who may work here but they live outside and are completely disconnected in a world of their own.

The big challenge for Blackpool is that so many on the council seem to have tunnel vision. They need partners to help them see beyond what is in front of them.

Carmen Conquer and her team radiate positive energy. She made a bold decision not to be part of the public sector. She decided that she wanted to do something entirely different. Her wish to be independent of the council so that AF can pursue and pioneer good practice is exactly how the voluntary sector should operate. She is, understandably, angry and frustrated about the negative example of Kids Co.

Conquer has also been successful in securing financial support from the public sector via the NHS and the Big Lottery Fund and has motivated local businesses to be supportive both with cash and in kind. AF is richly deserving of philanthropic support and yet finds it hard, given small and tight resources, to tap into charitable giving from the local population.

I was born and brought up in prosperous Lytham St Anne's, six miles down the coast from Blackpool, but we could have been on the other side of the universe. We had little idea about what went on in Blackpool. There is so much private wealth within twenty miles of Blackpool and only a fraction of it could transform the lives of those in the care of Aspired Futures. On the evidence I have, not enough of the prosperous either know or care about what is happening on the other side of the tracks. If only they knew what joy and fulfilment they could find by giving to those who need their help.

*   *   *

For someone working in the second most deprived LSOA (Lower Layer Super Output Area) in Britain, Simon Lawton is notably cheerful. He has seen many changes in the way that Blackpool tackles social problems associated with a declining economy and although he has some doubts about policy for the future, he remains positive and committed to supporting the deprived and disadvantaged. His focus is on the front line, somewhere that is invisible to many of us.

Lawton works for the Blackpool Council for Voluntary Services or CVS. CVS is a membership organisation mainly for small voluntary groups. It offers funding and governance advice and help with business planning, marketing and grant applications:

We do important work for residents' associations, luncheon and bingo clubs and small groups that bring people together and help with social isolation and associated health problems. These groups need help establishing themselves and to learn how to apply for funds.

Until quite recently, we were funded from the public sector via local authorities. When I first joined CVS, there were twenty staff and now there are three of us. Seventy CVSs have shut across the country in the last two years.

We are involved with Communities Can, a £1.2 million pilot scheme to build capacity in up to 750 small groups in five towns, and Blackpool is one of them. This is organised by the Young Foundation and supported by the Big Lottery Fund.

There is another Big Lottery Fund initiative led by Local Trust called Big Local, a £1 million ten year project in Revoe, the most deprived area of Blackpool on Central Drive. It is grim. The funding is to enable local people and residents to make their own communities and their areas better places in which to live. This is a challenge because local residents are not used to committees and spending a million pounds. The project is, however, going really well. We now have a community plan to commit £240,000 to various projects including funding two youth workers who will work with teenagers.

We are also looking at high-street regeneration. This will also be a challenge as there are lots of boarded-up shops and those that are operating are very small and with a rapid turnover. There is also environmental work, a health initiative around drugs, alcohol and smoking and a crime project working with the local police.

The Big Lottery Fund has committed around £60 million to Blackpool via Blackpool Better Start (babies, young children and families), Blackpool Fulfilling Lives (mental health, drug addiction, homelessness and criminal justice) and a range of other programmes.

Revoe is a desperately poor community. The Revoe project is going well but it is a bumpy ride because working with people in deprived neighbourhoods and making them leaders of community projects is hard work. Identifying leaders who people will follow is difficult but crucial.

Blackpool Council always tries to be optimistic because it is a tourist town and they don't want to talk about how grim it is. They have done good work in addressing these problems. The problem is that this kind of work is staff intensive because it needs feet on the ground and it takes time to get results. The council has neither the staff nor the time. There were twenty council people working on community development and now there are two.

The council now see itself as an arms-length facilitator. It has to look to partner organisations. Our funding from Blackpool Council finishes next month, having come down from a quarter of a million a few years ago to £50,000 this year and nothing next year.

This is the Big Society question. In places like Blackpool, people need help to reach out and help others. Nothing will happen otherwise. There is a misconception that because it is called the voluntary sector, then everyone must be volunteers so that means everything is free.

I have been working in the voluntary sector in Blackpool for ten years and every successful project must have at least one paid worker. People have neither the time nor the energy to run these kinds of things out of love. Volunteers do great things and we would be lost without them but it is unrealistic to imagine that a full-time operation involving very hard work in deprived communities can be done for nothing.

The charity and voluntary sector is very small in Blackpool and that is another reason why we need CVSs. It is not the case if you are in the leafy Ribble Valley where there are retired professionals. These kinds of areas have social capital. We don't. People who have worked all their lives in manual or low paid jobs often retire in ill health. With the rare exception, they have neither the experience nor the understanding to organise things without help. I am talking about basic things such as how to run a meeting.

And because transience is such a problem in Blackpool, it is harder to build communities and to build community spirit.

Local charitable giving is negligible. There are two Rotaries but they don't have much money to give. The demographics don't work. There is huge churn within the town.

There are lots of brilliant can-do people here but they are spread a bit thin given the level of need. The kind of change that Blackpool needs will take a very long time and needs people on the ground to bring it about. There are not enough of them.

Youth services no longer exist in Blackpool. There are only very few youth clubs and I like what I hear about OnSide Youthzones [see Chapter 23]. Perhaps we need one here.

*   *   *

Steve Hodgkins, the founding Director of Jobs, Friends and Houses (JFH), is also a serving police officer on a full-time secondment from Lancashire Constabulary. He told me that his record for arresting offenders was one of the worst in Lancashire. During his time as custody sergeant, he was much more interested in the background and life history of criminals and what circumstances had led them into crime. He wanted to help.

This led Hodgkins to found JFH in 2014, a social enterprise developed by Lancashire Police with local agencies in Blackpool to build and renovate properties to provide 'recovery housing' and in the process of doing so, rejuvenating the housing stock in the town and providing meaningful activities for a range of vulnerable and excluded people who become highly skilled.

Hodgkins has worked for the police since 1986, serving for twelve years with the Metropolitan Police in London, transferring to the Lancashire Police in 1997. He is a trained Crisis and Hostage Negotiator. He is an independent steering group member for Left Coast, a Lancashire-based arts organisation, and is chairman of the trustees for the local charity Carers Trust.

I met Steve Hodgkins about eighteen months after JFH had been established and asked him how he had come to change his own life so radically and to what effect:

As a serving police officer, it was becoming increasingly clear to me that the best way to reduce crime is to reduce re-offending and that means helping offenders rehabilitate themselves. That is the thinking behind JFH and why I set it up eighteen months ago. We support marginalised individuals who are recovering from addiction and/or offending and we support them by giving them accommodation, training and work.

I understood that ex-offenders need work but the key thing is to find them meaningful employment. People need motivation and the prospect of a meaningful career. So we have created skilled employment opportunities in construction. We start with an apprenticeship, we skill them up and give them a career and something to aspire to. And that includes a pension. Before they come to us, many of them would be unable to think about anything other than their next drink or hit of heroin. We are getting them to think thirty years ahead. Our employment is meaningful employment. Our accommodation is good quality. We are giving people security and a future.

Friendship is the glue that holds things and people together. Our people need peer group friends. We realised that for many of our people there was something missing: life skills and how to live. One of our team had a lot of bereavements early on, got into crime and drugs and from the age of fourteen to forty was in and out of prison and in and out of care. He was a heroin addict and he was the most prolific burglar in Blackpool. He has been with us a year now and we realised that to find a time when he had been out of custody for six months or more we had to go back to before he was fourteen.

He had become institutionalised. He asked me: 'Steve, how do you make a friend?' He could relate to other addicts, to handlers and to dealers, people who only wanted something from him. He had never learned how to make positive, giving friendships.

We provide that kind of support to people. They don't know the rules of life and work. So we teach people life skills, how to find a doctor, a dentist, to get a driving licence, open a bank account.

One of the key things we do is change a person's identity; we take them from being an offender and an addict and change them to be Mr X, the trainee plumber or Mrs Y, the health and social care professional.

I heard a former gangster speaking at a conference in Glasgow. He said: 'If you can imagine transporting yourself into a criminal fraternity, just think how difficult it would be for you to survive. To do that in reverse is really difficult. Criminals find it very difficult to live in a world without crime.'

We don't get rid of people the first time they fail; we actually put our arms round them tighter and love them that bit more because that is what they need. We are all about building and promoting a person's self-worth.

At the very start, when I was trying to find funding, I had to do this in my own time. People were not prepared to offer finance until I could prove that the project would work. However, we had initial funding from the Ministries of Health and Justice to get us started and we have since been supported by the Department of Communities and Local Government, Public Health England, the Police and Crime Commissioner and the Arts Council.

JFH is now the first social enterprise with the official backing of a constabulary as Lancashire police continue to pay my wages. Our turnover is almost £450,000 a year. We are not yet close to being self-sustaining but we hope to be by the end of the year. We are a business and a true social enterprise in that all profits are ploughed back into the business.

We are contracted to work on properties, converting them from offices or hotels into flats. We are contracted by the council and private homeowners to renovate properties. I had never envisaged that people would let former criminals into their private homes. But we now have credibility and a positive reputation. We are really proud of this.

We have been successful with a Reaching Communities application for funding from the Big Lottery Fund. Our construction business is making money for us. We have an eco-deal to replace boilers. We have a lettings company that started last year. This is the only lettings agency in the UK that employs a full-time police officer! We can provide wrap around support for vulnerable tenants and their landlords and we charge a management fee. We also maintain the properties and are an accredited training centre.

We are working with really challenging individuals. We have to adapt to each and every one. However old they are, they are often just like traumatised teenagers. It is hard work helping them to become positive contributors. But it works.

Hodgkins told me that JFH had commissioned an evaluation of its work from Professor David Best of Sheffield Hallam University. The report concludes that after one year, JFH

- provides huge savings to the public purse;
- leads to massive reductions in criminal justice involvement and acute health problems;
- stimulates pro-social networks and a powerful sense of community;
- challenges stigma and exclusion and generates a powerful social identity;
- evidences strong post-acute recovery across a diverse group of excluded individuals with a range of complex life problems.

Arts Council England gave JFH a grant to commission a book about its first year: *Rock Bottom*, by Len Grant. In the book, Deputy Chief Constable Andy Rhodes gives his perspective on JFH, why he supports it and what difference Steve Hodgkins' work is making:

> I want my people to be aggressively tenacious about hunting down bad people. But, on the flip side, I also want them to have more empathy and be less judgemental. Getting involved in projects like JFH helps us have a little more empathy for those in the criminal justice system with addiction problems. You start to understand the journey a bit more and ultimately the mindset changes. At best, the system makes no difference to the life chances of offenders. It often makes it worse. Criminalising young people sets them off on a path through life from which it is very difficult to recover.
>
> Culturally, the Police Service is nowhere near being able to handle this type of project because of the huge amounts of bias and stigma in its own culture.

I have done a lot of partnership work in twenty-five years of service and this is about as innovative and exciting project as I have seen. If I were to cost benefit Steve Hodgkin's job, he is paying for himself a hundred times over.

My argument is this: first of all it is a commercial venture. That is unique for the Police Service. And there is the knock-on effect it has on improving poor housing. I think that policing, done in the right way, can have a massive impact on reducing deprivation.

Don't forget that all these people employed to renovate houses are also paying tax. So the project has turned ex-offenders from what some would call the bane of society, costing the taxpayer money, into productive members of society.

JFH is actually informing how we develop our policing in Lancashire. It is helping us to understand the skills people need to bring to us, and how we deliver our service. Policing is now about the complexity of need within communities ... it is about unlocking the potential of the community for them to do it for themselves.

There is so much baggage in my workforce that is a barrier to this, I would like to be able to wipe it clean and start again. From now on, you won't be able to join Lancashire Police unless you have two years' experience of working with people with complex needs or from complex communities.

If JFH just stays in Blackpool, employing forty or so people, then that is great. It will have achieved a great deal more than most other projects. But this isn't a one size fits all model. We should only expand when we have the right people in place. It is not about the properties, it is about the people.

I asked Hodgkins if he needed or would accept private donations. This would require him to apply for charitable status or set up part of JFH as a charitable foundation to receive tax-efficient donations.

Do we need private money? Yes, we do. We are not yet self-sustaining. There is a lot of interest out there in what we are doing and potential for expansion because we are the solution. Lancashire

Constabulary wants us to expand into other parts of the county. We
need pump priming money to get started elsewhere. We are not
generating enough revenue to do that. But I don't think we are sexy
enough for private donors and investors.

I disagreed and said that people who provide solutions should
always attract funding. Hodgkins was not sure:

I believe in people and in humanity. I see these amazing people who
have previously been written off and it fills me with immense pride
to see their journeys: reconnecting with families, giving amazing
support and empathy to others, their passion and humility. There are
some amazing things happening in Blackpool but I don't think the
level of need is reducing.

Historians will look back at the Thatcher era and see it as the
death of the community and the rise of the 'what is in it for me?' culture. People are greedy and either spend their money on themselves
or hoard it. And there is too much competition for what charitable
money is available.

*   *   *

My final meeting in Blackpool brought me firmly back down to earth.
My conversation with Alistair Clarke and Tony Carr, chairman and
managing director of Social Enterprise Solutions, reminded me that
the private sector in Blackpool is no longer what it was. Moreover,
from their perspective, there is a downside to a dominant public sector.
I told Tony Carr and Alistair Clarke about a recent trip to Belfast
(see Chapter 17) and my optimism as a result of what is happening
there at grass-roots level. I also said how impressed I had been with
Blackpool Council's vision for the renaissance of the town. They
offered a different perspective. Alistair Clarke responded:

I would love to be as optimistic as Northern Ireland but we find that
although we have set up and supported a lot of social enterprises,

and they do thrive in deprived areas because they are trying to meet social needs rather than make money, it would be great if they could get work from Blackpool Council or do what the council used to, but the council and the health authority don't easily hand over services to the third sector.

Our clients are saying to us: 'The new way of doing things should be an opportunity for us to take on and run things that had been in the public sector but that just hasn't happened.'

Tony Carr added:

There has been some consultation with the third sector by the council but we expected social enterprises and the third sector to flourish as a result of cut backs in public spending but it isn't happening. There is a catalyst missing. The same is happening with the local NHS Foundation Trust. Our sector could be providing non-statutory services, the nice things to do that are, crucially, preventative measures. This may be a problem that is peculiar to Blackpool.

The fact that you have come here today is wonderfully synchronised because we have been looking at the big picture of developments in social enterprises as well as the local scene. In any deprived area, you are more likely to get social enterprises and third sector organisations springing up to fill gaps, led by passionate people who want to get things done. That happened here. We organised a conference in 2009 about collaboration between the town hall, politicians and the sector. A key speaker said that Blackpool is a social enterprise town. That resonated with me. We could have been a beacon for the rest of the country.

So we started the ball rolling in 2009 and only in the last two years have we collaborated with Social Enterprise UK and come up with a concept called Social Enterprise Places. There are now designated Social Enterprise Places in the UK and it is interesting that Blackpool isn't one of them even though the thinking started here. The idea was and still is that these places demonstrate the growth and development of the sector.

The key point is that a Social Enterprise designation is a demonstration of collaboration that can lead to significant social investment. If you go back to the early days of Blackpool, this was a collaborative effort involving other families and businesses in addition to the Bickerstaffes and Nicksons. They all bought into a vision for the town and collaborated to make it happen.

Institutions need to be on board. Universities are becoming interested. Social enterprise can be a career path for young entrepreneurs. Ideally, there needs to be buy-in from the public sector and that is where we are struggling in Blackpool.

I told Carr and Clarke that my research in other parts of the north of England had led me to new partnerships between the public, private and voluntary sectors that were achieving demonstrable results in terms of creating social capital and transforming lives.

Clarke: I do not think Blackpool's hope lies with the council. The area became too dependent on public sector jobs in Premium Bonds and the Department of Work & Pensions but these have shrunk by one-third. Manchester has invested in office space as a way of attracting firms. Blackpool should do the same and give the area more hope.

Carr: The current question is: what more can local business do for the community? Warburtons, the baker, became massive benefactors, by supplying bread to food banks. This was a local responsible business connection that actually worked. Many businesses want to do more but don't know how to do it.

We have a project running that gets businesses to sign a pledge to offer support in any way; that doesn't need to be money, it could be mentoring or volunteering, and there isn't one company that has not signed up to this. The largest Tesco Extra in the north is in Blackpool. They have said that they want to be even more involved in the community. This is a good business move, for obvious reasons.

Beaverbrooks, the jewellers, have bought a building and given a lease of one pound a year to the Carers Trust in Blackpool. That is a phenomenal example. We are trying to find new ways where the private sector can support the development of the third sector.

The reaction I am getting from the private sector to support the third sector *is* giving me hope. It is all part of educating people, and that includes public sector workers, many of whom have no idea what the third sector is or how powerful it could be in the town's development.

* * *

I was impressed and invigorated by my time in Blackpool. I witnessed leadership, vision, commitment and drive. There is a plan to address crippling poverty, including investment in communities with significant support from the Big Lottery Fund. The council's leading role is critical given the small size of the private and voluntary sectors. Investment in cultural regeneration has worked elsewhere and could work in Blackpool if communities become less transient and more rooted, resilient and prosperous.

Blackpool remains vulnerable unless economic revival brings more prosperity to the town and creates more jobs and, crucially, there is affordable, high-quality housing that encourages people to put down roots. There needs to be a plan to develop the private sector and reduce the town's reliance on the public sector.

Underpinning this, however, is the need to create a stronger voluntary sector, able to follow the lead of the pioneering and inspirational work being done by Carmen Conquer at Aspired Futures and Steve Hodgkins at Jobs, Friends and Houses.

The old Blackpool of my Victorian forebears has gone, but the way to follow their example and enterprise would be for all forces devoted to the common good to come together and work in partnership as is happening in other parts of the north. In addition to a revived economy and resilient communities, another sign that Blackpool has been reborn will be a thriving voluntary sector with more charities and more social enterprises, supported and funded by local people. That is the way to create sustainable social capital.

CHAPTER 17

NORTHERN IRELAND: HOW COMMUNITY, PHILANTHROPY AND SOCIAL ENTERPRISE MADE PEACE POSSIBLE

"Northern Ireland never went over the edge... There were times when we thought we were going over and we managed to pull back because of unique networks as well as the depth and intensity of community action at a time when there was no politics here."
JACKIE REDPATH, CHIEF EXECUTIVE, GREATER SHANK-ILL PARTNERSHIP.

* * *

Northern Ireland dominated the news in the UK from 1969 to 1998 because of the Troubles or the Conflict. What almost thirty years of virtual civil war should be called depends upon whether loyalty is to Republican Ireland or to the United Kingdom. Following the Good Friday peace agreement, Northern Ireland (not everyone agrees what it should be called) has been blessed with almost no civil conflict and has all but disappeared from the English media. That may change following the UK's decision to leave the European Union in 2016. Northern Ireland voted to remain in the EU, as did Scotland. Leaving the EU could have profound implications for the peace process and for relations with the republic of Eire.

The rest of the UK has much to learn from Northern Ireland, about how to create social capital and social enterprises, to build communities and persuade them to work together, to sustain and strengthen civil society as well as how to resolve conflict. Understandably, many will assume that national and international politics, backed up with mountains of public money, led the way to the Good Friday Agreement and it is true that the peace process in Northern Ireland seemed to bring out the best in UK and US politicians. But nothing could have been achieved without the people on the ground, not least the Northern Ireland Community Foundation. Philanthropy from outside Northern Ireland and community philanthropy from within made peace possible. Community philanthropy, community ownership and social enterprise have helped to heal a society rent by division and seared by violence, a society that is still coming to terms with its past as well as the challenges of the future. This is a story that needs to be told; it is directly relevant to the needs of the UK today.

I was invited to speak to a UK Community Foundation conference in Belfast in September 2015. A coach tour of the city was a shock. I was not prepared for vivid murals on the side of buildings showing warriors wielding automatic weapons proclaiming 'We Are Ready', for the portraits of the Queen as big as a house, entire streets a mass of Union Jacks as if it were a Jubilee every day, and the 'Peace' Wall. I saw and crossed the Berlin Wall but I was not prepared for the Belfast Wall, over three miles long and up to twenty-five feet high.

I was shocked and yet so exhilarated by my first short stay in Belfast that I resolved to return. On my second visit, I met people who had remarkably positive stories to tell. Here is a reminder of what the people of Northern Ireland have had to endure over the course of the Troubles:

- 7,000 parents lost a child
- 14,000 grandparents lost a grandchild
- 3,000 people lost a husband, wife or partner

- 10,000 children lost a parent
- 15,000 people lost a brother or a sister
- 30,000 is the estimated number of ex-political prisoners
- 200,000 is the number of those estimated to be affected by politically related imprisonment
- 500,000, or 31 per cent of the Northern Ireland population, is an
  estimate by the Victims Commission of those directly affected by
  the loss of a loved one, physical injury or trauma.

Andrew McCracken is the chief executive officer of the Northern
Ireland Community Foundation which played a pivotal role in bringing the Protestant and Catholic communities together into the peace
process. The Foundation was able to go where others would not:

> The Community Foundation did not start as such. It started as a
> government endowed trust, the Northern Ireland Voluntary Trust,
> in 1979 at the height of the Troubles or the Conflict.
>
> The government provided an initial capital donation of £500,000
> plus an undertaking to match donations of up to £250,000 per year
> to set up the NIVT. The trust was there to make small grants to pro-
> jects that were beyond the government's reach or too controversial
> for the government to fund directly.
>
> Avila Kilmurray was my predecessor for twenty years. She drove
> part of the peace process, including the engagement of women and
> the engagement of prisoners and ex-prisoners in the peace process as
> well as supporting prisoners when they returned to the community.
> Their role as community leaders was crucial. I hope Avila will not
> play down the risks she took.

I met Dr Avila Kilmurray in the Europa, once notorious for being
the most bombed hotel in the world after twenty-eight direct hits.
Dr Kilmurray was born in Dublin. After university in her home city,
she went to Australia for a Masters in International Relations and
was given a further scholarship for a PhD on comparative guerilla
movements including the IRA, the Tupac Amara in Peru and the

Red Brigade in Italy. At that point, she could not have known how relevant this was to be in relation to her subsequent career.

In 1974, she was asked to volunteer to support a conference at Amherst, Massachusetts, bringing together for the first time the combatants in Northern Ireland and some representatives from the Irish republic. This was during the second ceasefire. What happened next was to change Avila Kilmurray's life and transform Northern Ireland's prospects for peace.

Kilmurray came to know all the leading players during the conference. On her return, she was asked by the Quakers to continue encouraging discussions between the two sides. She was based in Derry where her flat was blown up. She became more involved in community action and the women's movement in particular:

> I didn't have a role. I just made it up. I was twenty-three. I was trying to get them to identify social and economic issues that could possibly provide a bridge between the two communities. They had problems in common.
>
> I had to ask myself, as an outsider, how could I do something useful? I could read and write which was more than some of the people I was working with. I was working with elderly people who were afraid to use the telephone. I became a de facto source of advice and support because there was nothing else. One of my priorities was to try to break down stereotypes. Derry was a city divided by the river and people did not cross from one side to the other.
>
> Some key issues were becoming clear and one of them was domestic violence. At that point, there was no refuge for battered women in Northern Ireland. Our laws were nineteenth century. I was working with a group of women to try to do something and in the end we squatted in an empty public building and were denounced from the Catholic altar for breaking up marriages. So community action became organic as we responded to emerging need, we started to campaign for legal change, against the inability of the housing executive to house women who were separated from their husbands, picketing the courts against reactionary judges.

All this was during Direct Rule. In effect, there was no local politics through the 1970s and '80s and into the '90s. The dead were buried, births were registered, rubbish was collected and that was about it. That was why the community and voluntary sector became so powerful.

The community sector was largely volunteers and very engaged with local politics at ground level. I remember one Loyalist paramilitary saying to me: 'Avila, we don't pack up at night and go back to the mountains, we are living next door to you'. So there was an interface between politics and community action.

Those of us involved had to duck and weave to get the space for community action. We weren't asking for permission from the paramilitaries but we were making it clear what we were doing and why so that it could not be misconstrued. When we opened the Women's Refuge, we had a guy turn up at the door with a gun saying 'I want my wife back'. We identified what paramilitary he was a member of and I had a meeting with them. It was a Republican group and they told me it would never happen again. The refuge looked after women from both sides. So we went round all the armed groups to tell them what we were doing. They left us alone.

This was 1978–79 when what became the Community Foundation was established as the Northern Ireland Voluntary Trust by Peter Melchett, a minister in the Labour government.

Kilmurray moved to Belfast in 1980 to work for the Northern Ireland Council for Voluntary Action on their magazine, *Scope*. She met Richard Hauser who was married to violinist Yehudi Menuhin's sister Hephzibah. Yehudi Menuhin funded the salaries of four leading activists in Belfast – two were Loyalist and two were Republican.

She was then seconded to run a European-funded anti-poverty programme and that was a partnership between a number of organisations. She ran that for four years in the 1980s and developed a trans-European network:

In 1994, I became director of the Northern Ireland Voluntary Trust which became the Community Foundation in 2000. The board was 50 per cent Catholic and 50 per cent Protestant in order for a divided community to see itself reflected in one organisation. The same applied to the staff and the allocation of grants. In contrast to the other UK Community Foundations, it was set up to serve the community rather than provide a donor service.

Following a ceasefire in 1994, there was the advent of a European peace programme in 1995. The EU was an established funder in Northern Ireland. An approach was made by Brussels to ask if the Community Foundation would manage a number of grants. One was for community development and one was for groups and another for the rehabilitation and integration of political prisoners and support for the victims of violence. So the Foundation now had a much more important political role in peace-building.

We had a huge consultation exercise to help us prioritise how to spend millions. We had to decide how the money would be spent. I went to see all the paramilitary heads to get their view on priorities and process. After that, the trustees agreed to set up ten advisory committees. The committees became the decision makers about how European money should be spent. Crucially, paramilitaries were making decisions about how the other side should be funded.

The great thing about the Community Foundation committees was that we were able to use them for back-channel discussion. That went on from 1995 to 2005.

During this time, philanthropy from the US began to make an important contribution to the peace process via Atlantic Philanthropies, although this was initially confidential. Atlantic Philanthropies (Atlantic) was founded by Chuck Feeney, an Irish–American businessman who decided in 1982 to devote his wealth, made as the co-founder of the Duty Free Shoppers Group, 'to the service of humanity'.

From 1991 to 2014, Atlantic invested nearly $570 million in Northern Ireland to support the peace process, address the legacy of violent conflict, protect and expand civil and human rights, spur economic growth through higher education, create a stronger sector to support the elderly and to transform children's services through prevention and early intervention. There were twenty-one grants to the Northern Ireland Community Foundation totalling $30.1 million.

Atlantic was investing in political, economic and social solutions when and where others were unwilling and at a level of funding comparable to what national governments might spend. In addition to imaginative grant making, Feeney, a shy and modest man who rarely gives interviews, was operating behind the scenes to bring President Clinton and the Northern Ireland Republican leaders together. Feeney's contribution to the peace process was of fundamental importance.

*   *   *

My journey to meet Jackie Redpath, chief executive of the Greater Shankill Partnership (GSP), took me down the Shankill Road, through West Belfast and the predominantly Loyalist working-class area known as the Shankill. During the Troubles, the Shankill was a centre for Loyalist paramilitarism, and was subjected to bombings and shootings by the IRA and conflict between the Ulster Defence Association (UDA) and the Ulster Defence Force (UDF).

GSP is one of five area partnerships in Belfast. It is a registered charity tasked with delivering regeneration projects in the area by focusing on programmes for neighbourhood renewal, children, community sports, health and well-being, tourism, arts and culture.

Jackie Redpath is eloquent, passionate and compelling. He gave me an insight into what life in Belfast was like, how peace came and the challenges that remain for his grandchildren. I was much moved by what he had to say:

I was born in the Shankill in 1951 and I have lived and worked here all my life. I was brought up before the Troubles broke out in 1969, lived through them and brought up my family here. I have five grandchildren and they all live in the Shankill.

I have been involved in community work since the 1970s. I was the first person in my family to go to university. I think the story of my children and grandchildren is the reverse of what is the normal story in the UK, of generation upon generation doing better, earning more and having more choice than the previous generation. My family is in reverse.

I attribute that essentially to bringing my children up in the Shankill and they have suffered because they were brought up in a troubled area where disadvantage is at its sharpest. This is mainly because of educational under-achievement which is the worst in Northern Ireland. It drives me on with some degree of anger.

The government here has measures of deprivation. There are 502 electoral wards in Northern Ireland and the Shankill wards are the worst three in terms of education. People say the Catholics are worst off but the Protestants here score worse in terms of education. Interestingly, we measure well in terms of proximity to services but in terms of both health and education we are almost at the bottom.

Research shows that the connection between poverty and poor education is a given in any community. People blame the parents, the schools or paramilitaries or the government and some even blame it on the children themselves. We look deeper. The fact is that Belfast is an old industrial city. Its economy was based on shipbuilding. We had the largest engineering works in the world. Men and boys found employment in those heavy industries. Girls went into the cigarette factories and the linen mills. Mine was the last generation when those jobs were accessible. There are now none of these jobs left.

The point is that you did not need an education to get into those jobs. They used to say that your education started with your apprenticeship. So when those jobs were lost within one generation, we were left with a gap in which education had not been valued. Since the loss of the great industries, the population of this area has dropped from 76,000 to 26,000 over twenty-five years during a time of great redevelopment. The third element was thirty-five years of the Troubles which blighted our community. The overall effect of all this was devastating.

Belfast was hit by a perfect storm: de-industrialisation, redevelopment and the Troubles. The storm left behind a swamp and we cannot get out of it without help. The effort to get out of the swamp means that different communities have a common interest. That means we have to build a new society here in Northern Ireland that offers new possibilities. And we need to do that together.

We decided to take a long-term view and tried to work out what and where the journey would be. That was an important and critical decision. That means you need to be patient and take time to take a long-term view and then to develop a strategy and understand that the rewards will be some way down the line. Interestingly, that is counter-cultural to working-class communities. Working-class culture is about an immediate reward. That culture was made by industrialisation. You got paid at the end of the week not at the end of the month.

Investing for the long term was a foreign concept, especially in a community that had made machinery and had made things. People understand what you can touch. The second important thing we learned was that we cannot do things on our own. If you need help you need to reach out for it. If you reach out, that means going into some kind of partnership. There is no good in closing in on yourself.

We started to bring people together from government, government agencies, and from the private sector, which was not in a good state, to think about what was the best strategy for regeneration. What were the priorities we needed to address?

Doing community work, it is very easy to spread yourself a mile wide but only an inch deep. The priority that we identified in this community was education. In 2001, the Northern Ireland government set up a task force for West Belfast and Shankill. The really big issues were unemployment and education but we would be challenged to solve unemployment without addressing education.

Two big things happened to us. We were working on strategy in 1993 and 1994. There was a Loyalist and Republican ceasefire in 1994. This was a time of hope. There was a new European Union regeneration initiative involving around seventy-five cities and Belfast was one of them. In all cities except Belfast, the project was led by the local authority. The local authority here was in disarray so it was the two community organisations that had been thinking about strategy who were in the right place at the right time.

This was when Loyalist and Republican cross-community action became concrete.

The two organisations made a joint bid to Europe under the banner 'Making Belfast Work'. One was the Shankill Partnership where I am still working and the other was the Upper Springfield Development Trust in Republican West Belfast. This was an alignment and a partnership between the most infamous Loyalist and Republican areas. We put in a joint bid through the British government. We got £6 million each over five years.

For Europe, it was a training and employment project. For us, the added value was about bringing change. This was a first big opportunity in years.

We were able to start the Shankill Partnership's Early Years project predicated on the notion that the first three years in a child's life are the most important. If you are thinking long term, that is where you want to begin. Springfield had a preponderance of young people who were rootless and they focused on 11- to 25-year-olds.

The programme lasted for five years and had a legacy. When Labour came in 1997 and they were thinking about setting up Sure Start, they were interested in what we had been doing for the very young. Sure Start was a legacy of our joint initiative in West Belfast. We did such a good programme of work here and it is operating today in Shankill. It had a real impact. The programme was evaluated by Queen's University in July 2000 and it was affirmative that we were making a difference.

One month later, in August 2000 we had the worst experience ever in our Shankill community, effectively a civil war between two paramilitary groups, the UDA and the UVF. Within one square mile, the conflict raged for three months, families were split, seven people were killed and 239 families were evicted from their homes. There was massive disruption to families and schools.

That scattered the gains of our Early Years programme. And because of redevelopment and unemployment, our gains were also limited. The trail of underachievement still exists.

Two years ago, I was still working on the notion that we have to integrate all the services. We are the worst in terms of education and almost best in terms of proximity to services; what we need to do is put those things together. That assumes that the services are right and we can do all that needs to be done to bring them together.

This is how we have changed. We are now talking about young people rather than problems and issues. Our view is that if we can get in at the earliest possible stage in the early years, and get children and young people and their families to tell us what they want their life story to be then we can work out how to get there. As the journey starts and progresses, and on the understanding that the child will not make the journey unaided, we draw in support from wherever it is needed, staying with them as long as it takes. That is a transformative process.

This thinking has come from within our community. A year and a half ago, this community designated itself as a Children & Young People Zone. We did this through a Community Convention. We made a declaration and a commitment to support this generation of children and young people.

We went to government and we told them that we did not want their money. They relaxed and were intrigued. Our work has been endorsed by seven government departments. We will need money in due course. I am employed by a community organisation that is funded by government. Our biggest enemy would be another initiative coming in. We have our zone and we could add to it. It is not that we will not need more financial resources, because we will; the key thing is to be clear about what we will do with more resources. Growth needs to be organic according to what we believe is right and to be long term.

What we do in our zone will happen whatever government we have. We have managed to create something that will happen anyway. Queen's University Belfast is one of our partners and helping with research. The Vice-Chancellor says if we want to make a difference, we will never make it through government.

Northern Ireland never went over the edge because of the community infrastructure. There were times when we thought we were going over but we managed to pull back because of the depth and intensity of community action at a time when there was no politics. Community action ameliorated the very worst and has been at the cutting edge of really positive developments.

My next appointment was in the city of Lisburn, eight miles from Belfast, and during a half-hour taxi journey in rainy darkness, I had time to reflect upon my conversation with Jackie Redpath: industrial collapse and civil conflict to the brink of civil war, the shocking failure of education, particularly to prepare the young for a different future, the resilience of community and the willingness to work with others across barriers of fear and hatred, initiatives that had come from within the community for long-term social commitment rather than short-term political fixes to support the young so that they may enjoy fulfilling lives, all the time learning lessons from thirty-five years of conflict and failure. Jackie Redpath was understandably angry about the circumstances of his grandchildren and yet spoke positively, with warmth, confidence and hope.

I was on my way to the Highway Inn, a community-owned pub in a working-class district of Lisburn, where I was to meet Philip Dean, chair, and Adrian Bird, director of the Resurgam Community Development Trust, a social enterprise that connects communities across Lisburn and aims to drive community, youth, social and economic development. Given intense and revelatory conversations with Kilmurray and Redpath, I had high expectations of Dean and Bird that they fulfilled. They believe that their commitment to community ownership and social enterprise could be replicated anywhere in the UK.

Adrian Bird led the conversation and spoke with such urgency that I was loath to ask questions lest I miss a word. He told me that there had been shootings in the bar where we were and that if I had visited ten years ago, I would probably not have got past armed men on the door.

Bird: My background was that I was in the army for eight years and then I was in prison for just over six years. I was released just before the Good Friday Agreement. I had learned a lot about life inside and outside prison. I was a founder member of the Lisburn Prisoner Support Project that was started with a £1,000 grant from the Community Foundation. The project was about split families, former prisoners, employment, social life, children, using my knowledge that would help to create an organisation to solve the many issues that we had.

I have been involved with the Voluntary Trust, which became the Community Foundation, for twenty years. Philip and I sat on the Peace Partnership and for twelve years, I chaired the conflict working group that brought representatives of all the former political prisoners around the table.

The Community Foundation played a crucial role by providing seed funding and creating groups that have grown substantially. I have a lot of admiration for Avila who took such risks and people like her who got involved with former prisoners. When I first got involved, the early work was going into prisons to prepare prisoners for their release and to reintegrate them into the community.

Ceasefires were announced but then they broke down again. Within Lisburn there were a number of community-based organisations that had been going for thirty or forty years. The Prisoner Support project began in 1997. Its aim was to integrate with other community-based organisations because they had the skills and connections that we did not have.

Lisburn is an affluent town but with pockets of deprivation. We couldn't get mainstream funding from our own government or the British government. It was all based around European funding. The importance of seed funding was that it enabled you to hire a room and hold meetings and get a committee together to make plans. It was all basic stuff.

That is where we started, with almost nothing. The most important thing then was to get people talking and talking to each other.

Dean: There were different attitudes in the communities in
relation to prisoners and to their release. Even though Lisburn is
a predominantly Protestant town, there was no great mainstream
support for Loyalist prisoners.

Bird: When we started to come out of conflict in the '90s and
early 2000s there was still a conflict mindset. By working closely
with other groups, we were not seen to be creating conflict. As a
former prisoners' group, we were reaching out into the community
and we were not seen as a risk.

From the early days, we had an entrepreneurial approach to community development. We knew that peace money was not going to
last for ever. Social enterprise was not a word we knew then. We got
a grant of £20,000 to create a community-based garage. That gave us
the money to employ a mechanic. The garage kept going for seven
years and at one point employed five people with a mixed workforce
of Protestants and Catholics. When we employ people, we don't care
about their background. We learned a lot of business skills at that
time. A lot of former prisoners were having difficulty getting credit so
we set up a credit union. A number of loan sharks had moved into the
area and we wanted to clear them out of the community.

I was approached by Avila to get involved in a self-build scheme.
Some years before, a Republican group in West Belfast had formed a
cooperative and had built five or six houses. They were former life sentence prisoners. Avila wanted to know if we could do something similar
in the Unionist–Loyalist community. I didn't think it would work in
Lisburn because it would go against the grain of what we were trying to
do in terms of integrating prisoners back into the community. It would
not have been accepted within our community if former prisoners were
seen to be bettering themselves and owning the house they had built.
There was also some political opposition to releasing prisoners.

We told Avila that we wanted to do this differently. We would
form a limited company called Lisburn Community Self Build Ltd.
The company would also be involved with education and training

for young people from Lisburn regardless of religious background. It would not be just for former prisoners, it must be much wider than that.

We went into a partnership with Avila and the Voluntary Trust, the Northern Ireland Housing executive and Ulster Garden Villages. The Housing executive gifted us land, UGV gave us a loan of £130,000 to build nine houses. The business case was that we build them, sell them to first-time buyers, train fifty or sixty people over the two-and-a-half years it took to build, sell to pay off our debts and at the end all debts were cleared and we owned three houses valued at £250,000 each. So our small community organisation had assets of three quarters of a million. We sold one of the houses and reinvested and that was how we began the journey to what we have and where we are now.

That is where the money came from to buy the pub and to create the taxi firm and to develop the small housing portfolio we have now. At this point, we were in 2008 and then everything went wrong.

The partnership had been run by a husband and wife team who were in control. There was a fear factor because paramilitaries were also involved. People were scared to challenge them. They were employees and yet were in total control of the funding. The directors decided to dissolve the partnership.

This was the crossroads in 2008/9. So we formed a new kind of partnership and that is how Resurgam was born. We asked our former partners, if we are to form something new, what would you like us to do and to be? We went back to the statutory funders where relationships had broken down, went to the police and to the health authority and asked the same question: what should the new organisation do?

We changed the name of the Lisburn Prisoners Support Group to Lisburn People's Support. The integration work had been done and it was now working with the wider community and families. We changed the common bond of the credit union to Resurgam And we formed a new positive relationship with the police as relations had been bad.

We have built up a portfolio of property, seven houses and a pub and two community centres. There will be more in future. We want government to pay for some of the services we are doing. We are planning a new youth centre with the money in place. In the early days, we bought two run-down properties in the centre of Lisburn. We have planning permission to convert a derelict building into five one-bedroom apartments with a commercial unit downstairs. £410,000 is in place to do it. We are only £100,000 short. This will be assisted housing but it will also give us five more rental incomes.

All this is in community ownership.

We have created a vision of having our core work self-sustained by 2020. We want to build up our housing portfolio of community-owned housing that contributes to the core activities of Resurgam. We went to government and said look at what we have done without any money from you. We said that if government could support what we are doing, we can create a model that could be replicated anywhere in the UK. Three and a half years ago, government invested £450,000 to pay for a core team of four members of staff: a social enterprise development worker, a regeneration manager, an administrator and a trust director. Government called it a social enterprise pilot. That funding finishes in March and the next project will be to ensure the sustainability of what we have done.

When we bought the pub nine years ago, there was a £380,000 investment. We put down an £80,000 deposit and borrowed £300,000. This will be paid off in six years. So our social enterprise will then be in in a position to fund our charitable work.

We can see the exit strategy where we won't need any more funding. Our assets will be generating income and we may be in a position where we are able to deliver some services that are paid for. We are continuing to develop new social enterprises.

We have created 104 sustainable jobs. The social enterprise network has a turnover of about a million a year. In salaries from employment, £1.9 million is being spent in the Lisburn economy. Others may be creating better social enterprises but what makes us different is our holistic approach to community regeneration. We are working with pre-school groups, we are doing youth development work with 600 hundred young people, we are a significant employer in Lisburn and perhaps should be a member of the local chamber of commerce. Our taxi firm is the largest in Lisburn.

We are still committed to our cross-community work. It is now normal for our Loyalist working-class Protestant community to work with the Nationalist Republicans. We also have excellent working relations with the police.

We said to government that we think this model can be replicated in other communities for a small amount of public money. We are also trying to get one of the universities to come in and do a study and evaluate what we do. We need to be clear why it is different here. We need an independent evaluation. This used to be a very violent place. There were a number of deaths in this bar.

We have put our own money into what we have done. We have put our own time and effort into everything. When we built our community centre next door, our community building firm built it for no profit. We involved the local kids in the building of it. So it is their centre. Nothing has been stolen, nobody breaks the windows. We now have a small number of community-owned assets. All the other pubs and clubs are closing. Ours works because it is in community ownership. It is our place and their place. We own it. If we are going to have a party, we will have it here. If we want to buy cakes, we buy them from here.

And this means we can attract government investment. We won a contract for £513,000 to go into primary schools. Early Intervention Lisburn is a group we created that will address educational under-attainment in the communities in which we live and work.

When we go to the bank to secure loans to expand our social enterprises and invest in our community, they ask why are you not doing it for yourselves rather than for a charitable social enterprise? We would not be able to bring about change if we were doing it for ourselves. There are also 500 volunteers who keep everything going all year round. Nothing would have been possible without them.

Because we have been so successful in what we do, local government is asking us if we can help them. We are being asked to do more and more and that is a risk. We are having to do more with less. We say to government: if you want us to manage assets and assist with the development of other communities, then pay us to do so.

Dean and Bird began their quest for reconciliation and renewal without knowing what social enterprise was and yet they have created an exemplary model. Resurgam has evidently benefitted from public investment but can anticipate reaching a position whereby it can be self-financing. Dean and Bird and their colleagues have a created a model for community ownership. Out of necessity, they have reinvented how things should and can be done.

None of this could have been achieved without the time and effort they have given, backed up by the essential contribution of their volunteer supporters. By giving so much of themselves, Dean and Bird are philanthropists as well as social entrepreneurs. This is how community philanthropy works.

*　*　*

I ended my return visit to Belfast with a second conversation with Andrew McCracken of the Northern Ireland Community Foundation. Having absorbed the history of Northern Ireland since the Troubles began, I wanted to know how the future looks with significantly less public expenditure and investment and the ending of the Atlantic Philanthropies commitment. McCracken and I met in the café in the Belfast City Hall:

Fifteen years ago, a small charity called the Now Project started, to support people in north Belfast with learning disabilities. It has since grown into the NOW Group, a number of social enterprises giving training and job opportunities and also running profit-making enterprises, ploughing profits back into the core work of the charity.

They won the tender to run the café here in City Hall because they were able to give better value for money and greater social value than their private-sector competitors.

This is a non-sectarian social enterprise. The woman who started all this, Maeve Monaghan, is now chair of the Community Foundation's trustees. Her appointment to the board signifies our need to support more entrepreneurial, sustainable approaches to our local issues.

The original grass-roots community development ethos has remained with us since our beginnings in 1979. The Community Foundation was a leader in building local community relationships and this work continues.

One recent example is work we've supported with the London-derry Bands Forum and how they've worked on the highly controversial issues of parading. In essence, some in the Protestant Unionist community feel they have the right to parade in certain places and some in the Catholic Nationalist community find that oppressive. It is particularly contentious in Belfast and in Derry/Londonderry. These standoffs have been resolved in Derry partly because of work done by Community Foundation staff.

Northern Ireland has been blessed with a lot of external funding since the peace process began, from the US and from Europe, mainly government and quasi-government public funds, as well as Atlantic Philanthropies and other donors. Tens of millions of philanthropic funding has come from outside over the last twenty years and the community and voluntary sector has mushroomed as a result.

Many positive things came out of that but there were also negatives, namely a dependency culture that skewed business models so that the question was always: where do I get the next grant from to do what I do?

Now that there is a big reduction in external funding coming into Northern Ireland, many organisations are folding, reducing their staff and questioning their business models and wondering where their funding will come from. Although there is a strong tradition of charitable giving here there is very little culture of philanthropic giving, at least in the way that community foundations traditionally work.

That means that, as a community foundation, this is a new chapter for us. In a normal society, there must be some sense of the common good where the more affluent give back to society and have some connection with the less well off. This is not happening yet.

The role of the Community Foundation in future must be about bridging the gap between the affluent and less affluent, getting money and resources flowing across that divide, and then helping civil society to have a coherent and confident voice.

We have comparatively few individual philanthropists. Private sector industry is limited. There are a few entrepreneurs but getting them to be charitable via their own foundations or the Community Foundation is as yet untested. A plan for more middle-class people to become involved should not just be about them giving more money to the poor. We should be striving to use giving to transform the lives of those who give as well as those who receive.

I left Northern Ireland with hope because I was inspired by the people I met and by what they have achieved despite many and complex difficulties, some of which remain unresolved. The history of the last forty or fifty years shows us what people can do when they take power and responsibility. Many related factors contributed to the peace process and Northern Ireland's emergence from conflict but without the resilience of communities, the courage and foresight of those who led and supported them and the generosity of personal and community philanthropy, there would have been no settlement and no peace.

Whilst the Northern Ireland Community Foundation considers how it can cross boundaries and create wealth for the community as a whole, what lessons can the rest of the UK learn about the role of community foundations in addressing local social needs?

CHAPTER 18

COMMUNITY FIRST:
A CRUSADE FOR MORE
LOCAL GIVING

"I believe the propensity of people to serve their communities has
been in decline since the Victorian era. It may well have rebounded during wartime but has certainly declined since 1945. That
reflects our consumer culture. Part of our role is to champion the
importance of commitment to community."

FABIAN FRENCH, CHIEF EXECUTIVE,
UK COMMUNITY FOUNDATIONS.

* * *

Community foundations are the link between local money and
local need. They collaborate with private philanthropists, family
trusts, businesses and the public sector with the aim of providing
permanent, flexible and growing sources of local charitable funding.

The community foundation movement began in the US in 1918
where they are well established and well known. The largest US
foundations have endowments worth billions.

There are more than 1,800 similar foundations around the world
and forty-six of these are in the UK. Collectively, the UK foundations have endowments worth half a billion pounds and give
away almost £70 million a year. It is too often said that community
foundations are one of the UK's best-kept secrets. Given the challenges facing our country, that needs to change.

I spoke to Fabian French, Chief Executive Officer of UKCF, in July 2016. French was formerly a corporate finance banker before becoming head of fundraising at Marie Curie, the charity providing care for the terminally ill:

> One of the things about Marie Curie that had a profound effect on me was community fundraising. So much of our donation income came from very active communities. That showed me how much people cared about where they live. Some of our very large donors were as concerned about where the money was spent as they were about the palliative care that was going to be delivered. That helped me to understand community foundations. They offer a brilliant way for people who have spare cash to put money to work for the community.
>
> Two generations ago, it was the family and an extended family of neighbours that looked after the community. For some reason neighbourliness has either broken down or it is not what it was. One generation ago, local authorities took responsibility. For this generation, there is little or no funding from local authorities which have seen their budgets cut by 40 per cent or more. So the burden has to fall on new shoulders. That is what community foundations are there to do.
>
> The floods appeal mounted in 2015 by the Cumbria Community Foundation is a good example of what can be done. £10 million was raised.
>
> Community foundations look in two directions. They look to donors to provide financial firepower. They also look to the community and to the voluntary sector that supports it. We are the bridge between the two. Community foundations know what communities need and how to meet that need. They don't have the resources to meet every need but they know what the priorities are. Our unique ability is to make a linkage between those who give and those in need. The obligation for supporting local causes falls on individuals and local businesses. We act as catalysts and as an agency to transmit donations to communities and to charities.

I believe that the propensity of people to serve their communities has been in decline since the Victorian era. It may well have rebounded during wartime but has certainly declined since 1945. That partly reflects our consumer culture. Our role is to champion the importance of commitment to community.

We have an ambition to increase our endowment from half a billion to a billion pounds by 2020. Under a previous matched funding initiative, the government put in £40 million and donors matched it with almost £80 million and as a result there is £130 million of community foundation endowment that wasn't there before. We are trying to find a replacement programme for that.

I am hopeful that the corporate sector will become more philanthropically minded and will do more than meeting current corporate social responsibility targets. My children's generation is demanding that the organisations they work for play a meaningful role in society in a way that I would not have dreamt of when I was a junior in the city. The view that the sole purpose of business is to generate profit that will return to shareholders as dividends will change if and when their staff demands it.

I believe that within ten years, we shall see community foundations much better known. There is poverty within a few miles of any postcode in the country. Even some of the wealthiest counties have pockets of deprivation, and as people begin to realise this it will make them more conscious of supporting their communities. The old adage is that charity starts at home and today, that should mean your community.

I needed to see how a relatively new foundation operates in one of the wealthiest counties in England. I met Helen O'Donnell, then Chief Executive Officer of Cheshire CF.

We are positioned between Manchester and Liverpool where needs are very obvious. So much funding goes straight from London to the two cities and Cheshire misses out.

David Briggs, Lord Lieutenant of Cheshire, and Joelle Warren,

Vice Lord-Lieutenant, believed the county should have a community foundation and set it up in 2012. At that stage, I don't think anyone had any idea what Cheshire was really like in terms of its needs. Going out to learn was quite a shock. It took about a year to develop the concept before the Foundation was registered as a charity and that was quite a challenge as funds needed to be raised to establish something sustainable.

There was an initial target of £350,000 to pay for three years' running costs and almost double that was raised from a mix of private companies, individuals and trusts. We asked: will you help us make Cheshire a better place? The response was heartening. Most donors pledged for three years. Since then, we have established an endowment of £4.2 million, helped by Community First, the government's commitment to match endowment fundraising up to 50 per cent over four years. We have given grants worth £1.9 million in that time. In 2014, the Foundation raised new income of £2.47 million.

We all knew that there was deprivation in Cheshire but I don't think any of us knew the reality. When applications came in, we had to admit that some came from places we had never heard of. It has been an eye opener. We knew there was scope for donor education in Cheshire, about what it is really like only a mile from your electronic gates.

At the beginning, the trustees were struggling to work out which grants should be made and to who. In the end, we said: who are we to say what people need? We need to listen to what people are telling us their needs are.

According to CCF's report published in 2014:

Too many individuals and families across Cheshire continue to face disadvantage and are unable to benefit from the area's success. There are stark inequalities in employment and in quality of health and life expectancy and too many people remain socially excluded and need support to help them out of poverty.

- Four per cent of neighbourhoods fall within the 10 per cent most deprived in the county, and 11 per cent fall within the top 20 per cent.
- Over 100,000 16–64-year-olds are economically inactive.
- In some areas, over 30 per cent of working-age residents are claiming out of work benefits.
- 23,500 children are living in poverty.
- Over 34,000 households are living in fuel poverty and have insufficient income to keep warm.
- The difference in life expectancy between people living in the most disadvantaged and least disadvantaged areas is ten years for men and seven years for women.

One of the most shocking features of life in Britain is that amidst great wealth, people go hungry. The Cheshire Community Foundation is supporting the West Cheshire Food Bank, part of the Trussell Trust's network. Demand for charitable emergency food provision in West Cheshire has grown rapidly over a two-year period. Problems with benefits directly account for almost half of all referrals from social and health workers. Those referred are given a voucher entitling them to emergency food provision for three days. In the last recorded period of twelve months, the local food bank distributed emergency food parcels to 5,000 people.

O'Donnell continued.

We are keen to support grass-roots initiatives. We had some difficulty in getting applications from Ellesmere Port because some of the voluntary groups are really tiny. They don't have the time or resources to fill in an application. We need to go over there and let people come to us there.

Wilmslow is one of the prosperous towns in the county but it has two wards that are amongst the poorest 10 per cent in the whole of the UK. Lache is a small estate surrounded by very grand houses on the waterfront at Chester and amongst the top 1 per cent of the most deprived wards in the UK. It is stigmatised because of that. Lache is ravaged by unemployment, homelessness and poor health.

We worked with the Lache Community Development Trust on a project for the kids to visit the local radio station where they learned about the media, presented their own shows, began to develop their communication skills and this has raised their aspirations.

The life expectancy for women in Nantwich is seven or eight years longer than that of women in Crewe. They are less than five miles apart. In Rossmore, Ellesmere Port, 100 per cent of children live in deprived households.

Most of our grants have gone to support the young. They fall into the following camps: health and well-being, poverty and deprivation, improving life skills, community capacity building. We are also aware of a big problem with the loneliness of the elderly. Macclesfield has the fastest growing elderly population in the north-west of England. These problems cross all socio-economic groups. The same is true with alcoholism and that affects all age ranges.

We are seeing projects that have become vulnerable because funding has been cut by local authorities. And there are smaller charities that are not now being commissioned because they no longer fit the commissioning criteria. Who is supposed to pick up the pieces?

Donors are turned off by the argument that the state doesn't fund things anymore. That is not an attractive proposition. They want to work in partnership with a community that wants to help itself. Giving locally is attractive because it is much easier to be engaged if you want to be.

We will give away around £600,000 this year. We aspire to give away a million a year. This may be a drop in the ocean but it can make all the difference in deprived communities. £1,000 goes a long way at a local level.

Most of the corporate funds are coming from small local businesses. We have switched them on because we offer them a way of being philanthropic locally by giving relatively modest grants.

Bentley's UK factory is in Crewe where there are pockets of real need. When Bentley, one of the UK's most luxurious brands, set up its fund to support need in Crewe, we took on all the administration and continue to direct their funds to where they make maximum impact, mainly supporting health and social deprivation projects. We provide this service to a number of other companies.

The biggest door opener for us is matched funding. The government's matching for endowment fundraising has stopped. If I knew now that we will have matched funding again, I could match it with up to a quarter of a million almost immediately. We have people who are waiting for match. They want to top up their endowments and create new ones. That is how we raised the £4 million endowment.

We initially struggled to sell endowment but now we can. The match has made the difference. Most of the people who we talked to were not prepared to give to endowment but now do because they are attracted by two things: matched funding from the government and the ability to go on giving in perpetuity. Also, donors come to understand that you can't fund something for a year and expect a problem to be solved.

Here is a good story. Two mums in Congleton both suffered severe post-natal depression and this had a significant impact on their families. They started a couple of mornings a week in a community centre letting other women talk to them about their experiences. They have now helped 900 families in east Cheshire. The guy who funded this was blown away by what these two strong, determined women have done. The initial grant was a couple of thousand pounds to develop a website and they made a brilliant short film. They call themselves the Smile Group.

Think about what that £2,000 private donation has saved the NHS.

* * *

Oxfordshire Uncovered is a report by Jayne Woodley, Chief Executive of Oxfordshire Community Foundation. The county's problems and needs are in stark contrast to the general perception of a green and wealthy county. Here is a representative selection of facts:

- Fifteen neighbourhoods are in the 20 per cent most deprived in England.
- The city of Oxford is the least affordable to live in Britain, with houses costing sixteen times the local annual income.
- The number of council houses available to rent has decreased by more than 75 per cent.
- 54 per cent of people can only afford social housing rent or below.
- About 600 people are homeless.
- One in five children in Oxford is living in poverty.
- Oxford's school results for children aged seven to eleven are in the bottom 25 per cent nationally.
- There were nearly 10,000 cases of domestic abuse involving children in 2013–14.
- Over 600 children are subject to child protection plans, 70 per cent of them under the age of ten.
- On average, two children in every Oxfordshire classroom are young carers, and nearly 40 per cent of them have special educational needs.

The report goes on to account for how the Oxfordshire CF is working with others to pool resources, focus on collective efforts and work in partnership to find positive and creative solutions. I asked Jayne Woodley, a former banker, how she sees OCF's role:

> People who give often don't have time to do due diligence. We do it for them, and quickly. Most of us procrastinate because something might be too difficult or time consuming and we can take that burden away and help them get things done.
>
> We are offering a similar service as a financial advisor. I realised that we should not be talking like a charity but as an advisor on the transfer of wealth. So we started to have these kinds of conversations that enable people to think strategically about what they want to do, who they want to be and how they want to be remembered.
>
> We are all about building an endowment. Originally, OCF did not believe that you could raise money for endowment. They thought

the work was about grant making. Well, it seemed clear to me that we would not be making grants in future without an endowment.

We can now see the benefit of creating permanent wealth. The CF in Cleveland, Ohio, recorded that the total donations they had received in their first 100 years amounted to about $975 million. In that time, they gave away $1.7 billion, and their endowment has grown to about $2 billion. Looking at those figures, you can see the value of creating permanent wealth. Community foundations are here for perpetuity. And that has changed the conversation we have with our prospective donors.

There is a dark side to Oxfordshire. There are pockets of deprivation in every county. So many people are oblivious to this. Our role is to identify what we believe are the most challenging issues and to use our convening power to bring together people who do care and who have the capacity to help. We need to persuade people that they can make a difference and they can change things by working together.

Bringing people together is our role – people who are motivated to give, who are passionate about finding solutions, people who have specialist knowledge.

Housing in Oxfordshire is a very serious problem and clear evidence of the inequality that exists. In terms of average earnings, Oxfordshire is the most expensive place to live in Britain. Buying and renting property is becoming unaffordable for the majority, but particularly for key workers such as nurses, teachers, social workers and bus drivers – people who typically play a vital role in keeping the county moving and thriving. This also impacts on businesses, who find it increasingly difficult to retain and recruit staff.

We don't believe there is one simple solution that will solve this housing crisis but we are now proactively seeking to identify local initiatives that could become part of the solution and we are using our influence to inspire others to get involved and add their support too. One of the most recent things we have developed is an Affordable Housing Fund and what is really encouraging is the number of people that are now coming forward with their ideas.

One such idea is to identify land assets that could be removed from the open market and to hold the land in a community trust specifically for the provision of permanently affordable homes. Eliminating the need to purchase the land would certainly improve the financial viability of such schemes and would enable community groups and cooperatives to be considered as potential developers. So we do need to think differently. Building more and more houses is not necessarily the solution. Community foundations are the ideal organisation to 'own' these properties in trust for future generations.

Oxfordshire County Council has had to cut their budget by another £60 million in addition to about £252 million since 2010. This has significant impact on all services but one in particular that has come under the spotlight is the closure of children's centres, there being a very active one in Chipping Norton called the Ace Centre. David Cameron happened to be the local MP and his constituents complained so he wrote to the council leader and said the service should not be cut and they should cut staff and running costs instead. However, the council has already done all the things government wanted, including cutting staff by a third.

We are considering if there is another way of providing these kinds of 'preventative' services. This is about children and a very emotive subject. We think this is an opportunity for community foundations to act. Could we inspire others from across the voluntary and faith sectors to offer a similar but alternative service? One that could be collectively funded by a combination of donors, the local authority, philanthropists, trusts and foundations, and charities? How willing are people to collaborate and form partnerships? If people want something that badly, then alternative solutions need to be found.

We all work within constraints but I do struggle to understand how politicians can accept the consequences of their short-term actions and that cutting these sorts of services will often cost more in the long term. We should use our community foundation voice in a positive way, not to say you cannot do this but to offer to help find community-based solutions. We know from our experience that early interventions and preventative measures really do help turn people's lives around.

We need to understand what the big issues are in our community. Rather than lots of sticking-plaster grants, we should concentrate on the bigger more strategic problems and use our convening power to bring people together. Donors find that motivating.

There is no point in just blaming the government. The only way of increasing social expenditure is by increasing taxation but people are unwilling to vote for that. We have to deal with the situation as it is and quickly.

We have to be more visionary and more strategic in order to attract more philanthropy. The OnSide Youth Zone model for young people [see Chapter 23] where the local authority invests on the charity's terms is exactly how we should run a new children's services model. Everything appeared to be going wrong with cuts and unemployment but the people who established OnSide Youth Zones have radically changed the way things are done. The key to success must be to establish partnerships.

Community foundations need to target major donors in order to build endowment as quickly as possible but we must also be the people's community foundation and encourage those who only give a very little. This confirms our legitimacy. Again, all this is about membership and people feeling they belong and can contribute.

We should try to be a national organisation and lead on things. We can then say we have hundreds of thousands or millions of members. This is how change is managed now. Look at the lead the Irish Community Foundation took on equal marriage.

Reviving a sense of community and commitment is an essential need in our fragmented and divided society. There is much talk of one nation but little evidence that it exists. Community foundations should be one of the nation's most effective and practical tools to renew and reinforce thinking about the common good. They are now well established and are in a strong position to benefit from devolution, and more localism should that happen. It might not be going too far to say that community foundations could represent the Big Society in action.

The primary financial objective of UK Community Foundations is to double their endowments from half a billion to a billion
pounds by 2020. This is necessary to meet growing demand and
is appropriate if more responsibility is devolved from government
to the regions. Any sensible fundraising campaign should initially
focus resources on securing the largest possible donations from a
relatively small number of the wealthiest donors.

Focusing on the wealthiest few is also prudent given that community foundations run a lean operation and resources are limited.
However, there comes a point in every fundraising campaign when,
for financial, tactical and even moral reasons, it becomes essential to
widen the campaign to ensure not only that financial but that social
objectives are also fulfilled.

Current thinking is that there is no need for the man or woman
in the street to know about community foundations. I understand
the reasons for this from a practical point of view. Any appeal to
a wider public would have significant implications for costs and
resources and would require a new strategy backed by major investment. However, I agree with Jayne Woodley that in the longer
term, the community foundation movement must become a moral
as well as a practical force that commands the support of all those
who wish to support their community regardless of their means.

Britain lacks and needs a new culture of giving appropriate for
the twenty-first century. This will only come about if people are
inspired to join a new, positive and non-political social movement.
UK Community Foundations could play a leading role in such a
movement at a local and national level. They would make the case
that voluntary redistribution should become a normal expectation
in an enterprise culture. Truly independent, locally and regionally
based, supported by a mass membership, community foundations
could be seen as prized institutions that help to solve problems,
provide opportunities for transformational change and act as champions of the common good.

According to David Sheepshanks, Chairman of UK Community
Foundations:

Our greatest challenge is apathy. When we talk about 'community', too many roll their eyes and think either 'that is the government's job' or worse still, 'why don't more people help themselves? Why should I help them?' Or, 'if I am to give money, better to give to a big charity in the UK, or overseas'.

This is the mindset we are tackling head on in our community foundations across the UK. And with considerable success because every new supporter or donor we engage finds his or her attitude to giving transformed. Most have no idea of the depth or variety of charitable enterprise that is undertaken with such energy by selfless people meeting the needs of almost every city zone, town ward or village. They have the rich satisfaction of witnessing close up the evidence of how their money can change lives.

We engage them and connect them with the causes that resonate most. We know it works because our collective grant-making grows every year; almost £70 million last year to over 20,000 causes.

We are on a crusade to open more people's eyes to the joys and rewards of local philanthropy, to become a much needed and ever greater power for good in our country, where local giving will be the norm rather than the exception.

CHAPTER 19

PIONEERING NEW CHARITIES: THE HEROES AND HEROINES OF TWENTY-FIRST CENTURY BRITAIN

"Charity and the not-for-profit sector will never be able to replace government but it can find new ways of doing things."
LORD STEVENSON, FOUNDING CHAIRMAN OF MQ:
TRANSFORMING MENTAL HEALTH.

*　　*　　*

The history of successful charities and charitable foundations tells us that they flourished because they were needed. They were led or guided by remarkable people who were attuned to the needs of contemporary society. The story of pioneering charitable initiatives continues in our own times and the need for them is as great as ever.

I call these people heroes and heroines because I believe that is what they are; they are motivated by the needs of others rather than their own. They are not in it for the money. This is notable in our consumer age that craves personal fulfilment, values material success and celebrity, thinks what celebrities do is news and encourages people to become famous simply for being famous.

In this chapter I focus upon relatively new charities and charitable foundations and upon those who have founded them or enabled them to prosper. I hope some readers may be persuaded to follow their example or encouraged to support their work.

* * *

TwentyTwenty

I guess that Andy Cook might call himself an ordinary person, given his modesty, but he is clearly not because what he has done is exceptional. In 2007, at the age of twenty-four, he and a friend, Mike Hughes, founded TwentyTwenty, a charity offering brighter futures to disadvantaged and disengaged young people aged 11–19 years in Leicestershire. I asked Cook how this came about, how the charity has flourished, and what the future of TwentyTwenty should be:

> I am from Yorkshire, Leeds originally and then Sheffield Hallam University where I did a sports management degree. I went to a Football & Church camp and heard about Extreme Team that offered a year out volunteering but you had to work on the side. The idea was that you went into deprived communities and played football with local youngsters. I don't know why I said I would do it but within a week I found myself in Loughborough. I joined a team that was run out of the King's Church Trust.
>
> I could not believe what I was seeing on those estates. I could not believe what was going on in my country. One of the first lads I met was Ash who had five siblings including two older brothers, one of whom was in prison and he hadn't seen the other for months. Ash was bringing up his younger siblings at the age of fifteen. Mum was depressed and spent her days on the couch with multiple addictions; there were four different dads, none of whom played any role, even though they lived close to the estate. Another lad, Terry, had four younger brothers, all had different absent dads, the same situation with the mother and Terry was bringing up the children. A few months after I met Terry, all his brothers went into the care system.

These were lives that were going absolutely nowhere in cycles of hopelessness. So the likes of Ash and Terry, who were bringing up siblings, and were not able to study, get kicked out of school without any qualifications, can't get jobs, have too much free time not doing anything, become lethargic and fall into drink, drugs and end up with a criminal record.

The thing that struck me most was how amazing these lads were: full of potential, full of life, bright and funny. They have seen and experienced such stuff that if I had had to cope with 5 per cent of it, I would have flat-lined. They seemed to have been destined for this and I was destined for something very different.

I am not one of those founder types who seem born with a mission. I had just witnessed something shocking and I felt I had to do something.

I was brought up in a happy middle-class family in Leeds and didn't see the kind of deprivation I have seen in Loughborough. My own father died suddenly and unexpectedly when I was starting up the charity and that taught me something about being without a father. We were lucky in that we had a network of friends and family friends to turn to.

These youngsters in Loughborough see their dads walking down the street and feel rejected. Rejection after rejection and then a new man comes in and they have another child.

Loughborough is a classic market town of 60,000 people. It has villages around it that are very affluent but it also has pockets of disadvantaged and deprived white working-class areas. The work we started was in the Warwick Way estate. In the 1950s, the estate won an award for its very cool design but it has now turned into a nightmare because there is only one road in and out. It has become a dumping ground. That was where I met Ash and Terry.

Mike and I felt we had to do something. We set up a charity called Charnwood 20:20. Did I know I had leadership skills at the age of twenty-four? No. I just knew I had to do something. Mike was involved with the King's Church Trust so we were able to get a few contacts and help from them and the church gave us a bit of cash. The borough council was also very good. I soon realised that relationships and networks are fundamental to getting anything done. Wendy Brown was the council's anti-social behaviour coordinator. I remember vividly walking around the estate with Wendy and Mike and we were all saying: this isn't right.

Wendy gave us £7,000 to set up the charity and to pilot our first project which was a mentoring scheme. We realised that none of the young people we were meeting had good adult role models. No one who was there for them through thick and thin, there was no unconditional love. I worked with Wendy to train eighteen volunteers in the first year who became mentors to young people on the estate. In the first year, we saw no ASBOs given out when there had been fifteen in the year before. We saw crime drop by over 60 per cent, and school exclusions were reduced simply by an adult spending time with a young person.

That was the first thing we did and my job was to support the mentors. This was a huge learning curve for me.

I approached the Tudor Trust and asked them for funding for a full-time salary for a mentoring coordinator to support forty young people, double the existing number. Not only did they do that via a grant of £25,000, they gave us an additional £5,000 to pay for consultants to help us build our capacity. That changed everything. That relatively small grant was fundamentally important because it enabled us to think and then to improve our offer and become more sustainable.

We started another project called Love for Life to work with vulnerable young girls to help them avoid sexual exploitation by building their confidence in order to make good decisions. This was funded by Children in Need. I was doing a lot of this in my spare time. The income I was raising was predominantly for delivery, but funders understood the need for proper management, and encouraged me to build management costs into later bids.

Things snowballed from there on the basis of our positive results. We became clear that our core mandate was to get young people into work. That is the real game changer. So we have developed Life Skills Centres with one in Leicester and one in Derby looking after kids who have been kicked out of school aged 11–19 (occasionally older) and those who are NEETs (not in education and training) and we teach them core skills in English, maths and IT. We also provide counselling.

I am spending at least 50 per cent of my time networking. I realise that my rhetoric is changing. Rather than asking for handouts, I say that the kids we work with need a hand to help them step up. We say that our young people are resources to be developed not problems to be solved. We can offer you these resources and they can make your business better.

We have just started working with Impetus, the foundation working on behalf of private equity companies [see Kawika Solidum, Chapter 20]. They are helping us to maximise the impact we can make. They have given us an initial £100,000 for core costs to see how we get on.

Out of every ten young people we work with, on average six or seven have their lives turned round. Impetus will help us to improve that. Those of us who demonstrate that we are making a real difference will succeed in securing more ever-stretched resources. The next three or four years will be devoted to refining our model to produce the best possible results.

I have given my all to TwentyTwenty but I understand that change is important. This is the right time for me to move on and so I have accepted an invitation to work for the Centre for Social Justice. I want to see social change nationally not just locally. Joining CSJ provides with me an opportunity to do that. And the future is bright for TwentyTwenty.

The work of Andy Cook and his colleagues has turned round the lives of the disadvantaged young in ways that are beyond the resources and skills of the public sector. This is not to disparage the state and local authorities whose contribution is indispensable. Cook points out, however, that some of the requirements of public funders are not always consistent with need or reality. Public funders need to be more flexible.

I am not surprised that Cook has been successful in attracting both public and private sector funding. Despite his modesty and insistence on sharing the honours with his co-founder and his team, Cook has a compelling personality. Contrary to his own self-assessment, Cook was born a leader and it did not take him long to find his cause. Since we spoke, Cook has been appointed chief executive of the Centre for Social Justice.

*   *   *

Greenhouse Sports

Greenhouse Sports is a London-based charity committed to using sport to help young people living in the inner-city to overcome disadvantage and to realise their full potential. The charity's professional coaches work full time in schools and the community to provide sports programmes that nurture social, thinking, emotional and physical skills, known as STEP, that equip young people for life. Sport is used as a means of empowerment.

Since Greenhouse Sports was founded in 2002, the charity has worked with over 38,000 young people and operates in forty mainstream schools and nine schools for those with special educational needs (SEN), and has four community programmes. All Greenhouse programmes are tailored to meet the needs of each school, its pupils, staff and the local community. There is also a Coach Core programme to nurture the next generation of inspirational sports coaches.

Greenhouse Sports has come a long way since it was founded by Mike de Giorgio, its first CEO, as he explained to me when we met in January 2016 in the charity's new headquarters, a former church in Marylebone, London. Although situated in one of the wealthiest parts of London, the poorest ward in London is only minutes away. He explained that he did not set out in 2002 to create what Greenhouse Sports has become. The charity has evolved in line with continual assessment of what works and what doesn't and with need:

Like all start-ups, you tweak it as you learn more. You should always learn from your mistakes.

I used to be in finance and in 2001 was fortunate to be able to sell my business. I decided to do something I enjoyed, which is working with young people. I am also passionate about sport. Originally, I thought I would set up a one-off programme, which I did in the summer of 2002. I thought I could help the community where my eldest son was at school in Barnes. There was some rivalry between the young people at his school and other local youngsters. The solution seemed to be to get the two to mix. We invited young people from the neighbourhood to play sport at St Paul's Boys' School.

This was a two-week programme that went well. After that, we decided to do more and so it grew with time. My idea was not to set up what we have today.

The first programme was simply about the local young people playing sport and using the facilities at St Paul's. The problem is that private schools tend to be in leafy areas where there are not many disadvantaged young people. So we had to bus them in. This was expensive and people don't feel comfortable leaving their own area. It took us a while to work this out and that we should go to the young people we wanted to work with.

At first, we thought that the magic point was having great facilities. Then we realised that the coach was the key. If you have an inspiring pied piper and you take people to the middle of nowhere, they will all turn up. The magic ingredient is leadership by an individual.

We are trying to use sport as a means to an end. This is not sport for sport's sake but sport for social outcomes. Originally, after I had realised that an inspiring coach is the key, I then thought that we needed to recruit coaches who were technically the best and could teach the young how, for example, to hold a table tennis bat at the correct angle. That wasn't the case. Inspiration is what matters, not technical ability. We need coaches who are role models and who can mentor young people.

We then went to the other extreme and thought the young people needed youth workers, but the trouble with that is that the youngsters got bored, as they wanted to improve at the sport. It took us a while to find that the right balance for leadership is 51 per cent mentor/ambassador and 49 per cent coach.

If a young person was sitting in front of me now, I would say that we can give you a high quality provision that the private school student takes for granted. PE involves large numbers of young people, but we have found that it is more effective to do a lot with a few. The key thing is to encourage the young to be with us regularly a few times a week rather than just the odd half hour when they feel like it.

We work principally with secondary school age children, generally with eleven- to sixteen-year-olds. We are working in schools because that is where the young are or should be.

We are trying to prove to young people that if they work hard they will get better at sport without telling them that getting better at sport is a byproduct. We have our STEP capability framework: Social, Thinking, Emotional and Physical. Resilience and self-confidence comes from that framework. We convince them that if they work hard at all of those, they will become better at sport but that they can also transfer that to their maths. They may not become a professional table tennis player but we tell them are likely to get a better job if they do better at maths.

We are not a youth club; we are not about recreation and play. We are about coaching and learning life skills. The aim is to get the young to believe in themselves. We are aiming for better people as much as champions.

I have been very fortunate in being able to help raise a lot of money for Greenhouse. With money, you can buy professionalism. It helps that people like me are not being paid. Some people have been exceptionally generous in providing core funding. Two organisations initially gave us £100,000 a year each, the Mercers' Company and Man Group. They realised that, although I was working for free, I needed professional management back up. These were classic capacity-building grants.

In 2011, Centre for Social Justice (CSJ) asked if I would chair a report for them into how sport could be used to transform the lives of disadvantaged communities. In our report, *More than a Game*, we concluded that the most important thing about any programme was the appointment of the right coach.

We launched the Coach Core apprenticeship scheme with the Royal Foundation in 2012. By providing 16- to 24-year-olds with the chance to train as professional sports coaches, Coach Core will improve the quality and availability of sports coaching in schools and communities, whilst simultaneously creating job opportunities when many young people face-long term unemployment.

We have recently received some money from Sport England. SE is funded by the Department for Culture, Media and Sport (DCMS). In the past they only funded sport for participation. SE then realised that sport for participation was not working. Regardless of how much money was poured in, half the country was not exercising. Why put money into people who are already playing netball? Surely it is better to put more money into the people who are not doing anything.

We agreed to do a short-term pilot for £72,000 which went well, and the new money spurred us on to develop a programme for young people over fourteen working outside the curriculum. That was a success and SE said they would give us a grant of £1 million over three years, amounting to 8 per cent of our £4.5 million annual budget.

We are blessed with an extraordinary board of trustees who not only concentrate on proper governance but are also very generous with their own funds, and help us with wider fundraising approaches.

I have recently announced that I will be stepping down. I will step down but not step away. I will remain a trustee and ambassador.

Technically, we are a charity but I am a bit prejudiced because I think a lot of charities are not well run. Charities need to be much more business-like in the way they run themselves and manage their finances. Many large charities like Kids Co. should never have been allowed to operate without reserves. This is why we always try to keep some funding in reserve. However, some people have not funded Greenhouse *because* we have reserves. These include business companies that would not dream of operating without reserves. Why should charities be any different?

The voluntary sector is a big part of our economy. Many of the established charities have been around for a long time. Nobody seems
to question whether they are doing good. The government needs
to recognise this and only fund charities that are efficient and can
demonstrate outcomes.

You asked why we are operating in London when there is also so
much more need outside. London is relatively privileged. Though
I originally came from Malta, I now consider myself a Londoner
rather than an English person. I have dedicated myself to my local
community and that is London. And I like to see our programmes.
The new CEO might have a different perspective.

We have just acquired a phenomenal building in Marylebone, a
decommissioned church that had been turned into offices, following
a donation by one of our trustees specifically for this purpose. We
will transform it into a community sports centre. There is a lot of
need here in this otherwise wealthy party of London. There is a
women's refuge next door and a huge estate up the road in one of
the poorest wards in London (Church Street).

I really worry about the 'Paris effect' in London, in that the poorest
people are being moved out of the centre. There is a lot of need in
London alongside obvious prosperity with Mayfair round the corner.
This will be an iconic sports centre in the middle of London but it must
not become a place for the wealthy. It will open in the summer of 2017.

The Greenhouse Sports 2014–15 annual report notes they engaged
8,000 young people in the fifty programmes they ran over that time
period.

In its mainstream programmes, on average, participants attended
four more days of school than other pupils in the same school. Six
out of ten young people also reported they saw an increase in their
leadership, confidence, self-reflection and determination.

Greenhouse Sports programmes are in schools where two-thirds
of the population are considered to live in areas of high deprivation.

More than 90 per cent of schools that responded to a satisfaction
survey agreed they opened up opportunities for pupils.

Greenhouse Sports' expenditure was almost £4 million in 2013–14. The majority of its income of almost of £4.9 million was donated by the private sector with a contribution of £312,000 from government.

Mike de Giorgio can look back having devoted almost fifteen of his middle years, without pay, to creating a charity that evolved to meet the needs of some of the poorest young people living in one of the wealthiest cities of the world. Not everyone has his leadership skills, his private means or his network but many working in finance do and those who are approaching mid-life would do well to consider following his example, not least as a way of finding fulfilment. De Giorgio is one of only a small minority of the most well-off who give something back to society in the hope that life will be better for those who do not have the opportunities he has had.

It is worth pausing for a moment to consider what our country would be like if people such as Andy Cook, young and with no money, and Mike de Giorgio, middle-aged and with no need to earn a living, had chosen not to be public-spirited and to do what they have done by giving so much of themselves.

*   *   *

UpRising

Social mobility, a positive feature of the post-war boom years, is in decline. Whilst Britain has undergone radical change and is one of the most diverse countries in the world, this is not reflected in those who hold power. In 2015, David Cameron, then Prime Minister, accused universities, the armed forces and Britain's biggest businesses of 'ingrained, institutional and insidious attitudes' holding some young people back.

According to the Social Mobility and Child Poverty Commission, 33 per cent of MPs went to private schools compared with 7 per cent of the public as a whole. Of MPs, 5 per cent are from a black or ethnic (BME) background, compared with 14 per cent of the population. Only 23 per cent of MPs are women, and only 13 per cent of FTSE 100 board positions are held by women.

UpRising was founded in 2008 to address this imbalance. The charity is a youth development organisation whose mission is to open pathways to power for talented young people from diverse and under-represented backgrounds. Those who participate are equipped with 'the knowledge, networks, skills and confidence to fulfil their leadership potential, find new opportunities and transform the world around them by social acts'.

The key to UpRising's effectiveness is intense mentoring by committed volunteers.

UpRising was serving 2,000 young people in 2014–15 from centres in London, Bedford & Luton, Birmingham, Cardiff, Liverpool, Manchester and Stoke-on-Trent.

UpRising is the brainchild of Rushanara Ali, Labour MP for Bethnal Green and Bow and a social entrepreneur. She is the co-founder and chair of UpRising and I asked her to tell me her life story because her personal experience explains why she felt compelled to empower young people with similar backgrounds and facing the same challenges she has had to overcome:

> I grew up in the East End of London. I was seven when I came to Britain from Bangladesh. I didn't speak much English. I went to local state schools. This was in the early 1980s. I grew up with this feeling of being stuck and powerless. We lived round the corner from the City and I could see the towers of Canary Wharf going up and I felt cut off from all that. Life in the East End was bleak at that point. There was a lot of racism and hostility.
>
> The path out of all that was education. My parents were encouraging. I was very lucky because I went to very good primary and secondary schools with great teachers. That was my passport to opportunity. Quite by chance, I had a lot of back up and support. One of the most influential chance encounters I had was with a group of people at what is now called the Young Foundation. Michael Young and his colleagues were doing their research into family and kinship in East London and I became a researcher for that book

which came out in 2005 called *The New East End: Kinship, Race and Conflict.*

So that is how I landed on my feet without realising it and there I was hanging out with the man who wrote the 1945 Labour manifesto! I was in my late teens and surrounded by all those extraordinary people. That was how I got first hand experience about how you do social entrepreneurship. Looking back, I can see that I absorbed more about how to do start-ups than I realised.

One of the first things I did was to help Michael do some social research in how to keep young people living in Tower Hamlets out of trouble. The first BNP councillor had been elected in 1993. We set up Tower Hamlets Summer University which was later renamed Futureversity. It's an education charity providing free courses and activities for 11–25-year-olds to help them develop the skills and self-belief they need to make the most of their lives. Their programmes have been proven to raise aspirations, reduce youth crime, break down racial tensions and get unemployed young people off benefits and into work. Over 120,000 young people have gone through that programme since the charity was established.

I also helped him develop an organisation called Language Line, a telephone interpreting company which provided interpreters in over a hundred languages in less than a minute. It was very successful and when it was sold, Michael left an endowment to what is now the Young Foundation. I was working on these great projects during my vacations from Oxford University. Looking back, it was an extraordinary kind of apprenticeship in social entrepreneurship, social research, policy making and politics.

I have always had this social entrepreneurship bug. I started my political life by working with my Labour predecessor, Oona King. I worked for the Institute for Public Policy Research (IPPR) and later worked in the Home Office and Foreign Office. I helped set up the Forced Marriages Unit in the Foreign Office. I was quite restless by 2005. I realised that I was not temperamentally suited to being a civil servant. So I returned to the Young Foundation. I worked there as an associate director leading on research and international projects and also focused on starting up new organisations.

By the time I returned to the Young Foundation, I had written a report for IPPR about the lack of representation of black, Asian and working-class people in public life and the barriers they face. I started to think about an organisation that would transfer the skills and instil the confidence needed to break down those barriers and get into positions of power and influence that are currently dominated mainly by white upper-middle-class men.

I started a pilot in 2008 and named it UpRising, but found it very difficult to raise money in the first year. The reaction was that there were lots of similar initiatives but that was not true. Today, there is little else that is dealing with power and teaching young people how to understand power, how to navigate through power structures and systems, power within political institutions, in business, community organisations.

The thing that so often holds people back is confidence about feeling or believing they belong. Britain has a particular problem in that people often feel they don't belong or fit in. People should not be prisoners of their background.

We started with helping young people understand themselves and what they want to achieve, to help them become self-reflective and to identify the big challenges they face and the challenges facing their city or town and to think about strategic issues. Then we focused on developing their skills and capabilities such as public speaking, media training, social media training and campaigning skills. If you build such skills, you are then empowering others to change things for the better. Our focus is to identify talent among 19- to 25-year-olds from ethnic minority and white working-class backgrounds, while not turning away those from middle-class backgrounds who make up about 20 per cent of participants. We are looking for people with fire in their bellies, who want to make a difference and to contribute to their community or beyond. They can be school leavers or university high fliers. Mentoring is only an element – but an important one – in the programme, but the overall aim is leadership development and training. At the end of the course, they mount a campaign either as a group or on their own. Of our alumni, 20 per cent have gone on to set up their own social enterprise.

People did not want to invest in our start-up without evidence of what it could do. I had a tiny bit of funding, so we started to recruit and then I looked through my address book and emailed everyone I knew who could become a mentor. They were the first group of mentors, forty or fifty of them. A number of people who later went on to become MPs became mentors including Tristram Hunt, Seema Malhotra and Sadiq Khan. Others like Zac Goldsmith MP, Richard Fuller MP and Chloe Smith MP have spoken in our leadership training sessions. One of the early mentors, my friend Alexander Stevenson, probably recruited up to twenty of his friends as mentors. In order to recruit UpRising participants, we went into sixth-form colleges, universities, community centres and advertised through local media and other community networks. All this was done by volunteers. At this point, I was an associate director of the Young Foundation. Once we got through the first year, we were off. We had started to establish our networks and credentials. But funding was still a challenge. Trusts and foundations have been very good to us but we have not yet managed to get enough corporate backing in the form of a critical mass of them donating say £10,000 to £25,000 a year. However, some corporates have been good at giving in-kind support such as donating office space. We have had government support via the Cabinet Office and that has helped us to expand. The Paul Hamlyn Foundation has funded us to expand into Wales. We are in Stoke-on-Trent and in Bedford where we are focusing on reaching young people from white working-class communities. We have our sights on going national and I would have liked to have seen the organisation expand at a faster pace. We now have over 2,700 alumni who are mainly in their twenties doing some amazing jobs and running campaigns as well as taking up leadership roles in their communities.

What do we need? We need more funding to help us build our

capacity in a sustainable manner. JP Morgan is one of the few banks that provided financial banking along with Canary Wharf Group and we are now working to attract more corporates who can see the impact we are having and the potential for their own organisations to recruit talented people from diverse backgrounds, through Up-Rising. We need a network of wealthy and well-connected people to help raise funds as that would enable us to scale up and transform the lives and prospects for thousands more young people from different backgrounds around the UK.

Britain is not good at preparing people for power. Other countries are much better at this. We need to create a bridge between those who hold power now and people who should be future leaders in all walks of life. There is so much talent out there and we need to focus on developing pathways for them.

My next big project is the idea of recruiting and training a Million Mentors over the next decade to help a million young people.

If we are able scale up UpRising so that we are working with many more thousands of young people, then growing and developing the mentoring element is key. We need more mentors to help open doors for young people to get into work. Careers advice and work experience is disappearing. Whilst it is not a substitute, if we have more trained mentors, we can help the young make the right connections. This could potentially make a huge contribution to breaking down social class divides and promoting volunteering on an even bigger scale.

Rushanara Ali's ambition to transform volunteering in Britain by creating a million mentors would be a grand thing if she can raise the necessary funding. This was our first meeting but it was immediately clear to me that she is the kind of person who if she asks you to do something, you do not say no. That explains the success of UpRising to date. She has won significant cross party support including warm tributes from Tory MP Sajid Javid, then Secretary of State for Business, at an UpRising gala in Canary Wharf in February 2016 that raised £100,000.

I talked to three UpRising alumni.

At sixteen, Poppy Noor was homeless. She went on to study at Cambridge University two years later. She is currently training as a social worker and works pro-bono for the youth homeless charity Centrepoint. I was struck by her awareness of an inherent danger in that by creating new elites, new inequalities may arise, an echo of Patricia Napier's experience in Zambia (see Chapter 14). Noor is grateful for her UpRising experience and endorses it but she is right to be aware that individual empowerment needs to benefit the many and it will be her responsibility and that of her fellow alumni to ensure that happens as a result of their own leadership. That will be one way of changing the world for the better. We talked in October 2015:

> I went to a state school. I am from Newham originally. My family was very poor. I went to Cambridge University where I read politics, psychology and sociology. I always felt 'behind'. By my third year when everyone was applying for jobs, I thought that the friends I had made there had so much more knowledge than me about the working world and applying for jobs. They knew what to do and had so many connections that I did not have.
>
> There is no doubt I would not have done what I did without UpRising. When I was a teenager, I could not live at home anymore and became homeless. I went into local authority care and I stayed there for three years until I went to University. I did my A levels when I was on benefits that paid for my food.
>
> I started with UpRising when all the anti-benefits stuff got really nasty. I wrote a piece for *The Guardian*. Although I did this on my own initiative, I wouldn't have done it if I hadn't had the UpRising experience. That helped me to believe that what I had to say was valid. Then Channel 4 news invited me to do a piece. The piece was about removing housing benefit from people who are under the age of twenty-one. That would have meant that I would be homeless until I could get a job and would have been at the expense of staying on at school and going on to university.

There is a catch-22 about UpRising because they help you to get all the networks and knowledge you need to become successful and which you would not have otherwise. However, there is a risk that problems become perpetuated by creating new elite circles. If you create a network for a new elite of working-class people, your success will depend on who you know and that is replicating what happens with middle-class people. UpRising is a sticking plaster but it is very good that is there.

The real issue is diversity. You cannot see yourself as a judge if there are no judges who are black or a woman or both. People become conditioned to a way of thinking that only people like you are worth talking to. We do need to try harder to become more diverse to counter what is a very natural way of thinking. If we don't, we are wasting talent. The trouble is that middle class is now synonymous with good.

Even with my background, I started to think, behave, dress and speak like the more privileged middle-class students who were my friends. And many of them went to get jobs starting at £50,000 a year. One of the reasons I want to be a social worker is so that if I go into politics, I can understand the people I will represent. I think it is very difficult to understand if you don't have that experience.

For example, when I was on benefits and I first became homeless, there was a rule that if you went to university outside your borough, you got taken off the housing register. You had to choose between whether you wanted to go to university or having somewhere to live. This discriminates against poor people who have the ambition and ability to get on. What people are really saying is that if your parents can support you, you can do what you like but if they cannot, then you should be a cleaner. The whole of the rest of your life will be determined at that point.

You may see more of this confident and challenging young woman on YouTube, being interviewed for Channel 4 News.

I was also impressed by the two other UpRising alumni I met. Alvin Carpio was featured in UpRising's gala programme as a

Most Outstanding Achiever. His parents were originally from the Philippines. He was raised in Plaistow, east London. Carpio has been involved with UpRising since the start. He is now twenty-seven and a public affairs officer for the Joseph Rowntree Foundation.

My dad died when I was nine. That was completely devastating and disorientating. My mum is a hero to me. She took over from my dad. She pushed me to go to the London Oratory School on the other side of London, where Tony Blair's sons went. That was a transformational experience. When I look at my mates in east London, many of them got into trouble. One of them got done for murder, another one for robbery. So going to the London Oratory was a defining moment for me.

I know that going to a really good school helped me to get to where I am now. I was the first in my family to graduate from university. I went to SOAS to read history and politics. That was great because it enabled me to learn about the Philippines, to learn about my family's history as well as learning about the Middle East, Africa, South America and east Asia. I knew so little about the Philippines and the struggle for human rights. Being at SOAS made me much more politically aware and active. I was shocked to hear about extra judicial killings. This was 2008–09.

I was accepted into an investment banking trainee programme when the financial crash came. I was interviewed by Goldman Sachs and Merrill Lynch, who accepted me for an internship but the crash put an end to that in 2008.

A week later, I saw an advert for UpRising on a SOAS notice board. I applied and got into the very first cohort of about sixty people.

At the time, I wasn't sure that investment banking was what I wanted to do. It could have helped me transform life for my family. I did have my doubts and joining UpRising reconfirmed and helped me to further realise that I should follow a different route and that I should be involved in some way with social change. UpRising encourages you to believe that you could become a top civil servant, a government minister or a leading business figure. UpRising helps you nurture that belief. You really can learn to change yourself by challenging yourself. The programme is for a year. We had skill sessions and networking sessions. We learned how to write a speech. We learned how to network and hold people's attention. We learned social and etiquette skills. Yes, UpRising has changed my life.

After UpRising, I became a community organiser for three years at London Citizens. I worked on the Living Wage campaign and became borough organiser for Haringey. I then worked for David Lammy, the local MP, before I did a master's in social policy at the LSE. I then worked for two years for Catch22 [see Chapter 21], helping young people who were involved with gangs. And I have been working for the Joseph Rowntree Foundation for a year as a public affairs officer.

I am not sure what comes next. I know I want to do something that really makes a difference, to address poverty and to help young people who are in catch-22 positions.

I have been selected to go to Davos in 2016 for the World Economic Forum (WEF). Every year they pick up to fifty young people to go. I am probably the only person from Plaistow who has been able to do this. UpRising has given me the confidence to believe that I could apply for Davos. If UpRising were able to offer more opportunities to many more young people, just imagine how the country would change for the better.

Sophie Richardson hails from what she calls the Las Vegas of the North, by which she means Blackpool, so we have local geography in common. We met in London in the summer of 2015 in the offices of the charity Free the Children, where she is a manager. She also volunteers as a governor at Thornton Heath primary school in London and continues to be involved with UpRising as a participant on its pilot leadership programme with Pricewaterhouse-Coopers (PwC). Introducing herself as a Master of Ceremonies at the gala, she described UpRising as her Oxbridge:

I was born in Blackpool twenty-seven years ago into a large and close family. I love Blackpool and enjoyed growing up there until I was eighteen. I was lucky to have a happy childhood. I was brought up to believe that I must go to university in order to get a good job.

I went to Queen Mary University of London (then Queen Mary College, QMC) to read French and Linguistics. I visited Cambridge University but did not think I would fit in. I realise that was silly but that was how I felt when I was seventeen. I had been on our school council and I was student governor at sixth-form college and that was the beginning of my understanding about power and money. I was ready for living a city life even though I cried the whole way to London.

QMC was great for me and I felt at home in east London. I became Vice-President of the Student Union, and then had a year as President. That was such a great and positive experience. I learned a lot about how charities work. I became a member of the governing council. All that ended when I was twenty-four. The power and responsibility were so good for me and I miss it!

I joined the UpRising Leadership Programme when I was at university. They approached me. I was attracted by its social action programme. I was particularly attracted by the prospect of learning more about how leadership works and opportunities for networking. I learned so much from my time with UpRising. There was a really diverse group of people, many who were a lot more disadvantaged than me in terms of education or family background. What UpRising teaches you is to find your own power within yourself.

I am still involved and in a year-long UpRising project with PwC. Eight PwC staff are working with eight alumni. We were invited to examine PwC's strategic challenges ahead and to come up with a project to tackle some of them. This has been a great opportunity to learn more about the corporate world.

I am now working for Free the Children, a youth empowerment charity. We are involved with the Barclays Life Skills programme working with schools in economically deprived areas, particularly in the north of England, including Blackpool. Another project is called Team London, set up post Olympics, designed to get young people volunteering and involved in social action, backed by the

mayor. The third project is our flagship 'Be the Change', partly
funded by Virgin Atlantic and partly by the Queen's Trust.

We are working with 2,000 schools in Britain. I am the Manager of
Speakers and Facilitators, meaning I lead on the delivery of our schools
programmes across the UK, leading a team which works with young
people to develop their skills and become involved in social action.

The young are being denied life opportunities. More and more is
being devolved. In 2013, I spent a day with the Director of Social
Services on Blackpool Council. Every school in the area is under
an academy. They were all willing to work with her but they are
under no obligation to do so. She said her power is very limited.
When education is no longer the responsibility of a public or local
authority, how can we guarantee that the same opportunities are
being offered to young people nationwide?

I have noticed since working here how desperate schools are to
teach more about citizenship and to encourage social action.

I was struck by the commitment to others demonstrated by all
three alumni. How effective is UpRising? Demos, the think tank, is
undertaking a long-term review and according to an interim report
published in March 2015:

- 46 per cent of UpRisers reported taking practical action to benefit others.
- 52 per cent reported taking on a leadership role since completing
UpRising.
- One in five reported setting up a business.
- 85 per cent thought the programme had improved their
confidence.
- Three in four said their career aspirations had been raised.
- 17 per cent reported setting up a social enterprise.
- 68 per cent reported gaining employment since completing
UpRising.
- One in four reported serving as a trustee or board member of a
non-profit.

UpRising needs more private sector support to expand its work, and deserves it.

* * *

Localgiving

Marcelle Speller is passionate about giving and equally passionate about persuading others to give online; after she sold her business, Holiday Rentals, she founded Localgiving. Her concern is the future of communities and her ambition is to secure the small local charities that make all the difference and where modest amounts of money go a long way. This is needed because 47 per cent of local charities estimate they will be out of business within five years.

To date, Localgiving has raised over £15 million for communities from more than 138,000 online donors.

Speller is an entrepreneur who has become a social entrepreneur. She has a genius for leveraging money and can show donors how they can create social capital by multiplying a donation fivefold through matched funding. She is looking for more philanthropists to leverage more online donations and so she is learning to become a fundraiser:

> When I look back, I can see that I was often keen to recognise opportunities and to follow them up from my student days. When I worked at American Express, it was the time of an appeal for the Sudan floods at the end of the 1980s. I could not get through to the Disasters Emergency Committee (DEC) on the telephone. I thought this was no good. I told a colleague who ran the Amex telephones. Two days later, we diverted the DEC's overload of calls to American Express. We took £54,000 on our first night. Call centre staff taught members of our management committee how to answer the calls. Amex is still doing the same twenty-five years later.
>
> We set up Holiday Rentals exactly twenty years ago. Looking back, it was fun but at the time we did not know we were going to be successful. We didn't pay ourselves for six years.

My approach to philanthropy has always been: what can we do about this rather than just write a cheque? So when there were major floods in Boscastle in Cornwall, we contacted the owners of all the houses in the area on the website and asked them if they could provide temporary housing for those who had been made homeless. Many responded. Localgiving is now doing the same in Calderdale. Since the Boxing Day floods in 2015, we have raised £220,000 for those affected.

My plans took off after I went to an event about fundraising at an INSEAD (business school) alumni event. What really fascinated and impressed me were the people working at the coalface, the people who were accountable. I realised that I had skills to offer that were probably more valuable than the amount of money I had to give.

This was 2007–08 and online giving was increasing. There were lots of very small charities that were too small to be registered. They could not claim gift aid tax relief and they couldn't register on other online platforms. I realised that a lot of important work was being done in local communities and what public money there was would go on decreasing. They didn't have fundraising departments. How were they going to survive?

I realised that they needed to be connected to the internet. I thought about our Holiday Rentals business model where we had moved holiday home owners from having a couple of lines on the back pages of one week of the *Sunday Times* to being able to post entire pages on a website.

I was trying to use technology to help these small charities to raise awareness about what they were doing, to create proper websites, to give them gift aid automatically. We were providing a lot of services to small charities and we were helping people to find charities in their area. We were using the internet to make these connections and to encourage people to give and to volunteer.

A third of the charities on Localgiving have a turnover of less than £5,000 and are too small to be registered. Yet they are making a huge contribution to their communities and society as a whole.

We teach the people who run local charities about how to use social media, about fundraising campaigns, and to have the marketing skills that the bigger charities have. They are also short of time to plan campaigns so we plug them into our ready-made fundraising campaigns like the Local Heroes fundraiser campaign, or Grow Your Tenner match funds. This gives them the confidence to go out to fundraise. Of the charities who fundraised through Grow Your Tenner, 80 per cent gained new donors.

The first big lesson was the need to train people. The other lesson that I learned is that I thought Localgiving would be just like Holiday Rentals in that it would just take off. It hasn't happened like that. We have 2,000 charities on the site and we are still losing money. I have eighteen staff to pay so of course we have to charge a small subscription to charities and we take a 5 per cent commission on donations. With Holiday Rentals, there is an entire industry devoted to telling people to go on holiday. We don't have the same thing to encourage people to give to charity.

What really makes the difference is matched funding. This gives everyone an incentive. It is such a good thing for donors because we can leverage their donations, via tax relief and matching, to be worth up to five times more.

We had a donor who gave us £200,000 and that was matched and went to 1,300 charities. How else could a major donor find and validate 1,300 charities in one single transaction? That was funding of small amounts to local charities that can literally keep the lights on. This is really important.

I am now working on how to persuade more philanthropists to support more of these matched funds. This is proving challenging, particularly with some foundations because decisions about how funds are to be used are delegated. Some foundations are saying that Localgiving needs to make the decision where the money goes.

John, in your career as a fundraiser, there were buildings, productions and exhibitions to fund. These are tangible things. I am dealing with charities all over the country working in a range of areas including disabled or bereaved young people, individuals who have been raped, environmental charities, mental health charities, ex-offenders, isolated and lonely old people. It is very hard to raise money for all these differing causes.

I took the person who gave us £200,000 round some of the charities he had helped and he was amazed by what they were doing in west Berkshire. There is a group called Community Responders. They live in villages that are a long way from hospitals. All these great, enthusiastic, proud guys are volunteers. They have basic first aid training; they are not formal paramedics but almost. They have a feed into all 999 medical emergency calls that come into their area. And as they are in a rural area far from the nearest hospital, they can get to the location many precious minutes before an ambulance – and those minutes save lives.

They have a car that was donated by Big Lottery Fund and Coutts. But they have to insure and maintain the car, they have to pay for petrol, bandages and oxygen. This is covered by Localgiving. Our donor worked out that an ambulance costs about £900 to bring out and these guys cost £9. They are able to save lives because they are trained to deal with people who have had heart attacks. This is such a cost-effective way of working. The local community can provide an effective and faster service than that paid for by public money.

I am an entrepreneur who has turned into a social entrepreneur and now I need to turn myself into a fundraiser. I have a machine, I know it works but getting the matched funding is a real challenge. We need funding partners. Who might they be? Could we connect with online shopping?

We have just done a study of the sustainability of local charities. 80 per cent think they will be around in a year's time but only 47 per cent think they will be here in five years' time. If we don't support the sector, there won't be the charities for us to support in ten years. The money is needed now. That is the problem with endowment. I can see all the advantages of building endowments so that good may be done in perpetuity but what about all the charities doing good work who will have to close if we don't fund them now?

Of donations on Localgiving, 50 per cent now come from mobiles or tablets. Technology has enabled that to happen. The key thing is to get people to understand what is possible and what they can do. Now other people are looking to follow our example. I want to give people the confidence that they can do things. I want people to understand the joy of giving. Giving is a two-way thing. Those who give also receive.

*　　*　　*

MQ: Transforming Mental Health

One in four of us, 15 million people in Britain, are affected by mental illness each year. MQ (Mental Health and Quality of Life) is a new charity funding research that will change the lives of millions for the better. The charity's vision is to help to create a world where mental illness is understood, effectively treated, and prevented.

I talked to Lord (Dennis) Stevenson, MQ's founding chairman, and to Paul Stein, Director of Development and Engagement, about the genesis of the charity, what it aims to achieve in the first years of its life and how it will raise money for what some might think is a difficult cause given the stigma associated with mental illness.

Dennis Stevenson's life has been divided 50/50 between profit and not-for-profit. He has mainly created start-up businesses but has also chaired FTSE companies and charities concerned with youth, art and the third world, and was founder chairman of MQ.

The key to my philanthropy is that I have deliberately divided my life 50/50 between earning money and contributing to society. A key influence was a paragraph in a book by the Dalai Lama in which he said that the main point of life was to be happy and the best route he knew to be happy was helping others. I originally thought this was soppy stuff but gradually realised he was right. Simple, almost trite as it may seem, the best way to be happy is to help others.

Stevenson has also been prominent in trying to change attitudes towards mental illness by being open about his own depressive illness:

I started to suffer from depression more than twenty years ago. I was happily married with children. I was not impecunious. I didn't make a secret of it and told a lot of people, which was unusual then and not common now. And then government asked me to be involved with a promotion that involved Alastair Campbell and me in a show that went round the country. That was one of the bravest things I have ever had to do. Melanie Reid wrote a brilliant article about me and depression in *The Times* about ten years ago.

MQ was not my idea. Mark Walport, who was then Head of the Wellcome Trust and is now Government Chief Scientific Advisor, told me that even if you take out all the unhappy Europeans and Americans who don't have a clinical illness, mental illness is a huge problem, not least because there is huge co-morbidity with heart disease and cancer. He said that science was ready to do things but the resources were not there. Even though Wellcome is the largest researcher in neuroscience, they didn't have the funds and resources to invest in this.

He said if Wellcome were to grant a £20 million dowry to establish the world's first serious mental health research foundation, could I be persuaded to take it on? With that working capital of £20 million, could I set up the equivalent of Cancer Research UK and raise millions more for it?

I did a lot of research and took about a year to make a decision. I wouldn't have done it as a subsidiary of Wellcome but they would not have done it that way either. We are now independent of the Wellcome, but they are like a wonderful godparent.

I have now stepped up to be founding chairman of MQ. We established a small board of specialists which is now chaired by Sir Philip Campbell, editor-in-chief of *Nature* and the Nature Publishing Group.

We had an interesting fundraising challenge. We didn't need money during the period when we were evaluating priorities but we did need momentum and credibility before we were ready to start calling on the Wellcome grant. So I went to five good friends and said: we don't need cash right now but would you be prepared to put money into this, blind and on a discretionary basis, if we suddenly need funding? They agreed and I raised about £2 million. Their commitment was vital at a point whilst we were deciding strategy. I put in £100,000 and the charity started life in my office.

We then hired Paul Stein as our fundraiser. He is typical of a new generation of professional highly talented and extraordinarily committed fundraisers.

The really big charities raise hundreds of millions by appealing to millions of people. This could be a five- to ten-year job for MQ although I now think that it will be easier to raise money for mental health than I originally thought. Paul is now researching and testing how we should undertake retail fundraising whilst he has been cultivating the big donors in my address book and beyond. The early results from both approaches are very encouraging. Charity and the not-for-profit sector will never be able to replace government but it can find new ways of doing things.

I asked Paul Stein how MQ will be funded in future:

Given the scale of what we are trying to address, we need to prioritise and focus upon specific objectives. Our first objective must be to identify where we can make the most impact with the £20 million start-up grant from the Wellcome Trust. We must make this money work as hard as possible and start programmes that will have long-term impact. These will focus on three areas.

The first will focus upon psychological treatments because that is most likely to make an impact soonest.

The second focus will be upon capacity, meaning empowering people to carry out this work. The first of these programmes is investing in post-doctoral research at a critical stage in the development of younger professionals. They are ready to move from working for someone else towards independent research but they need help to make that transition. We provide three-year awards to the people who are conducting the kind of research that is aligned with our aims and we support them through that transition to independence.

The third focus will be on future treatments for children and younger people. So many mental health problems start in childhood and adolescence. By focusing our research we hope to get a better understanding of mental illness in the young in order to develop treatments that may help prevent mental illness in later life.

MQ was founded on the understanding that it would be multi-disciplinary. Until now much of mental health research has been disjointed and this is one of the reasons why it has been held back. Research has tended to focus on narrow specialisms whereas the best treatments are those that work in combination.

What are the immediate challenges for the charity in terms of funding what we are planning to do? As a start-up, we need to go back to basics in terms of fundraising. As of 2015, there is little infrastructure, no track record and no income coming in.

This is enabling me to build the case for support for MQ from a major donor perspective. You and I know that major donors tend to like to give to projects that have not yet started, that will not start without their backing, and projects with clear, tangible outcomes and metrics for measuring impact. The critical question is always: what difference will my money make? What would be the difference between me giving you nothing and me giving you X hundred thousand? This is fundamentally important from the point of view of a philanthropist.

Asking for more money to do more research would be too vague and woolly. I am driving a document designed to ascertain what metrics we can measure and what programmes we could be putting into place and demonstrate what impact they could have.

A key element underpinning research across the sector is that of Big Data. If you want to understand how many people are affected by mental illness, what kind of treatments work, what are the demographics, this data does not exist in any one place. The biggest source of data is the NHS. There are other cohorts of data but coordination between them could be improved. MQ is looking to lead on mental health data science, not necessarily to house the data ourselves but ensure that data is more joined up and accessible to the public and all the other charities, specialists and researchers in the field.

This is a huge project and of crucial importance to everything we are trying to do. We are commencing it, but will need significant investment to fulfil its potential. We are now building the case for support for Big Data. For the donor looking for investment, leverage and making a real difference, this is a great project.

Our case for support for all the projects I have outlined will also say what is likely to be the situation should we not implement what MQ is trying to achieve.

The initial funding from Wellcome came with a caveat, that we should also work in the public sphere as well as with private donors, the idea being that a public campaign could help to tackle the stigma associated with mental illness. So our work will also be funded by the public and in the public arena.

As we develop the case for support and the detail of the programmes for which we are seeking funding, we have assessed which parts of our programme would be suited to a mass-marketing campaign. This will be our work with children and young people and this will cost £22 million over nine years. This will be the focus of our campaign.

We are doing everything we should to ensure that when we roll out a mass-market strategy, it is as successful as possible. We have been conducting market research about attitudes to mental health. We are testing how emotive our messaging might be, who it might be directed to and what media we should use. We have conducted a survey on mental illness on Facebook to determine attitudes and how people might respond to different messages.

This should be a cause that people will want to support given that one in four of us are afflicted by mental illness. No family is untouched. The challenge is to connect people with causes they care about. Seven thousand people participated in our mental health survey and more than 10 per cent indicated that they will be happy to donate in future. The omens are good.

Prior to MQ, Stein has worked for Macmillan Cancer Support and subsequently became the first Director of Fundraising, Marketing

& Communications for World Jewish Relief. As a former Director of Fundraising, I was naturally interested in the challenge of raising funds for a new and pioneering charity. I was also interested to hear from a professional what he thinks about current charity fundraising:

> There is too much pressure to achieve short-term targets and to squeeze everything you can out of donors. The mass-marketing approach is designed to get as many donors in as you can and get as much money out of them as possible. Aggressive high-street tactics are not the most effective forms of fundraising.
>
> Street fundraising is not targeted and there is very little if any feel-good factor. They have extremely high rates of attrition. As many as 60 per cent of those signed up on the street cancel their direct debit. Long-term fundraising based on real engagement yields far more.
>
> If charities are to take on more responsibility, they need to be seen as being able to do so. Many people feel many charities are a bit amateurish. Their structures are built organically and become unwieldy. They can lack focus. They don't have proper strategic goals. This means they face a challenge in recruiting staff of the highest calibre.
>
> The way to increase personal giving must be to deepen levels of engagement. The biggest reason why people do not give is because they are not asked. Too many fundraising operations in long-standing charities are too passive because the money just rolls in.
>
> Charities need to be focused on how much extra business they are generating. They need to be more proactive. Outside the higher education, medical and arts sectors, we are not that good at major gift fundraising in this country. This is because charities are not working hard enough to position themselves properly. The sector must appeal to the brightest graduates and persuade them that charities offer a fulfilling career. Charities need more professionalism in management and more competence in fundraising; only that will enable us to play an even greater role in society.

Those who have committed themselves to the foundation and

future of MQ are fulfilling a public service that could change the lives of millions. Those who have no experience of depression or of those afflicted may assume it is merely about being miserable. Depression is about fear. Depression can destroy people, those they love and those around them. Ignorance around mental illness and stigma condemns too many to misery and a wasted, ruined life. The cost to society must be significant.

Coming out as a depressive requires courage. Dennis Stevenson was brave to do this twenty years ago. I was not so brave and only now that I am no longer in the job market am I prepared to acknowledge that I have been in and out of therapy and on medication for forty years. I know from personal experience that it is possible for some depressives to live fulfilling, creative lives. Others are not so fortunate.

The work of all the pioneers who have featured in this chapter reminds us that although we tend to talk about charity and philanthropy in abstract terms, the reality is that we are talking about ourselves and our fellow human beings.

This is personal.

CHAPTER 20

ARE MILLENNIALS 'NICER'?: NEW THINKING ABOUT GIVING

"Our millennial generation is compelled by the wish to be empowered, to care for others, to be informed, and to work with others
through technology. People are using their job skills and harnessing
the passion of others around them to commit to a social cause. They
are not going to be private; they are going to give in public – with
their friends, family and colleagues, and be proud of it."
KAWIKA SOLIDUM, CHIEF EXECUTIVE, BEYONDME.

* * *

Sir Thomas Hughes-Hallett is a former investment banker and a
campaigner for more philanthropy. He is co-founder of the new
Marshall Institute for Philanthropy and Social Entrepreneurship at
the London School of Economics, launched in 2015.

The Marshall Institute was endowed with a gift of £30 million by
Sir Paul Marshall of Marshall Wace LLP, one of Europe's largest
hedge funds. The institute aims to improve the impact and effectiveness of private contributions to the public good by 'informing
and coordinating the efforts of private citizens, researchers, public
and private sector organisations and social entrepreneurs who are
working to tackle the world's most pressing challenges'.

I have heard Hughes-Hallett, a baby boomer born in 1954, say
that his children are much nicer than he is, by which he means

that they are even more charitably inclined, socially aware and committed.

Is this true? Are millennials, those born between 1980 and 2000, more socially committed and philanthropically inclined than their parents and grandparents and if so, what impact is this having now and what might be the implications for our future?

According to the most recent Deloitte survey published in 2016, millennials appear to be steered by strong values. This is apparent in the employers they choose, the assignments they are willing to accept and the decisions they make as they take on more senior roles. Deloitte surveyed 7,700 millennial professionals in twenty-nine countries in 2015.

Whilst they have softened previously expressed negative perceptions of business's motivations and ethics compared with prior surveys, millennials want businesses to focus more on people (employees, customers and society), products and purpose and less on profit.

According to the Deloitte survey, 'sense of meaning' was amongst the top factors mentioned by respondents when assessing job opportunities. With so much staff turnover, companies will have to meet this aspiration if they are to retain talent. Since the recession and growing unaffordability of property have put wealth accumulation beyond the reach of so many millennials, finding meaning and a sense of purpose in work assumes greater importance. In response to the demands and needs of millennials, companies may need to go beyond providing opportunities to volunteer by changing strategy, even by making philanthropic community investments. If so, this could change the nature of business.

Whilst all the available data suggests that personal charitable giving has not grown in real terms for thirty years despite increasing personal wealth, are there any signals that millennials are 'nicer' than baby boomers in terms of social and charitable commitment?

A report published in 2015 suggests that they might be. *More to Give: London Millennials Working Towards a Better World* is a report by Professor Cathy Pharaoh and Dr Catherine Walker for CGAP@Cass, a consortium of researchers linked to Cass Business

School (City, University of London), and was commissioned by City Philanthropy.

The report reveals strong motivation amongst younger city employees to support the work of charities and community groups through giving and volunteering. They have high expectations of how they, their employees and the wealthy could contribute more to building a more equitable and sustainable society. The youngest employees are looking for opportunities, not only to give money, but to apply their business and professional skills to help charitable organisations, in turn gaining new expertise which benefits their working and personal lives. According to the report's executive summary:

> A distinct millennial profile has emerged. The desire to get more involved in giving and volunteering is most positive for the younger millennial generation of employees and declines consistently across the older age groups. This particular age-trajectory, or age-linked trend, is repeated across almost all other aspects of philanthropy studied. Motivation to give more, expectations of what employees can contribute, the desire for more philanthropic information and for workplace and other opportunities to give time and money, are all highest in the younger age-groups … This is a strong indicator of the specific value of investing in the millennial employee's willingness to give.

BeyondMe was founded in 2011 by two millennial professionals, Adam Pike, then at Deloitte, and Michael Harris of PwC. BeyondMe is: 'All about empowering future leaders to be generous today. We believe that the generosity of millennial professionals like us can drive change. That is why we motivate and mobilise future leaders to form teams that give their time, skills and money to pressing social issues.'

As an organisation, BeyondMe motivates and mobilises teams of professionals to tackle causes they are passionate about. They build a portfolio of charity projects that need the skills and time of professionals, bring the two together by matching skills with needs and aim to build long-term relationships.

Encouraging potential philanthropists to start today rather than tomorrow has to be a good idea. I talked to Kawika Solidum, BeyondMe's chief executive. Born in 1982 of a Mexican mother and a father from Hawaii, brought up in Texas followed by university in the UK and now living in London with a British wife, Solidum embodies a generation at ease with travel, other cultures and, crucially, technology. I wanted to know how he became involved with philanthropy, how millennials think and how they see the future, for it is, after all, theirs:

> I grew up with a notion of philanthropy in the sense of being grateful for what I had and recognising that others might be in a position where they could use help. I now recognise that my mother instilled this in me because she grew up in Mexico and was the luckiest member of her family because she was able to move to the US. We grew up with things her family didn't have. My mother and father brought us up to know that we were fortunate.

Solidum came to Britain on the Mountbatten Institute exchange programme between the US and the UK, its purpose being to enable young people to appreciate different working environments. He worked at Clifford Chance on the graduate recruitment team and did a master's degree at LSE. He then worked in the communications team of the British Private Equity and Venture Capital Association:

> This is where I learned about Venture Philanthropy. I realised that this was where I wanted to go, using business skills and long-term commitment to achieve a social mission. This is how the best private equity operates with businesses, investing in something small that has the capacity to grow. I was head hunted into the Impetus Trust. Then PEF and Impetus Trust merged.

I asked Solidum to expand on the work of Impetus given its involvement with TwentyTwenty, the charity founded by Andy Cook (see Chapter 19).

To stick with a cause or a charity and give it your long-term commitment is the best thing you can do. As you build trust and understanding that sometimes unlocks more capital, skills and networks. This is what Impetus-PEF does.

The first step is understanding a charity's potential to grow. Before that, they need to be sure that both partners understand what the intended outcomes are and what the impact will be. This has to be in tune with a charity's mission. So when Impetus-PEF gets involved with a charity, there is an extensive period of due diligence. When Impetus-PEF does invest big bucks a few years on into the relationship, there will be confidence that whatever is being scaled up will deliver meaningfully to its intended beneficiaries.

As a CEO of a charity/social enterprise, I now understand more than ever the theory and principles that I learned at Impetus. Every charity or social enterprise must be focused on achieving its mission. Its business model must allow the mission to be fulfilled and sustained. Charities need to adapt because they are operating in a complex changing world. The fundamental question for any charity must be: are we making the impact we should and what do we have to do in order to make an impact in an environment that is changing?

At BeyondMe, we aim to motivate and mobilise professionals to give their time, money and skills to causes that are important to them. We choose charities throughout the country that are willing and able to work with us and to use the resources and experience we can bring.

We are democratising philanthropy which has until now been confined to the wealthy. A typical venture philanthropist in the 1990s would be someone who has made a lot of money over decades. We need people like this but we also need people who are younger and who feel that they can contribute even although they may not be wealthy – they are the future of our country's giving culture.

BeyondMe gives professionals at the start of their careers that opportunity relatively early as part of a team. They, and the charities they work with, discover untapped potential, as individuals and in the charities.

I do believe we are on to something. People of my generation want to be enabled, and also believe that there is a need to care for others. This is much stronger than wanting to care. We also understand that this is becoming a necessity for businesses. We are the first generation of technology natives. We have an internet connection in our pockets that gives us access to a great deal of information and to contacts. We know that these two things together can add up something valuable in terms of a career and supporting a charitable cause.

Our generation is compelled by the wish to be empowered, to care for others, to be informed and to work with others through technology.

I think we need to be humble; we need to be comfortable with contributing to progress or to the efforts of others in making the world a better place. We do feel that we are part of something greater. Surveys of millennials show that we are looking for a work–life balance. Now it is possible to move between your work and your personal life during the course of a working day. I can check Face-book at lunchtime to see what my family on the other side of the world is doing when they are waking up. On WhatsApp, I can get updates of my son being cared for at home. I can check my work emails in the evening or early morning. At any time of the day or night, I can move into any sphere of my life.

What is becoming clear is that those spheres are not separate. They are all part of me; they are me at this present moment – what I prioritise and value. This makes it easier for people to support a cause because they feel that cause relates to a part or several parts of the people we are. And, through technology, we can share this commitment and enthusiasm and be motivated to do so or motivate others. So that is why people wear a pin or a wristband saying they support a particular cause and if you look at personal entries on LinkedIn or changing your profile pictures on Facebook and other sites, people say they are a volunteer and proclaim their charitable and social commitments in order to say who they are.

BeyondMe has existed since 2011 and already we have people talking about us during their appraisals; they are proud of belonging to a community. People are using their job skills and harnessing the enthusiasm and compassion of their colleagues to commit to a social cause. They are not going to be private about their commitment to a cause. They are going to be public and proud of it.

The teams unite around a cause or a set of skills they want to use during the course of a year. The charities focus on what they would otherwise pay for except that they don't have a budget. The idea is that the volunteers would provide that for them. We are remedying a market inefficiency where there is untapped potential on the professional side, and obscure and often uncoordinated demand in the voluntary sector.

A team decides they want to have more front-line experience. For example, they might choose homelessness. Over the course of a year, they might run employability workshops. Then they realise they want to do a second year. The volunteers are then able to understand the challenges of running the centre and can help with business planning and sustainability. Volunteers then have to choose between helping on the front line and building capacity of the charity itself.

Since we started we have launched over 145 teams involving more than 1,000 people. We'd like to get to a point where we have 1,000 people participate in a single year – or better yet, 1,000 teams a year. We recruit by making sure that we are alive and well on social media channels.

We talk as if society is segmented into the public, private and social sectors but we are all stakeholders in the same society. If you are asking people to make a commitment, then that is a deeply personal thing. And if it isn't a choice, then that isn't giving, it is something else. Philanthropy must always be about personal commitment and personal choice.

*   *   *

Kawika Solidum is determined that BeyondMe will help to democratise active philanthropy.

Someone else with a similar claim is Dame Zarine Kharas, who with her business partner Anne-Marie Huby founded JustGiving as the new millennium dawned. Technology has since transformed our ability to give, although that it would was not clear at the outset. Formerly a lawyer and an investment banker, Kharas was frustrated that her wish to give back via charitable giving was thwarted by lack of information. JustGiving is the fastest-growing giving platform in the world. We talked in the autumn of 2015:

In 1999, I had recently left investment banking to seek a new challenge. I had always wanted to run a business, but not on conventional lines. I believe that business and ethics go hand in hand and I wanted to explore how business could operate both for profit and for good.

JustGiving is the result of a late-night phone call. When you have been earning well, there comes a point when you think about what you want to give back to society. But there was no one place I could go to find out about charities and where I might give. When an ex-colleague of mine said that he and others were setting up an incubator for internet companies in 1999 – this was at a time when Amazon was only a few years old and Facebook had not even been thought of – he suggested that I should do something in the charity sector.

I knew nothing about the sector or setting up any business but the one thought that occurred to me from my experience was this:

Charities need a way of communicating their mission, their needs and how to give money in an efficient way. I had no idea that payment online was such a nascent thing and what it would become. The wonder of ignorance! No one was giving online. To the best of my knowledge we were the first.

Searching for inspiration, I remembered that in my City days I had wanted to support a girls' education charity but I could not find a single place with information on different charities and how they could be supported. I wondered if there was a space for an online portal for charities – a digital market place where people could learn about charities and make donations online.

I went to the States to find out what was going on. The initial idea was to found a portal to enable people to make informed giving decisions. I had been introduced to Anne-Marie Huby, who was running Médicins Sans Frontières in the UK. She had also been trying to find an online fundraising solution for UK charities. I convinced her to join me and together we hit the road.

We experimented and despite the market crash of 2000, we did a deal without any cash involved with an internet service provider and went live in February 2001. At the time, most charities believed the internet was a passing fad but a few of the more visionary ones placed their trust in us. By the end of our first year, some seventy charities had joined the site.

In 2001, we were lucky to meet a very patient investor with an incredible long-term view. His vision enabled us to experiment in radical ways and continues to do so today.

A key breakthrough moment was the 2002 London Marathon. The organisers were brave enough to let us loose on their runners, so we created a prototype 'online sponsorship page' to help them galvanise the support of family and friends.

It was an amazing success with one runner raising £10,000 for the National Autistic Society. This got us thinking. At this point, we had focused on enabling people to make individual, personal donations. What the Marathon taught us was that we could leverage the power of the web to change the way people give by 'democratising' giving.

We tried lots of different things and the thing that took off was the old-fashioned sponsorship form that we put online. It was a hit because the eternal truth is that people give to people. You have to make an 'ask' of people you know. That was our first insight. We also learned that the web was full of people interested in causes and causes looking for supporters. The common factor was people. We realised that giving is not a money business. It is a people business.

People give in response to the stories of others, including people they have never met. Stories unite us and are contagious. Look at the extraordinary outpouring of support generated by the distressing images around the Syrian refugee crisis. In the face of injustice, illness and tragedy, it's easy to feel powerless. However, if we can help people unite in response to the stories of others, then together we would all have the power to be a force for change.

This understanding of the social nature of giving has shaped our business. We focus on helping organisations and individuals garner as much support as possible for their causes, not just from family and friends, but from the broader community, by finding ways to share their stories with like-minded people.

If you think of asking, you can do it in increasing circles, initially friends and family, then your wider circle via social media, which JustGiving enabled. We were the first business in the charity sector to enable a close integration with social media sites and we were enormously successful.

I think a lot of people who would like to give don't because they don't where to start. They don't know how to and this is why the 'ask' is so important. I wasn't giving on any significant scale before JustGiving because I did not know where or how to begin.

So social media enabled people to increase their social reach in order to ask more people to give. And now we use data science and machine-learning to match people with the causes they are most likely to care about. Over fourteen years, we have created the world's first social giving network. As of August 2016, there are 18 million active users on JustGiving and the platform has raised more than £4 billion.

There is competition now and that is good for business. The best thing that happened to us was when Virgin Money arrived. That stopped us being complacent.

We have seen three big developments at JustGiving over the years. More than half of visits are by mobiles; 55 per cent by mobiles, 32 per cent by desktop and 13 per cent by tablet. The second is the use of Big Data. The third is crowd funding.

Crowd funding is interesting because this where people take the initiative into their own hands. As distrust in institutions grows, people will do things themselves. Personally, I think crowd funding has the potential to be massive. We have only just started and we are growing 20 per cent month on month. At the end of 2015, individuals will have raised up to £11 million via crowd funding on JustGiving this year. Millions of people visit JustGiving each month and will discover these crowd funding pages so the potential is huge. Individuals will have created over a million fundraising pages on JustGiving this year. Each page reaches fifty or sixty people, and, typically, seventeen of these will give. We have created a virtuous circle. People come to us because they know they will find the people and causes they want to give to.

I believe crowd funding will change everything.

I also believe that most people are charitably inclined. I think people may look back and say that charitable giving has fallen or is not growing but what they may not be able to do is add all the crowd funding, where an individual raises funds that go a cause that is unrelated to a charity; for example, where a parent of a sick child raises money to fund a particular form of treatment that's not available on the NHS; or an individual raises funds to transform waste land into a community garden.

The response to the current refugee crisis shows how the nature of giving is evolving. Whilst people continue to support charities in their missions to do extraordinary work, there is an increase in individual fundraising and giving for causes. From wheelchairs and life-saving operations to community gardens and junior football strips, people are increasingly using the power of the crowd to generate funds for social and community projects that don't involve charitable institutions.

Long before government became more active, we had thousands of pages on JustGiving to help the refugees. Almost £1 million has been raised on JustGiving alone in the last three months. This is evidence of a healthy charitable impulse and is going into crowd funding rather than to charities.

We saw a huge response: over 750 people have now created a page to directly help refugees, with one page raising over £150,000. We think this represents a shift in people being empowered to directly help the causes they care about and, together, they have raised over £500,000 (as of October 2015). Through these pages, the JustGiving community has pledged to help refugees in a number of ways – from food and shelter support to care rucksacks for children.

This is about individuals deciding themselves where the greatest need is. And increasingly, not wanting to give to established institutions. This is often all in the moment; think about the ice bucket challenge or the no-makeup selfie campaign. People are not necessarily giving to charity but they do want to be part of a movement.

JustGiving demonstrates that charitable giving is changing in line with the values and expectations of millennials whose commitment to causes seems greater than to charities and institutions. Kharas agrees that change will require new kinds of partnerships with implications for business as well as for charities:

> Partnership between government, the private sector, the voluntary sector and donors is fine where there is clarity of objectives and about who is responsible and who is funding what. This must be the way forward. However, this kind of partnership leads me to ask: what is business for?
>
> At JustGiving, we have a flat structure without much hierarchy, and we take a very long-term view of the business, so rather than extracting profits, although we are a for-profit organisation, we have re-invested in the business. We strive to build true partnerships with our charity clients. But above all, we simply trust everyone to do the right thing, because in a knowledge economy we believe it brings out the best in people and therefore works best for the company.

In 2009, Kharas was awarded the Albert Medal by the Royal Society of Arts, and made a speech in which she said:

> The guiding principle by which most of us in the industrialised world live our lives today is a separation of our working and personal lives. Work is the thing you do to make a living whereas our 'good' life, our 'moral' life is lived elsewhere – with family, friends and, quite often, charity or voluntary work. JustGiving users often echo this dichotomy – they talk about the things they do for charity as profoundly meaningful, whilst the world of business can sometimes be so meaningless.

Now that our financial system appears to be in ruins, and our politicians in disgrace, I believe we have an opportunity to reopen the debate and question the accepted wisdom that business must and should be 'a-moral'. I believe we have not only an opportunity but a duty to do so.

Dame Zarine Kharas believes that business and ethics should be inextricably linked. You will find the text of her Royal Society of Arts speech as an appendix.

My next conversations were with three business leaders about the relationship between business and society, being in tune with the ethos of millennials whose views and behaviour are becoming increasingly dominant and how to encourage more of those in business to commit to society.

*   *   *

Maurice Ostro is the chairman of Ostro Minerals UK Ltd and founder and chair of trustees of the Fayre Share Foundation. He is also vice-chairman of the Council of Christians and Jews. He is a passionate advocate of philanthropy and is planning a new campaign to encourage new entrepreneurs to be philanthropic. The campaign has the working title of Entrepreneurial Giving and I met Ostro in February 2016 to explore his thinking.

Every time I started a company, I put aside 10 per cent for charity. The companies were private and the donations were anonymous. This is in accord with the Judeo-Christian tradition. There is zero ego in this. There is no kudos because no one knows you have done it. That was what I thought good philanthropy should be.

Around 2004, two of the companies that I had created were acquired by a company listed on the London Stock Exchange of which I later was appointed CEO. Knowing that my shareholdings in the public company would have to be disclosed, it seemed sensible to set up an official structure to do so. We could then use it to fund things like a community project in north London that I wanted to contribute a seven-figure donation to, which would not be able to be given anonymously. This structure then became the Fayre Share Foundation.

It then became apparent that staff in my companies did not know that 10 per cent of their effort was going to charity. By not letting them know, I was failing to do something positive. This was not good for the charities because I could have been galvanising the staff to do more. Also, from a business perspective, involving the staff in what we were doing charitably would have been a positive from every perspective.

I resolved to do things differently. Many entrepreneurs choose not to talk about their philanthropy and I now believe that is a missed opportunity.

Having sold all my businesses before the financial crash in 2007/8, I chose to focus on my charitable activities. It soon became clear that the voluntary sector was going to be squeezed at the moment when they were going to be most needed.

Getting charities to be more effective is great but we must also get more resources too and going to the same people time after time is not the way to do it. I hate doing it to other people and I hate it being done to me. We need new donors and to increase the number of people who give. So I am now thinking about how to persuade people who are starting new businesses to think about the value of philanthropy to their businesses. When they are setting up a new business and are giving whatever percentage, it doesn't cost much because the value of a business is next to nothing at the beginning.

The suggestion that we are making is that when one sets up a business, one should set aside a proportion for charity and put that purpose, that mission, at the heart of the new enterprise. There are some other wonderful initiatives like the Giving Pledge in the US and the Founders Pledge in the UK but they differ in that they focus on those businesses most likely to contribute the largest amount on a liquidity event or the death of the owner and these organisations also get more involved in the giving process.

Our initiative is not about people at the top of the pyramid and success will not be defined by the amounts given and raised. Our objective is about changing behaviour. We are focusing on people who are starting out. We want smart people to understand that it is in their interest to change the way they think and behave. We need to find new ways of providing more social investment and new ways of involving donors in the effective distribution of their charitable funds.

There are 600,000 new companies registered in the UK each year. Entrepreneurial Giving will be campaigning to introduce entrepreneurs engaged in start-ups to the idea of philanthropy and to introduce them to the benefit of embedding a mission in to their companies from the outset. This is not about talking to philanthropists; it is a platform for entrepreneurs and about giving them access to an online resource as well as a network of like-minded individuals. These are commercial rather than social entrepreneurs. The idea is that they make their pledge in the early days of their start-up to donate at the point when they sell their business and in the meantime give them tools to make their philanthropic and entrepreneurial journey more successful.

They don't need to commit to a particular percentage, but we do say that it should be meaningful so anything over 1 per cent and that is for them to decide. If they don't sell, they don't give. Nor do we advise what causes they should support, this is for them to do in the fullness of time.

We help them to understand how such a pledge can help their business and motivate their employees. As there are so many start-ups every year, philanthropy can be a way of standing out amongst the competition.

This is something that we believe will appeal to today's entrepreneurs. They can download a form from our website, sign it, witness it and send it to us with minimal fuss and expense. Simple, easy and, most importantly, effective.

*   *   *

JustGiving may well be responsible for persuading people to give who have not given before and, as a result, it is possible that personal charitable giving in Britain is growing and greater than recorded. We cannot be sure because we know that some online crowd funding goes to causes and projects that are not registered charities.

One thing we can be sure of is that giving by the growing numbers of the very rich who are becoming ever richer is not increasing. One man who is determined to change this is Ben Elliot, the cofounder of Quintessentially, the luxury lifestyle group which offers a 24-hour global concierge service to the world's wealthiest, and chairman of the Quintessentially Foundation. Elliot is a child of the establishment and has an impeccable pedigree. What is interesting and unusual about him is that he sees little if any distinction between his business and its charitable foundation and will use all his considerable advantages and connections to further his charitable as well as business interests, by bringing them together.

Ben Elliot just misses out on being a millennial but many of those who work for him will be and so will some of his wealthy clients. Elliot's foundation gives away £3 million a year, primarily to empower charities that he and his fellow trustees believe will be even more effective as a result:

I was brought up to be a good neighbour and a good citizen. Even when I was at Eton, I was helping a club in Slough for Mencap. When I left school, I was a rather idealistic young man. I went to Romania to work in children's orphanages just after the overthrow of Ceauşescu. I knew that I was lucky. I was always OK at cajoling. Everyone at Eton thought I was mad for going on an Aids walk for Ian McKellen. I was fifteen. I just felt compelled to do stuff even if it was in a rather clumsy and chaotic way.

I then started my various businesses. In 2006/7, the world was a much more confident place even though I think there is a lot more money around now. Because we have a rich membership and a brilliant events team I thought we should do extraordinary events to raise money for charity. We started with very big charities doing ostentatious and over the top events. We did one for the Soil Association where all the food had to come from within ten miles. It was all very expensive but we did raise over £700,000. We would then hand a cheque over to the charity and I found the whole thing deeply unsatisfying because we were dealing with charities that had become huge organisations. Some charities are so big that it is almost impossible to have a meaningful relationship.

I wanted to do something that we could be proud of. We decided to change the way we work with charities to bring out the best of us and the best of them. Each year, we choose four or five charities for a relationship of two years, or sometimes it may be just a year. We ask them what they are trying to achieve from a profile point of view, from a donor perspective and we sit down with them to work out a plan to help them achieve their objectives.

I get really personally involved in the things that we do. Some of the best projects have been outside London. One was a treatment centre in Hull run by the Rehabilitation for Addicted Prisoners Trust (RAPt). RAPt works to help people with drug and alcohol rehabilitation dependence, in both prison and the community, overcome their addiction and lead lives free from drugs and crime. In 1992, RAPt set up the first drug treatment facility in a UK prison. We all went to town helping them and they were great.

We have also worked with Place2Be. We raised a million for them to provide schools counselling in Enfield and Croydon after the 2011 riots. The kids were having a terrible time. We have also helped Maggie's which supports people with cancer. We have cycled from London to Edinburgh and to St David's Head for them.

We have an infrastructure to do stuff. Last week, we did our sixth poker tournament. We are going to India at the weekend which sounds like a jolly but 500 kilometres in a rickshaw will be a challenge. We are doing this because Mark Shand, my uncle, died and people worry about the future of his charity, Elephant Family. This will be much more appealing than the usual charity gala with an auction. Forty-five beautifully designed rickshaws will race 500 kilometres across India. We hope to raise £2 million for the charity this year. My uncle was very good at fundraising. He used to say: 'You are so fucking rich, don't be so fucking tight.'

We also do a bicycle ride which gets more difficult and more expensive each year. We recruit people from hedge funds and the corporate sector; sixty to a hundred people will be involved. This is how we raised £600,000 for Greenhouse Sport.

We are aiming to create partnerships with charities. We do proper due diligence. We meet the trustees, look at their leadership, examine the finances. We decided not to support Kids Co. We need to feel confident in the leadership of a charity. Benita Refson founded Place2Be. I trust her completely. I would trust her with my own children. I am impressed with her integrity and ambition and that is what I am looking for in the people we work with.

We helped to get the House of St Barnabas in Soho into shape. It was originally a refuge for desperate women but it had fallen into disrepair. We turned it into a private club where people would be properly trained to support a vocational scheme that helped people get jobs. We raised all the money and helped them get planning permission.

I am spending more and more of my time on this. I think this is what a successful business should be doing, particularly a business like ours that is working with very wealthy people. What we do through the Foundation goes way beyond the usual corporate social responsibility programme.

We want to engage our clients in what we are doing and we want them to enjoy it. It remains to be seen how they survive in a rickshaw in India for five days. It is my job to come up with innovative and attractive projects. We have some billionaires in rickshaws. There is the bragging factor. They will go home telling people that they have had the experience of their lives. Good things will come from that. This kind of thing also generates business. This is serious networking. This is the way people work today; get out of the office, be in the market place and make things happen.

Next year, we will think about the long-term future of the foundation and what we want it to be. I feel that success is not just about the money raised and donated. Success is about helping charities and those they support to develop in order to prosper. I also see it as part of my job to persuade the very rich who come to live here to do their bit. If they are going to live here and not pay tax then the way to be a good citizen is to get your cheque book out. You cannot be a good citizen and not give back to the place where you live. It is all very well making a fortune in Russia; if you are living here, you have to pay your way. I have never been afraid of asking these people to give.

Wouldn't it be great if we lived in a world where all who had the means to give did so and were then championed for it by the media? Otherwise, if the rich don't give, they will be regarded as undeserving and rightly so. I wish I could find more people out there who could do what I am doing and with whom I could work.

*   *   *

Dame Zarine Kharas asks: what is the point of business? Should business be a-moral?

We know that some of Britain's most successful companies and their principal shareholders have had social objectives since the industrial revolution.

Necessarily, corporate social objectives change with the time and according to need. When I started fundraising in the 1970s and 1980s, the focus of the banks and financial services was upon the arts via performance and exhibition sponsorship and corporate membership that enabled company executives to entertain clients. Then sponsorship for cultural organisations had to be linked more directly to marketing in support of developing new business and profit. More recently, the focus shifted to 'corporate social responsibility' (CSR) in order to reflect a relationship between companies, society and their local communities, but with a clear link to the bottom line.

The financial crisis and recession of 2008–09 has forced companies to think again, particularly in the financial sector. CSR has become somewhat discredited as a means of 'box-ticking'. As we know, there is also pressure from those entering the workforce for companies to be more socially responsible.

Damian Leeson is Director of Group Responsible Business for Lloyds Banking Group. I first met Leeson and some of his senior colleagues in early 2016 during a fact-finding visit to Poplar and to the Olympic Park in order to see the extraordinary transformation and regeneration of this part of east London.

Lloyds Bank, Britain's largest retail bank, has form, having been around for 250 years and with four long-established corporate charitable foundations that donated £17 million in 2015. Lloyds has recovered from the recession but is operating in a different world of lower returns so it is time to think again about what a successful bank needs to be in the first part of the twenty-first century and what its social responsibilities should be in the age of millennials.

I read the 2015/2016 update of the Lloyds *Helping Britain Prosper Plan*.

> Britain ... still faces some serious social and economic challenges. We are using our scale, reach and influence to tackle them:
>
> - More affordable homes: We are helping to achieve this by supporting the construction industry, providing funding for social housing and offering affordable mortgages for more first-time buyers.
> - Supporting enterprise: The UK's five million Small and Medium Enterprises are the bedrock of the UK economy. We are helping them to start up and grow by providing finance, support and mentoring.
> - Becoming more digital: The Group's Consumer Digital Index tells us that 3.2 million people in the UK have low digital and financial capability. We are helping individuals, businesses and charities to improve their digital capability
> - Tackling disadvantage: Too many people still find themselves trapped in a cycle of disadvantage. Directly and through our foundations, we are helping them change their lives and their communities for the better.

- Saving for the future: The pension market is evolving and life expectancy is rising. It has never been more important to save for the future, yet almost one out of five people are saving nothing for their retirement. We are helping by providing much needed financial education and advice.

Lloyds's ambition is more than aspiration and a public relations exercise. The plan sets out clear outcomes with specific targets and metrics to be achieved, such as supporting one in four of first-time buyers in the UK mortgage market or increasing the amount of new lending to small and mid-market companies.

I was grateful to Damian Leeson for agreeing to a meeting in May 2016. Leeson had been brought in fourteen months earlier to develop Lloyds's thinking so he was not in a position to make any announcements of new plans. Rather, this was an opportunity to share thoughts because Leeson and I have a mutual interest: the future of the voluntary sector and civil society. Is there a role for Lloyds to help to strengthen the voluntary sector?

One of the things that attracted me to Lloyds was not only the *Helping Britain Prosper* plan but also the possibility of partnerships with the Lloyds Foundations to fulfil the Bank's objectives.

I am thinking how it may be possible to build a more sustainable third or voluntary sector. There is the traditional grant-giving model, where charities are wired up to the drip of continual grants. Is it possible to break down the cultural barriers on both sides? There are parts of the third sector that view business and capitalism with suspicion. They would prefer to keep business out of the process and simply write a few big cheques. We need to build bridges between business and the third sector to build more effective and sustainable models. Look at what Lord (Andrew) Mawson is doing in east London: he embraces business and fuses social and economic benefit. That is the future [see Chapter 22].

Our greatest secret is our four foundations. Collectively, they have had a billion dollars from Lloyds over the last thirty years.

We are thinking about how we move company volunteering away from a metric that measures hours devoted to painting a wall or mowing a lawn, valuable though those things are, towards asking if volunteering can make a more meaningful difference. We are now much more interested in skills-based volunteering which will also develop the skills base of our workforce.

Lloyds Banking Group employs 70,000. Not all will want to volunteer or do skills-based volunteering although 32 per cent of volunteering in Lloyds is now skills based in our first year of moving towards this model. We won't parachute an IT specialist into a charity unless the charity has a clear need for an IT strategy.

So directly via investment in social enterprise and indirectly by grants from the Lloyds Foundations, we are trying to develop a more sustainable third sector via skills-based volunteering. We also have an important relationship with the School for Social Entrepreneurs. We are investing £1.5 million a year matched by Big Lottery Fund.

We have just launched a Green Loan Fund, a £1 billion fund, which offers preferential rates to commercial building developments that are carbon free. We are incentivising the right behaviour. Developing products which are socio-economic hybrids is really interesting.

Lloyds is the largest funder of housing associations with loans of over £10 billion. We are also the largest provider of social banking in the UK.

The *Helping Britain Prosper* plan is essentially looking at the socio-economic challenges facing the UK. I was really impressed with the Prosper plan when I arrived but I wanted to know how we could make it more outcome-focused. So instead of referencing the fact that we give £1 million per annum to credit unions, we focus on the fact that this money goes into core funding and leads to an extra £5 million a year being leant by those credit unions across the UK.

My job is to rethink what Lloyds has been doing in terms of CSR and to help redefine what we do in order to address the country's needs and opportunities. We are not the ministry of good works for Lloyds. This about how we do business responsibly. This is about change that makes responsible business drive everything Lloyds does and how it does it. It is not a choice between responsibility and being commercial. We have to be both. We are aiming to do things that might seem counter-intuitive but that are not necessarily counter-commercial. I would like the Green loan fund to be a huge commercial success. And that would also deliver environmental benefit. This is not just a community affairs approach. Neither is it philanthropic.

I think millennials will look for particular things when thinking about employment. They hope to be able to identify with the values of a company and its societal impact. We are not aiming to capture some kind of moral high-ground. That is very risky. But we do want to be a responsible business that is committed to sustainability.

Many of our employees were not aware that we had a foundation tackling social disadvantage. When managers understand this, they see that under certain circumstances, this could give Lloyds a competitive advantage. We are now saying to the charities we support that, in addition to giving them funding, we will also partner them in terms of skills-based volunteering.

The dialogue goes like this: We have noticed over 250 years that when Britain prospers, we prosper. There is a mutuality of interest. What we are doing is social investment. Until this year, the plan did not include an external apprenticeship programme. And yet we have this groundbreaking initiative in Coventry where we provide £1 million per annum to the Advanced Manufacturing Training College (AMTC). We fund 120 students in a three-year rolling programme. We had not really recognised its value, or included it in a plan that is about socio-economic benefit. It is a perfect example of that indirect benefit. This is smart manufacturing. It is precisely the sector where the UK needs to compete globally. I asked what they were manufacturing and they said they were manufacturing solutions. The traditional titanium hub for a jet engine for an airliner took twenty-five days to hollow out with a laser and cost £250,000. The new version took twenty-five hours and cost £25,000. The laser builds the hollowed object rather than hollowing out the object.

This is something we were doing of great socio-economic value that we had not hitherto factored in, or recognised its real value and incorporated it.

A key challenge for us is to work out how to get this kind of achievement to resonate on the shop floor. So we have this new metric about skills-based volunteering. Wherever you are in the country, you can opt in and become involved. Internal awareness of the Foundations is very low but interest is very high. The signs are that when people hear about skills-based volunteering they want to do it.

We cannot return to the status quo. We have to create new models. How do we take the inherent talent of the British people and help nudge it in a different direction? That is the challenge for us. We have to open windows and doors so that our people can see what the opportunities are and how they can be involved through volunteering.

Motivating and mobilising the work force to support society through volunteering could be a powerful means of engendering a culture of giving in Britain. Some business leaders now acknowledge that volunteering can be a smart form of corporate social responsibility, giving a commercial advantage in an era that values social commitment. Whilst business must adapt to change, so must charities.

CHAPTER 21

CATCH22:
CHARITY'S DILEMMA

"We are interested in how you can organise public services that
enable people to thrive. Services should be enabling, supporting
and encouraging rather than being overbearing, instructive and
dictatorial. We want to see a shift from the state delivering people
services to organisations like ours which are less remote, less trans-
actional, and underpinned by philanthropic entrepreneurialism.
That is what good looks like."

CHRIS WRIGHT, CHIEF EXECUTIVE, CATCH22.

*   *   *

The challenge facing charities is how to survive by adapting to
meet the needs of the twenty first century. Catch22 for some
charities is this: if survival means working with the public sector
and delivering public services, how do they do so without compromising their independence and pioneering role which is their
fundamental purpose? Moreover, if charities need to evolve, how
radical should evolution be? And where will the additional funding
come from in order for them to meet more demand?

This begs the question: how do you define a charity? We could say
that a charity is an organisation devoted to doing good and registered
with the Charity Commission. However, Steve Hodgkins' Jobs, Friends
& Houses in Blackpool is doing a great deal of good in its work with
ex-offenders but it is a social enterprise and not a registered charity.

How do we define a social enterprise or a social business? We could say that it is an organisation without charitable status that re-invests profit to enable it to do even more good. However, some social enterprises have charitable status.

The charity sector is now so large and embraces such a diverse range of roles, responsibilities and activities, a comprehensive understanding based on rigorous analysis requires a book, rather than a chapter, and John Mohan and Beth Breeze have written one, *The Logic of Charity: Great Expectations in Hard Times* (see Chapter 11).

The remaining chapters illustrate how the common good might be best served by some charities and social enterprises working in new ways with the public sector and other partners without losing their independence and creativity. This could be the way forward for some charities but not for all. My first example will be Catch22, an organisation with charitable status and a history dating back to 1788 that works in and with the public sector and calls itself a social business.

Before exploring Catch22, some explanation about social investment is needed because the future has to be about collaboration, including social entrepreneurs and social enterprises. Moreover, social investors have the potential to provide and leverage much needed additional funding as demands on the voluntary sector increase.

There is nothing particularly new about people investing in social projects that may or may not return their capital. What is new is that there are now formal, government-backed initiatives to encourage more social investment and these are able to make an even greater impact when working with others.

One of these initiatives is Big Society Capital (BSC). BSC was established by the government as an independent organisation with an investment fund of £600 million in 2012, the world's first social investment fund of its kind. Most of the investment fund comes from dormant bank accounts. I asked Matt Robinson, head of strategy and market development at BSC until April 2016, to help me understand how social investment works in the twenty-first century, its significance and the role of BSC:

Social investment as we know it today is about fifteen years old and has been in some ways a cottage industry. We were founded in 2012 to invigorate the movement and provide a dollop of capital to accelerate the growth of social investment.

You have to buy in to the idea that civil society and the voluntary sector need to use their revenue as a way of generating more finance to make more impact. Broadly speaking, there are three models for this. The first are charity and social enterprise to government arrangements, where charities can compete for government money to deliver services; the second are charity and social enterprise to consumers; third, charity and social enterprise to business. These are the models that can repay investment.

Social impact bonds are used to engage with state contracts in terms of payment by results. Teens and Toddlers is a charity that helps teenagers who are at risk of dropping out of education because of pregnancy. They get the girls to look after a toddler so that they realise the consequences of their actions. The results are tracked with regard to re-engagement with education, GCSE pass rates and employment. The results are impressive. Government pays if targets are achieved. The results will not be known for a year and if the charity trustees are not prepared to take the risk, they raise the finance via a bond. Social investors now take on the risk and take the hit if there is one. There is also now attractive tax relief. Social investment can also be used to service a public service contract. Up to two-fifths of charitable income is from the state, and most of that is in the form of contracts not grants.

One of our investments buys properties for St Mungo, the homeless charity, on long-term leases. The impact there is that they can get much faster and greater access to property than they could from their own resources. Because there is rental income and the prospect of capital gain, this is an attractive investment. This model is not right for some charities. Charities supporting asylum seekers, for example, are unlikely to have the revenue streams against which they could repay social investment. They are most likely to be supported by grants.

One of the constraints on social enterprise is whether or not those who run charities buy into that model and see it as their future. Will there be enough of them and will they have necessary entrepreneurial and business mindset and skills? Some charities, such as Catch22, are wonderfully entrepreneurial but a lot aren't and don't want or need to be.

There can be a clash of cultures between public services, charities and market makers. Last year we tried to help some of the larger charities compete for Ministry of Justice Probation service reforms. Charities are good at rehabilitation. The price offered by government did cover costs but none of the charities were successful in the bids despite spending millions of their charitable resources. The problem was their inability to provide the kind of guarantees that would not have been a problem for a big corporate.

There is a total of roughly a billion pounds available for social investment now for charities and social enterprises to access. Loans are typically for eight to ten years so we are not seeking to raise more capital for the time being.

Ultimately, we might want to do ourselves out of business. We try to pull in as much investment as possible from other sources when we make a loan. We are trying to build a much bigger market of a diverse range of investors such as pension funds and insurance companies or indeed the man or woman on the street.

Immediately after my meeting with Matt Robinson, I talked to Seb Elsworth, Chief Executive of Access Foundation, which manages part of the BSC portfolio:

Many smaller charities and social enterprises are at a point where they want to diversify their model, their income or trade more. It has been difficult for them to access relatively small amounts of capital. They need capital to grow but they don't have security. For many social investment funds, it has been difficult for them to provide smaller sized debt of less than £150,000. The average loan needed by smaller charities and social enterprises is around £60,000.

Access has been created to address this issue and so we are managing a ring-fenced pot of the BSC portfolio and blending it with grants from the Big Lottery Fund. Grants can take losses and subsidise operating costs. Grants are allowing these investments to be made to organisations and at a scale which otherwise would not happen.

We have £45 million in the pot to support fifteen to twenty investments.

In future, it might be possible for community foundations to create loan funds to support what that they do. Some CFs are interested in working with social enterprises to develop their business model by thinking of themselves as trading entities that can take on debt. In addition, more charities are evolving from the grant-dependent model to develop a trading function or deliver public services. They are seeking growth finance like any business.

We are also talking to Credit Unions and other lenders who haven't previously lent to charities or social enterprises.

The innovation in terms of philanthropy is that we are using grant to unlock debt that will allow it to finance organisations that are more high risk and that would not normally have access to debt.

There is a sense that the new generation of wealth is more likely to understand enterprise so that the concept of being an investor is something they are comfortable with. We see Access as a catalyst to help bring this about. We see ourselves as adding more tools to the toolbox.

Social investment is never going to trump philanthropy. There will be a limited number of charitable organisations and social enterprises that have an appropriate revenue model. But some charities will be able to achieve a mixed model and social investment could be a starting point for younger entrepreneurs who might move on to more traditional philanthropy.

* * *

For a view of how some charities might evolve, I turned to Catch22: 'As a social business, we have the heart of a charity and the mindset

of a business. We work at every stage of the welfare cycle, supporting 30,000 individuals from cradle to career.'

Catch22 is a new model charity designed to meet contemporary need but its origins go back to 1788 with the formation of the
Philanthropic Society whose members aimed to 'unite the spirit
of charity with the principles of trade for prevention of vice and
misery amongst the poor'.

Catch22 was formed in 2008 following a series of mergers
between the Philanthropic Society and the former London Police
Court Mission, the Rainer Foundation and Crime Concern.

Chris Wright has been with Catch22 and its predecessor for ten
years and chief executive for the past five years. I wanted to know
how a charity working so closely with the public sector can maintain its independence and contribute to social change by acting as
a pioneer. Wright is thinking about what charities should be in the
twenty-first century, how they should operate, and with whom:

> We see ourselves as alternative service provider and a pioneer for
> social change, running some services that had previously been run
> by the state for sixty years or more. That forms the basis of our
> proposition.
>
> We think that the state should be an enabler and facilitator but
> it is not always good at delivering. We are interested in how you
> can organise public service that enables people to thrive. The service
> should be enabling, supportive and encouraging rather than being
> overbearing, instructive and dictatorial. This is our ambition – we
> want to see a shift from the state delivering people-facing services
> to organisations like ours which are less remote, less transactional
> and underpinned by a philanthropic entrepreneurialism. This is
> what good looks like.
>
> We have been operating a system that is largely transactional and
> process driven, where people are driven from pillar to post.
>
> We trace our roots back to the enlightenment and the beginning
> of a conversation where there was genuine concern from merchants
> about poverty. Our founding fathers were concerned about the

children of felons and initially set up a school in Hackney Fields designed to expose them to the discipline of work and to apply the principles of trade with the spirit of charity.

When I moved to Rainer, I had not thought this through from a philosophical point of view. I thought my job was to ensure the services we delivered were as good as they could be. I didn't at first realise that I would have to fight to win the right to deliver these services and to secure the necessary funding, primarily from public funding commissioners.

Although we have this philanthropic past, by the time I got involved in 2006, we were no longer a fundraising charity in that we had a very small donor base. We were principally talking to government. It was only when we merged and created Catch22 in 2008, and I took over in 2011, that we decided to stop pretending we were something else and call ourselves a social business, delivering social services in partnership with the state.

My thinking has evolved over the past five years. I moved from thinking that we take on the responsibility of the state to a position where we should do that in partnership with others, with the state in its new configuration as an enabler but also with business and philanthropy. We are trying to work out what that would look like. The challenge is to get others to be excited by the potential to do something radical.

Are we vulnerable to public expenditure cuts? Yes, but it's a risk we're prepared to take because we think if we can demonstrate capability and a track record we can influence how services can be reformed.

In the first five years of the so-called austerity programme, we grew our business by 25 per cent. What we have tried to do is diversify our delivery so that we were not dependent upon one aspect of public funding. We looked at four different social markets: children's social care, education, justice and employability.

There is a risk for being totally dependent on state funding. The answer is to attract new diverse sources of funding by enthusing foundations and business. I would like to see more business involvement with corporate social responsibility radically redefined to support system change rather than specific projects, welcome though that kind of support is.

It is up to us to create the conditions where this comes about. Think about this. We were the founders of the probation service. The state did not found the probation service, we did. These are services that were appropriated by the state when the welfare state was established.

How things evolve interests me. We are perhaps now in the next stage of the process as the state redefines its role. I agree that the borderline between the state and the voluntary sector can be murky and it is not always clear who is funding what. Some of these well-established larger charities are not always transparent about what they are doing. There is no doubt that they are using donated money to subsidise public services. That makes it difficult for organisations like ours that price services in a way that allows us to deliver them effectively and efficiently.

We are absolutely transparent about the kind of charity we are. We are a social business. I am very proud of our charitable status and our governance. There is a very febrile atmosphere around charities but it is almost passing us by. This is not because it isn't important but it is not directly relevant. We are here to carve out new territory.

We aim to create a second and third generation of public sector provision where the funding package looks different. We are looking for finance that allows us to change systems so that we can make a difference at scale by redefining what public service looks like.

We are trying to meet the needs of the state and of those the state supports. My big frustration is that so much of what we are commissioned to deliver looks remarkably like they were delivered by the state or anyone else. They are overly specified in the tender process and in their delivery. The outcomes for many of the people we are working with are often appalling given the amount of money that is spent on these services. We think many services need to be redesigned in order to secure better outcomes.

I never think about us being muzzled because we are delivering public services. We use our experience to say to government that services need to look different because they are not working. We do not openly criticise government policy. We suggest improvements.

Governments and policy makers tend to be lazy and prefer working with the people they know. The people they know tend to be the big names which command public attention. These household name charities also get a lot of money from the public via donations without the public really understanding what they do. They automatically get a place at the table but they are not advocating system reform. All they are interested in is running existing programmes.

I don't want to run what is currently being delivered. I want to move on from being a public service provider to being an enabler where we are located in communities where we can enable them to assume much more responsibility. The state's role should be to funnel the cash to a local level where decisions could and should be taken.

We are asking foundations to fund us in a way that would be new for them. We are asking the foundations to fund system change, to fund us to build our organisational capacity to influence and deliver public policy. We would be delighted if they want to fund projects but the priority is to build our capacity so we can deliver services more effectively.

We are also having this conversation with social investors. Effectively, I want to sell equity to foundations and investors so that they can invest in what we are trying to achieve and get a return on that investment. We would have to define the metrics about what that return looks like.

We won a competition last year that Big Society Capital launched, called the Business Impact challenge. The motivation for the competition was to stimulate different thinking amongst companies with regard to corporate social responsibility. We had to be in a partnership with a company to enter so we teamed up with Interserve (UK-based support services and construction company). We came up with a product we are calling the Lab.

The idea is that we are going to incubate ideas that will be designed to enhance the ability of communities to take on the responsibility for delivering some services and to persuade government and local authorities to let them do so.

We don't know what people want to do until they are asked. The first Lab will be in Liverpool. If it works there, it will work anywhere. The idea is to bring those who control public money together with community groups and their leaders to work out what the future could look like. The initiative will be funded by Big Society Capital. Interserve will support with debt and equity and we will provide equity. Ours will be an enabling role. This is not just about Catch22, our ambition is much greater than that.

Charities and philanthropy will never be able to provide the comprehensive services that the state aimed to provide. The state has not been that successful either. We at Catch22 cannot and don't want to do it all. If we did, we might end up replacing one flawed model with another. The answer lies in our communities. The state has become so controlling in its desire to give people the conditions in which they can thrive, it sometimes denies people the ability to do that because it is not nuanced or subtle enough.

Look at child protection. What we have is a totally risk averse culture. We are operating out of fear. The approach is far too negative. We should look at people and children as assets rather than as problems. We are contributing to a conversation about what a good society looks like in the twenty-first century. How do we translate the vision of our founding fathers in 1788 into a contemporary context?

I passionately believe that most people and the communities they live in have innate strengths, and that we must find a way to unlock the capacity of people to serve the public good. If we succeed, we will create an environment where people feel they can make a contribution and support those in less fortunate circumstances.

We have overcomplicated things and dissipated our effectiveness. We need to simply process and value people more and enable then to live more fulfilling lives.

I have always thought of myself as someone coming from the left but I won't put a political label on myself now. I know the state is not the solution although it does have a role. I don't think the left genuinely values people – it's too didactic in its efforts to deliver fairness. I am not presenting some kind of simplistic neo-liberal argument, but I do believe the state has to change by adopting an enabling role, as long as government knows and understands what that means.

Chris Wright has set out a vision for how a significant part of the charity sector could thrive, and bring about positive social change via transformed public services, by working in partnership with both the public and private sectors. This will require all parties to change thinking and practice.

In the next two, final chapters, we will examine the roles played by a social entrepreneur in the regeneration of east London and a philanthropist who has pioneered best new practice by transforming opportunities for young people in the north of England in partnership with local authorities, the private sector and local volunteers.

CHAPTER 22

COMMUNITY POWER: THE REGENERATION OF EAST LONDON

"The Poplar Housing and Regeneration Community Association, which I helped to found, is a social enterprise and we operate like a charity. All the profits go back into the St Paul's Way community. That allowed the company to build a £16 million health centre. Welcome to an entrepreneurial community business! We are about building communities but not based on fantasies coming out of Downing Street called the Big Society."

LORD MAWSON, SOCIAL ENTREPRENEUR.

* * *

The first indication that east London has changed was, for many, the opening ceremony of the London Olympics in the summer of 2012. An area once blighted by poverty, neglect and deprivation has been and continues to be transformed. The Olympic Park is only a part of what is Europe's largest regeneration area.

Regeneration began more than thirty years ago and involves a cast of thousands but one man, Lord (Andrew) Mawson, can claim a leadership role that has been consistent from the moment he became a United Reform Church minister in Bromley-by-Bow in 1984 until the present as a peer in the House of Lords and chairman of one of Britain's leading consultancies specialising in urban regeneration.

The regeneration of east London has been made possible by remarkable leadership and vision. Private and public sector partnership has not only transformed the local infrastructure but also had a positive impact upon employment, education, housing and health. What has happened in the East End could be a template for regeneration in other parts of Britain. This was once an area where there was little if any hope. Now there is optimism.

Mawson's adult life has been all about the regeneration of east London with a particular focus on Poplar and Bromley-by-Bow. His ability to bring together local people, local authorities, businesses, trusts, foundations and others who shared his vision has transformed the lives and prospects for thousands and is an outstanding and pioneering example of community philanthropy.

Mawson is a force of nature. I was introduced to him by Professor Brian Cox, who is also part of the east London story. Mawson lost no time in starting a conversation that began in the House of Lords and wound its way to Bromley-by-Bow, round Poplar, and to the Olympic site in Stratford, east London:

Government and civil servants spend too much time looking down at things from 30,000 feet and they don't look at the detail. I have been on this journey for over thirty years. We have created and built a thousand projects in this time, working with the private sector. I and many others have worked with six governments to date. I am an independent crossbencher so I am not for or against anyone. I am a practical Yorkshire man and only interested in what works.

The question we should be asking government, the public and the voluntary sector is: does this work?

We live in an enterprise economy and that is good, but how do we make big institutions relate to a more integrated modern world and to those who they serve or who are their customers? This is one of the challenges of our times, making sure that the interests of the consumer and the public are foremost.

My way into big things is: start small and focus on the detail of what works and what doesn't. Governments make statements about building scores of hospitals and health centres without really under-standing how even one works.

The beginnings of the transformation of Poplar and Bromley-by-Bow were not auspicious. Mawson left school at sixteen with no clear idea of what he should do with his life. After a spell as a Post Office apprentice, he read theology at Manchester. In the early 1980s, he became a minister in a church in Bromley-by-Bow. On his first Sunday, he found himself in front of a group of twelve elderly people sitting in the same places they had sat in for years.

He asked himself what he should do and realised that he didn't have the faintest idea:

> I decided to be the nosy Yorkshire man that I am and investigate exactly what was going on in the area. I realised that 97 per cent of everything there was run by the state. Anyone who could get out had got out. I looked at the local voluntary sector and I saw that religion had moved out of the churches into that sector; it was dom-inated by people who believed two things: that the public sector and charities were good and private sector and business were greedy capitalist pigs. When Tesco moved in with 300 new jobs, this was seen as terrible. Local unemployment was running at 47 per cent.

Mawson and his congregation considered giving the church build-ing away but they were approached by a young dance teacher who wanted to build a dance school.

> I had an unused Sunday school room and suggested she used that, and so we had a dance school. I wanted to work with her because I wanted to rebuild relationships within a community that was break-ing down.
>
> So we began this dance school long before anyone thought of social enterprises. The response was fascinating. Some people in the voluntary sector jumped up and down and complained that this woman was going to charge for classes. I realised that East

End mums wanted the best for their children just like every other mother on the planet. By year six, we had 150 children; some went on to the Royal Ballet.

This modest venture was to prove seminal. Lord Mawson and his wife had made their home in east London but other professionals were leaving because they wanted good schools for their children. He came across a group of families running a nursery at home who were looking for extra space. He realised that they should form a partnership. They did all the work themselves and created a nursery within the church for £70,000.

> We didn't call it a social enterprise but it was one of the first in the country. We had created a business model that worked. Some of the children were paid for out of public funds. My wife and I paid the going rate. There was a real mix of children.
>
> The expert from social services turned up and told me we couldn't have a church, a nursery and what became a theatre in one place because of rules and regulations. Smoke was coming out of the ears of these East End parents who were very blunt. I said her rules were driving poverty in our community. I told her I had to see her boss. He was supportive, asked us to make a few changes and so we built the first integrated model of nursery care in the country that made a small profit which was returned to the project.
>
> It was interesting that in this community where there was a massive dependency culture and much suspicion about meaningless promises from politicians, a strange new word had appeared. Integrity. People were promised a nursery and there it was. Perhaps there were other things we could do together. There was a derelict park behind our building, one of the lungs of Victorian London. It was tarmacked. It was a place for violence. It was a war zone.
>
> I told the new chief executive of Tower Hamlets that she was taking over a basket case. She said: 'I have a nursery nearby that isn't working and if you are so good at running nurseries why don't you take over this one. And whilst we are at it, why don't you take

control of the park on a lease for thirty years for a pound.' The deal was done. Everything we have done and built just started by starting.

I told her that we were running a community care programme for vulnerable people on a local housing estate which was controlled by a tick-box culture. You couldn't mend your toilet without ticking a box. We said we were not going to follow that culture. If people want do things, we shall say yes, let them get on with it and see what happens.

If you give people a sense of ownership and responsibility, then everything changes for the better. So we built a beautiful park and that that led to a landscape business called Green Dreams which ends up partnering with a major multinational and after seven years, we have twenty-six business sites across Poplar creating jobs and opportunities. If you go there today, we have created a new business culture with more than sixty companies in the Lea Valley, in partnerships with Barclays, Investec and JP Morgan. This happened because we started to form relationships with those companies who had come to Canary Wharf.

The future must be about relationships between business and social entrepreneurs. Government and councils need to step back. We can also teach business because some of their corporate social responsibility programmes are naïve and simply tick boxes. Governments like to talk to big business but small and medium enterprises (SMEs) are the key to the future. We are growing sixty SMEs in Bromley-by-Bow. They could be graphic design or social care companies and they are all driven by people who are self-motivated.

We have grown an entrepreneurial culture in Poplar and Bromley-by-Bow through finding dynamic people and forming relationships between them. In the early days we learned by doing. And so we began to challenge the status quo and the way of doing things in silos.

Health and social care has its priorities the wrong way round because too often the patient does not come first. We did a deal with Tower Hamlets on three acres of land and decided to build the first integrated primary healthcare model in the country. We built a cloistered building made of the kind of handmade bricks that were used at Glyndebourne opera house. We wanted to build something beautiful with an attractive garden. This would be a place for health, not just illness. We decided we would own it as a community development trust. The patients would own the building, not the doctors or a pension fund. After a few years, it would make a profit from the asset that would be ploughed back into the centre.

I set out this vision twenty years ago in the naïve belief that it would be supported by the NHS. Wrong. It was as if I had decided to build a nuclear weapons site. The response was not 'how great to have an opportunity to improve healthcare where there wasn't any', the response was 'we run the health service and we are going to stop you'.

Mawson had a difficult eighteen months until he persuaded Brian Mawhinney, then health minister, to visit. The minister was impressed and overruled his civil servants. Today, as a result of that intervention, Bromley-by-Bow has a network of four health centres and 37,000 patients, the biggest primary healthcare list in London.

About that time, I was asked to create a housing association in Poplar. I said no because the state was involved. There was too much bureaucracy and the customer interface was appalling. I said we would create the first housing company in the country that would focus on one area relentlessly for thirty years to solve some big issues and that we would not operate in a silo because we would connect housing to education and to health, and this would be the kind of company where the residents would have a controlling hand.

This company now runs a £1.7 billion regeneration programme and has 9,000 properties. What began as small began to scale up.

I have been involved in the housing association movement for many years. Early associations were run by innovators and entrepreneurs. They did really interesting things, including buildings of quality. What happened, and this is the danger for social enterprise, is that government got interested. This was a mistake. The point was that housing associations are meant to be independent.

There was excitement about government getting involved and pumping in money. But housing associations came to look like and behave as local authority housing departments. The result was the same old mediocrity, the water doesn't work, the grass doesn't get cut and the rubbish is not taken away.

We set a company called Poplar HARCA, standing for housing and regeneration community association. We were determined not to create a quasi-government body. Our company was going to be community owned. Instead of blaming the council, they own the issues themselves.

The partnership with Poplar HARCA today includes a school, the health service, Countryside the builders, and local doctors. This is how a community is recreated and transformed by housing, health and education coming together and sharing interests. When it came to building the new £16 million health centre opposite St Paul's Way School, we tried to do it with the NHS but it was a nightmare because they were so slow. So the housing company, which was concerned about the health of its residents, took responsibility for building it.

This was a great example of the NHS failing to work in a business-like way with local partners. The housing company created the new centre working with the school, local doctors, pharmacists and this was a demonstration of what joined-up behaviour means and what can be achieved.

I sat on the board of Poplar HARCA for ten years. Everything we did started small. Innovation should be like that. The key thing was how we assumed responsibility for some local authority properties. We did a deal with the local authority and then there had to be a democratic vote by residents. As we built everyone's confidence, including our own, by starting small, we could then talk to banks and do deals with them. And so after twenty years, we are now looking at what is almost a £3 billion redevelopment project.

Our housing company in Poplar is a social enterprise and we operate like a charity. All profits go back into the community. That allowed the company to build a £16 million health centre. Welcome to an entrepreneurial community business! This is what entrepreneurial public service looks like. We are about building communities but not based on fantasies coming out of Downing Street called the Big Society or the Third Way.

Initially, the first properties were transferred to us by a democratic vote. Some of these were substandard and we wanted to knock them down. 97 per cent of property was locally owned. We wanted to create a variety and mixture of housing, including shared ownership. This takes time and some of this was new development but we were now able to do deals with banks. All profits were returned to the company to improve quality of life locally.

Our new chairman is Paul Brickell, who is Director of Regeneration and Community Partnerships for the Olympic Park, who has worked down there for twenty years. He is building five new housing developments in the Park so all the experience we have built up in Poplar HARCA is transferring into a 240-hectare development on the Olympic Park. This is how you grow initiative.

In 2009 the CEO of Tower Hamlets contacted Lord Mawson to say there had been a murder on St Paul's Way, just north of Canary Wharf, and asked him for a report on what was going on. He found that the local school was ranked in the bottom ten in the country, there was a failing health centre next door with 11,000 patients and there was acute racial tension in the area. Mawson said that although the school was in trouble, its problems were more to do with its external environment. He said he would take fourteen people away to a conference centre for two days and see what happened. These included the head teacher, the Director of Children's Services, and an Asian entrepreneur who ran a local pharmacy. At the end of two days, there was unanimous agreement: no one could cope with the scale of the difficulties on their own but that together, there was an opportunity to rebuild a community.

I said we would do this brick by brick and it would take ten years. And to start, I had to get all the local health, housing and education and children's services leaders signed up to the same narrative otherwise we would fail.

As a result, we have rebuilt a £40 million school that had been on the point of closure. Previously, only thirty-five families had applied for places and 1,200 families applied this year. We were awarded 'outstanding' in every regard. In addition to the housing company building and a new health centre across the road, we have built a £1 million science lab with the Wellcome Trust because there has been an epidemic of diabetes in the area and we want the young people understanding the science of it.

I met Brian Cox five years ago. He told me that science education in the UK is broken. Biology, physics and chemistry are taught in silos and he believes they are all interconnected. I told him about the integrated world we were trying to create at St Paul's Way and he asked to see it.

I asked Brian to become the first patron of the school. We agreed to try to make it the best place to study science and we would do that in the middle of a housing estate in Tower Hamlets. We decided to do a Science Summer School for two days in the summer. This year was our fourth. Jo Johnson, the science minister, opened it in our 250-seat theatre in the school. Brian Cox was the host. The kids did practicals. Brian interviewed some top scientists including one from NASA. He interviewed her about possibilities for going to Mars.

Brian is very committed to the Science Summer School and to St Paul's Way. He is focused upon the ambition that Britain becomes the best place in the world to study science and engineering. According to Professor Cox:

Science is a force for extreme good in education, socially and economically. But there are not enough women in science. There should be 50 per cent. It is not just a sense of moral obligation about equal opportunity. It is about the talent pool. St Paul's School has been transformed in five years from one without a sixth form to one that now sends most of its students to top universities. By focusing on east London, the hope is not only to cover the national shortage of scientists but also to bring greater diversity to the science industries that is sorely lacking.

For Lord Mawson, the challenge was to move from dependency to enterprise.

> J. P. Morgan were moving into east London and were wondering how best to play an active role in the communities. I said: 'Don't give small grants to everybody; find the entrepreneurially minded people in the community you want to work with and establish long-term relationships with them. Help us build an enterprise culture and develop skills.'
>
> A lot of the J. P. Morgan people have degrees in STEM – science, technology, engineering and maths. Brian Cox and I are interested in those million jobs that could be created because we believe science should be a major part of our economy and J. P. Morgan understands this. So the question is: how do we link their staff and their skills with science and technology business development in the lower Lea Valley and the development of science education? This is something we will be exploring with J. P. Morgan.
>
> This must be a way forward: a major finance business forms relationships with local entrepreneurs and thinks beyond dispersing relatively small grants to do something really innovative. This is what organic and creative growth looks like, a million miles away from public sector silos.

*   *   *

When Andrew Mawson arrived in Bromley-by-Bow in the 1980s, the lower Lea Valley was a little-known wasteland. The loss of tens of thousands of jobs in the Royal Docks meant that the population of Docklands had fallen by 20 per cent, the local unemployment rate was 17.8 per cent and 60 per cent of the land was derelict, vacant or underused. The Lea Valley, which contains Bromley-by-Bow and St Paul's Way, had become an industrial desert.

Today, the Bromley-by-Bow Centre sits 150 yards from the Olympic Stadium. Mawson was one of the first to see the potential for the Olympics to be held in east London in 2012. He is a director of the London Legacy Development Corporation which is responsible for the long-term planning, development, management and maintenance of the Olympic Park.

The 'Olympicopolis' project will ultimately deliver one of the Olympic Park's most important long-term goals, the creation of an education and cultural initiative providing a new metropolitan centre for east London. The Victoria & Albert Museum working in partnership with the Smithsonian in Washington DC, Sadler's Wells, University College London, and the University of the Arts will be amongst those involved in a project valued at more than £1 billion funded by both the public and private sectors.

The Foundation for FutureLondon will be responsible for the funding and fulfilment of Olympicopolis and sees as its mission the delivery of the London 2012 promise to be the first host city to regenerate an entire community for the direct benefit of everyone who lives there. I talked to FutureLondon's chairman, Sir William Castell. Bill Castell, former chairman of the Wellcome Trust and a former director of General Electric and BP, has to raise the £180 million philanthropic and private funding needed but, as he explained, the vision and ambition of FutureLondon is far greater than meeting a financial target. For Castell, Olympicopolis is an opportunity to think about society today in the context of its needs in the future, for business to recognise the imperative to contribute more to society, for all to celebrate diversity and community in order to create a new way of urban living. I asked Castell about his ambition:

With over 75 per cent of the world adopting an urban lifestyle, it is critical that we create the best possibilities for 21st-century urban living that can take on the challenges and opportunities that lie ahead. Here in east London, we have a rare opportunity to consider how excellence and society's most advanced thinking to date can be applied to a diverse community.

Community and diversity are two important words. I was in Haarlem in Holland a couple of days ago. I went around an extraordinary museum that in the sixteenth, seventeenth and eighteenth century served the purpose of not only housing the guilds, but housing the women folk who looked after the aged as well as being the HQ for the defence of Haarlem, in a beautiful building that is a real statement of quality that has endured until today. And with contemporary pictures painted over 200 years ago of the extraordinary events that the city witnessed: the ending of a great war with England, the Spanish occupation and its atrocities, and I thought how good it was that the people of the guilds put in their own money to fund it and to support the community by paying for what today we would call social welfare. These people had a real sense of social purpose and I thought it was both beautiful and wonderful.

The key question is whether we can build the Foundation for FutureLondon in such a way that it can endure and have presence in perpetuity so that whatever local politicians decide, we can still operate and get things done. We need an income of between £3 million and £8 million a year, to be sufficient to break the silos and to provide funding that helps to activate programmes and projects across disciplines and institutions.

I would also like us to own some of the cultural and educational assets in the Park that are devoted to supporting our mission statement: that assets must be used to facilitate the Queen Elizabeth Park as the metropolitan centre for the east London community.

The Olympic Games showed us a degree of ownership of the games by London which not many people were expecting. That demonstrates that if we put our minds to it, we can encourage teams of people to come together. People then realise that they have skills and that they can contribute. And that contribution gives pleasure, pride and fulfilment. Giving people self-belief and dignity encourages them to participate in society rather being isolated.

The initial idea for our funding strategy is around the concept that the City invests in what we might call the 'United Way'. It is in the interests of the City that they see the two million people who live here are an asset, as is the land. There will be housing, entertainment, security, but most important of all, it can take the vigour and energy of east London and see it as a population they can employ in the years to come.

We are looking to major city institutions, the Corporation of London, the Livery Companies, the banks and financial services and, possibly, some of the high-tech groups.

We will say to investors: if you give us your money, we will create cultural and educational assets and facilitate schemes where we can help millennials, who are in danger of being lost because even forty-year-olds don't know how they can buy a house or get a decent pension. The current government has not facilitated affordable housing and pensions that will be large enough. There will be social housing. The plan is for 55,000 to be living in the Park by 2031 and that 35 per cent of homes should be 'affordable'.

The security and ownership model that has worked well over centuries is gone. We have to find new ways of doing things. So the message to the City will be: if you bring me your brand, I will connect you with what we are doing here; I will connect you with the Carpenters' Company that supports 1,000 young people a year in vocational trades, who get paid by Tottenham to take on their most difficult kids to enable them to become contributors.

We have a unique opportunity, given the scale of the park, the mix of offices, housing, sport, education and culture, to say that we can recreate east London as a place to be truly proud of, in a way that reflects east London and its culture rather than something that has been imported from the west. This has to be a local initiative that sees a diverse population as an asset rather than a problem. If we succeed, the reverberation will be global because of the Olympic tag. We will also be an early adopter of technology and will be seen as a pioneer of what 21st-century urban life can be.

We have to raise £180 million gross of private money of various kinds. This is to pay for infrastructure. This investment will trigger a £1.3 billion scheme. This will bring 10,000 graduates and undergraduates to the park, in fashion, business, mathematics and health.

Those educational assets are all business-facing and therefore will be looking towards the local community. The cultural assets will include the V&A with the Smithsonian, Sadler's Wells, and there will be others. All of them will be involved with the community.

On the educational front, we are looking at how we might create more apprenticeships and training that will lead some towards the city. How do we do all this? We are aiming to create a Faculty that will made up of all those who have invested in the park. I want the Faculty to meet twice a year so that we can encourage people to leave their silos and create partnerships.

Our ambition is that the Foundation for FutureLondon will be here in 150 years. And that we create measurement that has nothing to do with GDP and much more to do with quality of life, quality of engagement with society and to enable more people to enjoy and appreciate living in the great city of London. That is my ambition.

We prosper in London because we are a global city. We need to be seen as a city of the future as well as of the past and the present. This Olympicopolis project gives us the opportunity to make a statement about London in the future and our wish to experiment and to explore and to look towards new horizons.

Look at the ancient Egyptians who did the same thing for three thousand years because it worked but they missed out on the wheel and many other things on the way. This is an opportunity to recreate a significant part of our great city so that it becomes a place where people want to live and visit as well as work.

I think London could have a population of 20 million in a hundred years. The key thing is to create an environment where young people believe that they can achieve.

I think the private sector is fighting for its life. Political extremes and populism of the left and right are becoming more apparent. We must make sure that isolated boardrooms realise that they have a responsibility to society. The lack of accountability in globalism is a problem. Business will need to have much more meaningful engagement with communities and society. If they don't, we will lose what underpins Western society. The extremes of reward are too much. Business must do two things together: reward shareholders with profits and make a contribution to society.

We are under-calling the intellectual assets of this country. I do think it is deeply disappointing that none of our politicians seem to be prepared to think through and plan for the key components of a life: housing, job and pension. All their decisions are short term.

I have a 500-year vision, based on creativity, energy and sustainability.

Sir William Castell is unpaid as Chairman of the Foundation for FutureLondon. He told me that he has always been philanthropic with his time and, in their different ways, so have Lord Mawson and Professor Brian Cox. All are committed to the common good.

Mawson is now trying to work his magic in the north of England through the Well North initiative. I hope someone will invite him to Blackpool. I could not fail to be impressed by what social enterprise and philanthropy is achieving in London but I continued to search for projects where philanthropy performs a more catalytic role. I needed an example, preferably outside London, of something that demonstrates how philanthropy can transform lives at a local level by supporting communities, in partnership with local authorities, local companies and volunteers. Could such a model exist?

CHAPTER 23

FROM OLDHAM TO THE UNIVERSE: THE PATH TO YOUTH EMPOWERMENT

"We need to focus on communities. Many of our communities are becoming increasingly divided and intolerant. That is why it is important for charity and the private and public sectors to be working together. In our Youth Zones there is a reflection of all parts of the community. When everyone works together the results are unbelievably productive. Youth Zones could change Britain."

BILL HOLROYD, FOUNDER AND CHAIRMAN,

ONSIDE YOUTH ZONES.

* * *

In 2015, I received an invitation from Sir Norman Stoller to 'An evening with Professor Brian Cox: Exploring the Universe from Oldham'. A helpful intermediary had approached Sir Norman on my behalf to ask if he was willing to be interviewed. Not only was I invited to the lecture in Oldham but I was also invited to stay at the Stollers' hotel near their home overlooking Lake Windermere for an interview.

Sir Norman asked Professor Cox to give a lecture to 1,000 school children because he wanted to attract more young people to join the youth project in Oldham of which he is a principal benefactor and President, Mahdlo. Mahdlo (the sharp-witted will have noticed this is Oldham spelt backwards) is part of charity called OnSide

Youth Zones. I was to discover that Youth Zones, of which there are seven in the north of England, have the formula I was seeking.

OnSide Youth Zones aim to build a network of 21st-century youth facilities that give young people quality, safe and affordable places to go in their leisure. So far, they have 23,000 young members. On my way to Oldham in October 2015, I met Bill Holroyd, OnSide Youth Zones chairman, at his home in Cheshire.

Holroyd is heading a nationwide initiative to raise £600 million via a public and private sector partnership to build 100 Youth Zones, to empower the young and to combat deprivation and unemployment.

The public/private partnership engineered by Holroyd and OnSide is pioneering because the public sector buys in to a charitable objective on the charity's terms. This is significant because philanthropy is convening private and public resources at a local level to meet local need.

Holroyd made his money by selling his food service distribution business and appears in the *Sunday Times* Rich List. He has been a director of and investor in twenty-five companies in the past fifteen years but as he explained to me, he had reached a point in life where making money was no longer enough. He was looking for more meaning in his life and found it in a youth club in Bolton. This was the genesis of OnSide and the creation of a pioneering charity for which Holroyd is an evangelist.

About ten years ago, I felt something was missing. Life didn't seem balanced when it was all about me. I was not feeling fulfilled. People said I had done a good job, I had made money but it didn't feel right.

I had a phone call from Bolton Lads and Girls Club asking me if I would like to be chairman. I was not from Bolton, I had never worked with young people and I had never been involved in charity. I said yes immediately and that I would do it for three years. One of the best bits of advice I was given was that you should say to this kind of proposal that you will think about it for forty-eight hours to avoid making stupid decisions on the hoof. Something deep in my soul erased all those circuits! And so I took it on and then the minute I walked in I knew that this was it. There was a 25,000-square-foot modern building, with 300 young people doing sport, art, drama, dance, gym etc. I was seeing what the young are like when they do have somewhere to go rather than hanging about the street looking threatening.

The club was doing such an obviously important job by filling a vacuum left by a public sector in retreat. We cannot leave young people in a vacuum and simply moan about the situation and about young people being a problem.

The good people of Bolton had invented this modern iteration of youth club. The very word 'Youth Club' has been stigmatised. No kid in his or her right mind would want to join one and put up with rubbish premises. Bolton was different. There were 300 kids involved in a place that was equipped to an adult standard with a gym, a dance studio, a music room, football pitches, all fit for purpose.

Immediately, I saw the benefit of volunteers and kids all working together. Instead of the community moaning 'why doesn't somebody do something?', there was a realisation that 'they' were not going to do anything and we would have to do it ourselves. All we did was tap leadership and create the catalyst that brought these four disparate groups together: the public and private sectors are always bickering about each other, volunteers are full of desire and good intentions but they are disorganised and not a group and the young are too often dismissed as a problem rather than an asset.

The youth club was originally in an old mill and my predecessor wondered what would happen if they did this properly to the highest possible standard. That is what they did and the membership went from 600 members to 4,000 and there are now 6,000 members. The cost of running it is £3 million a year, all found within the community. We had to put a lot of private money into starting it up but the normal model now is 40 per cent of revenue comes from local council, 50 per cent from the local community private sector (this amount includes trusts and grants too, not all of which are sourced locally) and 10 per cent from the kids through membership. It is important that the kids feel they are members. The clubs belong to them and the adults cannot take them over.

My Damascene moment was when I saw the need, saw the solution and within the first year, I must have shown the model to hundreds of towns but no one had replicated it. This was unique: private sector, public sector, volunteers and young people all working together. We needed an enabling organisation to make sure we replicated this successful model because these things don't happen in a vacuum. And so we created OnSide.

The key thing is partnership. If each sector tried to create a Youth Zone on their own, it would fail. The combination of all four partners makes a great community effort possible.

In creating OnSide, we discovered this latent and massive desire for people who wanted to do things in their own communities. Bolton has 350 volunteers and a waiting list. People do want to give back but they don't want to be abused. They want training, uniforms, schedules. They just want to be treated the same as staff. It is all too easy to treat volunteers like cannon fodder. We have a ratio of 50/50 staff and volunteers.

In the north-west, we have raised about £75 million for seven Youth Zones. They cost £6 million each to build. The capital costs are divided 50/50 between the public and private sector. There are thirteen or fourteen in development, three of them in London. It is important to have flagships in London.

My life since I sold my original business is looking for business opportunities that need replicating, so Bolton triggered all my electrodes. This is what I do. I invest and grow things. I look at OnSide as a business that needed to grow. We had to get the best people. We run this charity like a business. We put together a board of really talented people. They are all activists and each took on one aspect of the work. And all are involved in monitoring financial management and performance measurement. We are very tight and we are not scared of spending money.

Can the charity sector learn from this? Are there transferable skills? I look at a lot of charities and the main lesson that I have learned is that charities should be run like a business. Look at Kids Co. Camila Batmanghelidjh was badly let down by her trustees, who should have insisted there were reserves and by her management team. No business could operate like that.

Are Youth Zones addressing, indirectly, some of the problems we know are afflicting vulnerable young people?

Young people are like blotting paper. If you put them in a positive environment, they will respond accordingly. The same applies to a negative environment. I am sure that our young people have benefited hugely because of the positive environment provided by Youth Zone. Statistically, where every Youth Zone has been created, youth-related crime has been reduced by a minimum of 50 per cent, in some places by more.

We helped close to 600 young people into jobs in the last two years. We measure our outcomes to prove to government that there is a reduction in anti-social behaviour and an increase in employability. Local government, for the most part, has been hugely receptive at a time when money is being sucked out by central government. They are contributing 40 per cent of running costs at a time of severe cuts but they see the benefit. There is a real return on investment. Overall running costs for each Youth Zone are around £1 million a year and the savings are circa £2.4 million using only anti-social behaviour and employability as the savings metrics. Based on the council's investment of £400,000 a year gives a six times return and if government was to contribute £200,000 a year, that would give a twelve times return.

The state has a leadership role to play but it is retreating fast. Currently, there is no leadership for philanthropy. We realised that we would have to do this ourselves. That is how we started the charity. We were asked to do all sorts of things that would have ticked boxes or enabled us to fit into a slot but we knew that they were wrong for us. We had to be pioneers and do things in the way that we believed would deliver the results.

I have had to put a huge amount of time into this, perhaps 80 per cent.

My wife and I have also made a commitment to put 20 per cent of any capital we make into charity. That was a big decision and it has to come from your soul. However tough it is, we must do it. But we didn't get much happiness out of a scattergun approach. We are much happier being focused because we are achieving more. I am working just as hard as I was when I was in business but this has been the most fulfilling thing I have done in my life.

We need to focus on communities. Many of our communities are becoming increasingly divided and intolerant. That is why it is so important for charity and the private and public sectors to be working together. In our Youth Zones, there is reflection of all parts of the community. When everyone works together, the results are unbelievably productive. When raising money, I have very seldom been turned down. I have been astonished by the response. Our donors are on a different level. They see how Youth Zones could change Britain.

I spent a morning in Mahdlo, the Oldham Youth Zone, before going to the Brian Cox lecture and immediately understood Bill Holroyd's response on his first visit to the Bolton centre. First impressions are important. On arrival at an airy, light-filled contemporary building, I was warmly greeted at reception before meeting Helen Taylor, then Chief Executive:

I have been involved for four years, joining before we opened. I set up the organisation and recruited the team. A group of young people did a lot of work on helping us design the building and they suggested the name, Mahdlo.

OnSide was set up to replicate the Bolton model. They asked the local community in Oldham if this was something they needed. There was a consultation in schools involving several hundred young people. This was how they started a steering group with over thirty young people and they drove the project from the outset. They visited Bolton and thought it was very sport-biased and they wanted more of a focus on the arts in Oldham.

Oldham was a key area of the textile industry and that has gone. The town has gone through bad times but there are now some large businesses and new industries and they are keen to support us, often in ways that are about helping our young people prepare for being employed and so that helps to make Mahdlo a more attractive proposition.

We have nearly 4,000 members who make 5,000 visits a month. They pay £5 a year and 50p to visit. All our Youth Zones charge 50p to create a sense of value. They can pay their £5 in instalments and we have a hardship fund so the young are not turned away.

We have a sports hall, a fully equipped gym, a boxing studio. We run archery courses and girls' karate. There are creative programmes involving training, performances, a dance studio, a digital media suite, an arts and craft area, a music room and a dance teacher. There is a really broad arts offer. We work with other organisations and groups, including the Oldham Theatre Workshop where we are introducing the young to drama.

We also have canoeing, riding and we also offer the Duke of Edinburgh award. People respond really well to this. We think about what skills they can learn from this environment, particularly communication, team-working and leadership skills.

We cater for people with particular needs around health and well-being. We offer counselling in partnership with Mind. There are workshops around issues that are important to young people such as child sexual exploitation, drugs and alcohol, respect and body image.

We do a lot of one to one work supporting the more vulnerable young, working with other local partners. We run courses for young people who are becoming ready to live independently and who don't have positive role models to support them at home. We have a number of young people who are homeless. We allow them to have showers here, we give them deodorant, they can use our clothes washing and drying machines. We provide a food bank. So there are lots of different ways we support young people's health and welfare.

We prepare our members for training and employment. We involve employers to help to inspire and empower young people by letting them know what jobs are out there. They give the young insight in how to access some of these opportunities. We do some of the programmes in schools.

We also help the young to relate to their own communities, to develop their leadership potential and to become involved in community projects. This all about giving young people a role, responsibility and opportunities to develop. We are giving opportunities to those who lack all of that at home. We are supporting a lot of young people who are disclosing previous abuse, much of it historical. They feel more confident in this environment. We are working with other charities on this, such as NSPCC.

I was impressed and moved by what I saw and everyone I met at Mahdlo including two smiling members of staff who were supposed to be on leave. The commitment of the executive and those who run programmes was palpable. I was struck by the quality of what was on offer in terms of both programmes and environment.

* * *

Professor Brian Cox was born in Oldham. When he took to the stage at the Civic Theatre in October 2015, he was given a hero's welcome and treated to a barrage of screams and squeaks by 1,000 youngsters as if he was the rock musician he once was. Silence, however, reigned as Cox held his audience transfixed for an hour as we examined the universe from the perspective of his home town.

All this was made possible by Sir Norman Stoller. Stoller has helped build and lead a successful public company in Oldham but making money for the sake of it has never been his goal. He told me that he has never been interested in buying rich man's toys. He had recently made a great deal of money from one of his investments and thought nothing of providing a further £50 million to enable his charitable trust to do so much more.

Stoller's gifts to diverse causes, which can be counted in multiple millions, will benefit many, but millions more around the world have reason to be grateful for the source of his generosity: the tubular bandage.

In 2008, I had the incredible honour of being given the Freedom of the Borough of Oldham. I seem to have been fortunate enough to have been showered with all sorts of honours. However, when a borough adopts you, it isn't just nice, it is almost unbelievable. I was very touched and remain convinced that no honour can be more important than to be adopted by the town where one was born or worked.

Our business grew from very small beginnings in Oldham in 1952. I would not be where I am today if it were not for my late father, who, almost by accident, discovered a new way of bandaging. He, and the various nurses and doctors who gave him their advice, brought up to date a technique of bandaging that was used by the Ancient Egyptians in the creation of mummies. Together they invented the technique of the tubular bandage and designed a clever system of frames or applicators to help bandage fingers, arms, legs, in fact all parts of the body.

After receiving news of the Oldham Freedom Award, Sheila and I went on holiday and I had time to think of ways of giving something back. Then I had a great idea – why not start a youth club in Oldham that would be warm, safe and modern to attract young people away from the street corners where they usually gathered because they had nowhere to go and nothing worthwhile to do? But how would I do it?

On returning, I received a letter that has undoubtedly changed my life. It was from an old friend who was doing his bit for society as the Chairman of the Bolton Girls and Lads Club. Bill Holroyd discovered that giving young people somewhere to go and something to do had an amazingly beneficial effect not just on the young people themselves, but on the local community too. Comparisons on subjects like good behaviour, reduced crime – especially juvenile vandalism – were clear to see. But it didn't stop there. Better attendance at school and higher achievements were clear markers as well. This led my friend to conclude that a club such as his was too good to be available only in Bolton; there should be one in every town and city throughout the country. That created a spark in me. I knew what I wanted to do but I didn't know how to do it. But my friend did.

Youth crime in Oldham has been decimated; vandalism is almost non-existent. Absenteeism is dropping like a stone; kids are more attentive and academic results are improving. Young people now see the point of education and work. There was a time when apathy reigned in Oldham; poor housing, mean streets, unattractive schools and teachers, and high unemployment. Young people could not see a worthwhile future and, worse, could not make a connection with school, attainment, training and apprenticeships to worthwhile careers.

I believe that the positive effect that exemplars have is very important. Young people can spot a phoney very quickly and can take to genuine people equally quickly. This was well demonstrated in the immediate effect that Professor Brian Cox had when he came to Oldham. The more that we can bring successful people into face to face situations with young people, the easier it becomes to convince them to follow positive examples.

Starting from very small beginnings can have very positive effects. For example, when I started my business I was under-capitalised and cash flow was a real problem. What this has taught me is the importance to those who are struggling to stay on the ladder to success, to get paid quickly after a job is completed. One of the great business crimes of today is how the large businesses take advantage of the small. It is a crime because it ruins opportunities to grow employment. We need a law that protects those who are not given the chance to succeed simply because they are not paid on time.

Another of the initiatives that we work hard to develop in Oldham is 'Young Enterprise' which is a mentoring and development organisation of experienced business people who come together with adolescent boys and girls and provide them with an opportunity to develop successful companies. We show how important it is to create and monitor the business plan and to enable them to experience the dangers and pitfalls along the way. We provide the money for them to learn the hard way because I would rather them lose two or three thousand pounds of my money than twenty or thirty thousand of their own. In all of this, partnerships created with people of different and complementary skills are so important. None of us can be good at everything but unfortunately, that is a lesson that few learn the easy way! What we look for in helping others is sustainability and everything we do is directed to that.

You have asked why my charitable trust has a particular interest in supporting healthcare initiatives. The answer to that is that my commercial life has been involved in providing better healthcare solutions to traditional problems that satisfy the needs of the Health Service for quicker, safer, less expensive healthcare. The best example of this is our invention of Tubigrip. But I have experienced what goes on in hospitals as well.

I had cancer of the colon in 1997 and I had prostate cancer in 2012 as well. It was tough, but I learned how to cope with leading as normal a life as possible whilst having hospital treatment. I also realised how much more difficult it must be if the patient doesn't have the support of a good and happy home life.

I was visited by the chairman of an organisation that builds recreational centres at some of our cancer hospitals to enable patients to have a cup of tea or chat to healthcare professionals on their way to having treatment, or before going home afterwards. The name of the organisation is Maggie's after Maggie Keswick Jencks who was a cancer sufferer in the 1960s. Since then her dream has become a reality with over eighteen centres having been built around the world. Maggie understood the need that a cancer patient has but didn't receive in terms of how to tell the family, who to talk to, where to get emotional and practical help. Maggie's Centres answer all these needs and I was asked whether my trust could help to create such a centre at the Christie Hospital in Manchester. Having visited such a centre in London, I realised its importance to the whole community and I am proud of our decision not only to help create a Maggie's Centre in Manchester but in Oldham as well.

Providing a helping hand to those in need has been a way of life for fifty years. This increased when my company became publicly quoted in 1990 and I provided shares to the Stoller Charitable Trust so that we could start to do really good work. This year we celebrate our Silver Jubilee and I look back on our past twenty-five years with a great deal of pride in what we have achieved, and a great deal of gratitude to my fellow trustees.

But all of this charitable activity was able to advance through several gears as a result of doing a good deed fifteen years ago.

I was asked by a friend if I could help his son whose business was about to fail as he could not afford the following month's wages bill. So I saw the young man, whose abilities struck me immediately. That meeting ended with my writing a cheque to keep the activity going. What followed was even more remarkable because I became involved, joined his company as a non-executive director, brought in others who took a similar role and together we created a fantastic organisation that has gone from strength to strength.

There are a number of very pleasurable outcomes to this story. Firstly, to have seen this young man grow in stature and maturity and to see how his abilities have developed. Then to see how he was able to grow his company to become a leader in a new area of activity – sales to the public via the internet. Then to grow a really able management team and grow a workforce from a handful to over one thousand people. Finally, to launch his company into public ownership, which was achieved in 2014.

I resigned from the board the night before that event – job done! – and AO World is now a household name not only throughout this country but becoming well known in Europe as well. My reward was to be able to put £50 million into my charitable trust and to pledge it into so many really worthwhile causes in this, our Silver Jubilee Trust year.

How do we persuade others to see the light? That is a very disturbing question. The answer is obvious. If you don't get an enormous amount of satisfaction from saying yes, and seeing the benefits that you can provide to others, then what is your life?

I am eighty-one years of age and although I haven't finished yet, I feel very satisfied with the benefits that I have been able to provide throughout my life as I grew my business to become known and respected throughout the world; by providing direct employment in an organisation that valued and invested in its people; by providing opportunities to so many to demonstrate their own abilities; and seeing them rise in importance and have really worthwhile careers is also a great privilege.

I am satisfied also in recognising that true happiness comes from giving and not receiving.

The OnSide Youth Zone model of the public and private sectors, donors, charities and volunteers all signing up to a clear set of aims and objectives ought to be one that is replicated to support other aspects of the common good. OnSide has its critics who claim that the charity is soaking up and diverting charitable giving in parts of the country where philanthropic funding is scarce and the voluntary sector is weak. Others say OnSide Youth Zones are unsustainable. Nothing is perfect but I am not convinced by this criticism. I would be more impressed if those charities who feel hard done by were to try to form a relationship with their local Youth Zone. Moreover, I would be surprised if the trustees of the Garfield Weston Foundation, who know all about due diligence, would give a capital grant to a project that is unsustainable. Bolton is still growing after fifteen years in Youth Zone format. Indeed, all Youth Zones are growing.

Being backed by a consortium of partners and diversity of income is one sign of sustainability. Local authority investment is crucial and impressive when their grants from government have been cut by 50 per cent or more. However, some local authorities are not prepared to pool their 'sovereignty' and support the objectives of a third party, in this case, a charitable endeavour. When a local council is not prepared to be a partner, there cannot be a Youth Zone. There are no Youth Zones in Liverpool and Newcastle.

OnSide is also a catalyst for more corporate social investment as I discovered when I talked to Charles Mindenhall, who is heading up the campaign to establish Youth Zones in London. Mindenhall is the founder and managing partner at Blenheim Chalcot. He and his business partner Manoj Badale have co-founded more than twenty technology-related businesses:

> When I heard about OnSide, and heard what business people were doing in the north-west working with local authorities to address youth deprivation, to counter a lack of ambition and aspiration, and to do this at scale, I was impressed. This chimed with me. I could identify with the pain and the problems they were addressing because you can see it all around you in London.
>
> The OnSide concept also fitted with our business perspective. We build businesses. We look for problems to solve, for the pain points around customer and client problems, we then try to solve those in an innovative way, and then we consider if the business can grow. This is the way we operate when we consider the businesses we want to invest in.
>
> We take a similar view of our philanthropic activities. We examine the issues and the challenges that need to be solved and overcome and consider if we have something to contribute. We also consider if we can do something 'at scale', if there is potential for replication and growth. That is often quite difficult in the charitable sector. When we consider scale and impact, we often think about the time and money we can contribute. We have to think whether or not the social return will be worth our philanthropic investment.
>
> Business and local government have come together in the north-west as partners and the Youth Zones they have created are very much part of the community. Business, the local authority and community leaders take joint responsibility for making sure the interests of the young are looked after and particularly those who are disadvantaged and at risk. It is crucial that responsibility does not just lie with the local authority.
>
> OnSide Youth Zones are perfect for those who have done well in life and are looking for ways to give back and to do so at scale. People struggle sometimes to know what to do with their money and entrepreneurial energy. Lack of awareness about what is possible may be holding some people back from being philanthropic.

OnSide Youth Zones are a way of supporting the local community. The people who started the charity put their names and reputations on the line in order to develop the charity and to prove its sustainability. These local champions have taken responsibility for what is going on in their communities. Many people and businesses who are supporting Youth Zones have never done anything like this before.

Bill Holroyd asked me eighteen months ago if I would be the chairman for OnSide in London. Our business has relationships with local authorities in London and also all over the country. OnSide were keen to be in London so I volunteered to lead the discussions with local authorities. One key message for local authorities is that trusts and foundations and individual donors are keen to be involved.

We are asking local authorities to provide land and put some money in and we will find the matching capital. We can give local authorities the confidence that these private funds can be found. The proposition should be attractive to forward-thinking local authority leaders as the OnSide model is now a proven model for empowering the young. Otherwise, as youth services have been cut, local authorities could be sitting on a powder keg. Resources are limited in London, the streets are a natural place to go after school and Youth Zones offer a much more positive alternative.

Local authorities are bearing most of the cuts. They have no choice but to cut services. We can offer an alternative. We have encouraged some local authority leaders to visit Youth Zones in the north-west and they have been impressed. They realise that this is a serious project that is achieving positive results. And these results are because of a public–private partnership.

These efforts are now coming to fruition, with five Youth Zones in London on the cards. Barking & Dagenham was the first authority to agree to launch a Youth Zone. They hope to open in a couple of years. The Queen's Trust is underwriting Barking and Jack Petchey has agreed to match the funding of the Queen's Trust through his foundation. Barnet and Croydon have also now agreed to launch Youth Zones, and we are hopeful of finalising arrangements very soon with Haringey and Hammersmith & Fulham.

Local authorities have been managing budget cuts to their youth services and thinking what their strategy should be for the future and we are in a position to help them solve this conundrum with extra capital and revenue. What is good is that the OnSide project is bringing local business leaders and the local authority together. They are not natural partners – but bringing the two together can create something very effective and impactful.

There is a recognition in local authorities that support for young people today in deprived areas is not enough. There is a time bomb ticking in some communities.

I find the OnSide vision very compelling, particularly the partnership between public and private, as both have something to contribute. And people who are in my position who are able to give money are also giving significant time and experience. Time is also more important than money. It is the contribution of time and quite a lot of shoe leather that – as elsewhere in the country – is unlocking London for OnSide.

I am forty-four. It is very exciting at this time of life to be involved in creating charities as well as businesses. It is equally interesting trying to address thorny social as well as business problems. The best charities are supposed to be innovative and it is great to be in a position where I can help them.

I have seen the future and it works – in Oldham, Bolton and those other towns with an OnSide Youth Zone. Might it be possible for there to be Youth Zones in Blackpool and Belfast?

Note the involvement of volunteers in Youth Zones. They are an essential part of a partnership which is empowering the young. Youth Zones could not flourish without volunteers. We all have a role to play regardless of our means. All involved are jointly taking responsibility for their communities and for the local common good. Is this an example for us all that could be extended to other aspects of society? If so, what should happen next?

CHAPTER 24

CONCLUSIONS: OBSERVING ETERNAL TRUTHS

"As you know, there is no such thing as society. There are individual men and women and there are families. And no government can do anything except through people and people must look to themselves first. It is our duty to look after ourselves and then, also, to look after our neighbours."

THE RT. HON. MARGARET THATCHER,
PRIME MINISTER, 1987.

"When one among us falters, our most basic human instinct is to put our own self-interest to one side, to reach out a hand and help them over the line. That's why the central tenet of my belief is that there is more to life than individualism and self-interest. We have a responsibility to one another. And I firmly believe that government has a responsibility too."

THE RT. HON. THERESA MAY, PRIME MINISTER, 2016.

*　　*　　*

Since conceiving the idea for this book in 2014, conflict in the Middle East has intensified, the refugee crisis has exploded, asset inequality continues to increase and housing has become ever more unaffordable. Nationalism, protectionism, racism, xenophobia, intolerance and populism are growing rather than diminishing. The US has elected a media celebrity as President, a billionaire who has been declared bankrupt six times, who does not pay federal income tax, who is not known to be philanthropic and whose campaign was notorious for inciting hatred and division.

According to a paper by Yascha Mounk of Harvard and Robert Stefan Foa of the University of Melbourne published in the Journal of Democracy, a quarter of American millennials considered democracy to be a 'bad' or 'very bad' way of running the country.

What have we learned that may give us hope that civil society and liberal democracy will survive and prosper in the UK?

On the basis of the evidence and opinions I have gathered, I will answer the questions I asked in the first chapter.

Q: As the state provides less, how will the voluntary sector meet increasing demand because charitable giving is not growing despite a colossal increase in personal wealth?

A: The voluntary sector will only be able to meet more demand by working with partners in the public and private sectors and by seeking new, diverse sources of revenue. The ability to meet demand will continue to be constrained unless a way is found to encourage significantly more giving and volunteering. There is currently little prospect of this happening despite many well-intentioned campaigns to increase giving.

Q: Is it realistic to assume that philanthropists and charities will be able to compensate for less state provision, and is it desirable that they should?

A: No. Neither philanthropists nor charities have the capacity to replace public funding and philanthropists are not prepared to pick up the government's bills. If philanthropy were to take over too much of what was the responsibility of the public sector, democracy will become plutocracy.

Q: Is it true that future generations will be less well-off?

A: Yes, and for the foreseeable future unless public policy changes; see the Resolution Foundation reports and David Willett's book *The Pinch* (see Chapter 3).

Q: What are the facts about inequality and poverty in the UK? And what are the implications for the future of civil society?

A: We are a very much more unequal country than we were forty years ago and social mobility is in reverse. Although income inequality has not grown for some years, except at the very top, asset inequality continues to increase. According to the Joseph Rowntree Foundation, 1.25 million people in the UK are destitute. If these trends continue, we should expect greater feelings of alienation, less commitment to civil society and more extremist politics.

Q: If wealth and power continue to be held by the few, will future generations inherit a plutocracy rather than a liberal democracy? How do we uphold liberal democratic values in a world where democracy may not be predominant?

A: Some say the US is a plutocracy because politics and government are dominated by the interests of the rich. Moreover, the liberal democratic West is losing its global dominance as the focus of economic power shifts to a more autocratic and plutocratic Asia. We will only be able to uphold our liberal democracy if its future becomes part of public discourse and by debate about what will make it stronger. The lack of trust in politicians and the poor quality of political leadership cannot be good for the future of liberal democracy.

Q: How do we ensure and respect human dignity in a more impersonal world? How do we defend liberty and encourage personal responsibility when authority has lost respect and power is unaccountable?

A: We must devolve political power, revive the concept of community, personal responsibility and a belief that individuals can make a difference. All of the charitable and philanthropic work described in this book is about empowerment. Encouraging more people to support society by voluntary commitment to local causes and to community foundations could help to invigorate our liberal democracy.

Q: Who will provide the moral leadership to persuade the rich and powerful to follow the example of their forbears by supporting human endeavour for the common good as well as for personal gain?

A: I do not know.

Q: How do we ensure that all of us, not just the rich and power-ful, understand that we have a personal responsibility for the health and vitality of civil society?

A: We need a new culture of giving and creating it will be a chal-lenge. Teach ethics and citizenship so that all young people leave school knowing what it is to be a good citizen. Leadership by ex-ample should also change behaviour but we need more role models.

Q: How are today's philanthropists and social entrepreneurs responding to current challenges and how do they see their role evolving in the future?

A: The best are being as creative, innovative and pioneering as philanthropists and social entrepreneurs have always been. Bill Hol-royd and Andrew Mawson are changing how we tackle social and economic challenges. They are persuading the public and private sectors to reconsider their roles and responsibilities and how they work with others. They are establishing best new practice and by doing so, they are empowering the lives of those without power.

Q: What has been the impact of recession upon charities? Do they have the capacity to meet increased demand?

A: The impact on smaller charities, particularly those dependent on local authorities has been severe. One survey suggests that 47 per cent of local charities do not think they will be in business within five years. Big Lottery Fund, leading charitable foundations such as the Weston Foundation and some community foundations are helping vulnerable charities to build their capacity. However, some charities have seen their income grow in this period: Catch22, for example.

Q: Do charities need to adapt to meet changing circumstances, the needs of society and of those who fund them? If so, how?

A: Undoubtedly. If charities do not adapt, they will lose support. Some think there are far too many charities but how does anyone know how many is enough? It may well be sensible for some char-ities to merge. Charities operate in a market and will survive only if they attract sufficient support. Charities need to respond to the real-ity that, increasingly, donors prefer to decide for themselves where the greatest need is by donating to causes online. Many donors wish to give to causes rather than to charities.

All donors should insist that charities are well managed and run as a business. Everyone should do due diligence. Kids Company failed to provide what is expected of a charity in the twenty-first century because it was badly managed. Trustees are ultimately responsible. It should be a moral imperative for trustees to make a financial commitment in addition to the time they give. The amount given is not necessarily the point. When potential donors ask if all the charity's trustees are giving, the answer has to be yes.

Q: Should charities be providing public services and if not, why not?

A: There is no reason why charities should not provide public services but they risk becoming agents of government, thereby losing their independence.

In the interests of transparency and accountability, major charities that are delivering public services should establish a social enterprise for the purpose. Contracts for public service provision should also be structured to enable small local charities to contribute, if only in an advisory capacity.

Q: Do we need to define the role and responsibilities of the public, private and voluntary sectors and the citizen?

A: Yes, not least because regardless of whether or not the state becomes smaller or bigger, the state is changing what it does and what it provides and that requires a response.

In addition to the state's role as guardian of national sovereignty and guarantor of our security, politicians need to acknowledge the state's enabling role. There is very little public debate or discussion about these matters which should be the concern of all of us.

Q: Does the concept of the common good meaning anything in an era of neoliberalism or is there an irreversible trend towards more inequality and social fragmentation?

A: The notion of the common good seems almost quaint in a post-socialist world. Cycles come and go but we remain in one that deems private is good and public is bad, in which paying tax seems to be an anathema, thus indicating that commitment to the common good is not high. There are signs of dissatisfaction with the current model of capitalism. In 2014, Mark Carney, the governor of the Bank of England, defined 'Inclusive Capitalism' as 'delivering a basic social contract comprised of relative equality of outcomes; equality of opportunity and fairness across the generations'. He argued: 'Unchecked market fundamentalism can devour the social capital essential for the long-term dynamism of capitalism itself.' He called for individuals and companies to 'have sense of their responsibilities for the broader system … market participants need to become true stakeholders, that is, they must recognise that their actions do not merely affect their personal rewards but also the legitimacy of the system in which they operate'.

The future for the common good is not promising until we move into an era of more socially responsible capitalism and the fruits of wealth creation are shared more equably.

Q: Is it possible to imagine a future in which all those who contribute to the common good work together? If so, what could partnerships between the public, private and voluntary sectors look like and what could they achieve?

A: Yes. However, we must be realistic. The examples of OnSide Youth Zones, Andrew Mawson's work in Poplar, and Catch22 represent only a fraction of what needs to be done. They have been successful in abolishing a bunker mentality in some local authorities, but not all. There is a long way to go before others will be persuaded and it is hard to imagine that the Treasury will be easily persuaded to relax its grip on public spending.

If we need to re-create a culture of giving in Britain, should we be following the example of the most generous nation on earth, the USA? Whilst the generosity of some Americans is commendable and the effectiveness of professional fundraising in the States may be admired, the cultural and political differences between our countries suggest Britain should create its own culture.

Attitudes to wealth and perceptions of personal wealth are more positive in the US than in the UK. There is no welfare state in the

US that can be compared with the UK which has a more mixed economy. The US, a federation of states, is historically committed to limited government. The giving culture in the US is so far removed from the UK because there are different motivations and peer pressure and there is also a cult of the individual.

As concentrations of wealth have grown in the US, so has the scale of philanthropy. This has led to accusations that the purpose of some philanthropy is to exert influence rather than to give back. Over the last fifteen years, the number of foundations with a billion dollars or more in assets has doubled to more than eighty.

Those who are not familiar with how philanthropy works in the UK may assume that all benefactors are seeking influence to advance self-interest. In the US, the boards of universities, colleges, hospitals and cultural institutions are dominated by donors, and there can be little doubt that these positions are sometimes used to pursue personal ambition and agendas. Because of our mixed economy, this is much less likely to happen here.

There are, however, American philanthropists from whom we could learn. Bill Gates and others have invented a form of activist philanthropy, bypassing corrupt government in Africa and empowering people directly, particularly women. The focus is on community development rather than doling out aid to third parties, creating structures and programmes that meet the real needs of people, thereby giving them a sense of belonging, fulfilment and identity.

The positive aspect of active philanthropy in the US is when benefactors like Gates and Zuckerberg empower their managers to deliver change. Managers are given objectives to deliver and performance measures to achieve. It is up to managers to overcome inefficiencies and to deliver transformational change. Philanthropists don't tell their managers what to do. They listen to what they want to do. This was how they made their fortunes.

Their philanthropic objective is to fix what is broken and they hire the best people to do that. The most intelligent and progressive philanthropists understand that effective managers need to be empowered and equipped with a set of values and skills that enable them to understand what needs to be done to achieve progressive social change.

This aspect of the USA's culture of giving is worth emulating or adapting to our circumstances and culture. Could we develop a culture in our universities, law and business schools and consultancy firms that will produce these kinds of leaders and managers who will work for them? These are the people we need to lead in initiatives for social progress and they could transform our voluntary sector.

There is a problem with accountability. Who is Bill Gates accountable to? This is less of a problem in the UK because most philanthropy is supporting projects in partnership with others, often the public sector. Although a philanthropic initiative, the Onside Youth Zone model requires that all sources of funding are accountable to each other.

There is another difference between the US and the UK. In the US, the most enlightened philanthropists recognise that the creation of so much wealth and its concentration in the hands of so few is a serious problem. They are coming together to work out what to do about it.

There is no such discussion in the UK. The media will occasionally publish the latest statistics about inequality, report a shareholder revolt about chief executive pay or publish a list of those who have the most money. There will be stories about failing charities and occasional condemnation of overly zealous and inappropriate fundraising. There is very little joined-up thinking and analysis in the media because the voluntary sector barely registers with even the most well informed. This confirms that if we have a culture of giving in Britain, it is not understood and makes very little impression.

At this point, we need to remind ourselves that millions of people are volunteering every week or cycling, running, swimming or walking all night for the sake of others. Some people are exceptionally generous with their time and their money. Charitable giving and volunteering is alive and well but not sufficient to meet need and not truly representative of our wealth and our ability to give.

I believe we can and must do better if we are to tackle poverty, empower the disadvantaged, sustain civil society and invest in its future. This requires us to be honest about the state of our country. We need to do much more by creating more social, cultural and intellectual capital to ensure that our descendants inherit a healthy economy and liberal democracy and the ability to lead fulfilling lives. We know from the examples of the men and women in these pages what is possible and how inspiring leadership can bring people together to achieve even more.

So what needs to be done to create and develop a culture of giving?

The voluntary sector must take responsibility for ensuring the nation understands why its work matters and is deserving of support. No one else will.

Government and the public sector have a leadership and enabling role to play even though some believe that politicians should 'get out of the way'. There are times when government endorsement of projects and programmes is essential.

Government and local authority cash should be used to leverage matched funding from the private sector. There are successful examples from the past, notably in higher education, and more should be invested, particularly in a campaign to grow the endowment funds of community foundations in order to stimulate more giving at a local level to support local and regional needs.

Government must give up command and control and be more flexible in the use of public money by following the example of those local authorities investing in OnSide Youth Zones.

Government could alleviate concerns that the sole purpose of some private charitable foundations is to avoid taxation by requiring that they donate a percentage of the asset value annually to an independent charitable cause or organisation.

Government should enhance the value of voluntary commitment by requiring business leaders to demonstrate significant charitable giving and volunteering before they are considered for a national honour. The same should apply to all those receiving the most senior honours. There should be more honours for those who volunteer and give at all levels.

Whilst current initiatives to encourage the young to volunteer are welcome, they are inadequate for building a culture of giving. There needs to be an initiative in all schools that requires, as part of the curriculum, that young people are taught ethics and 'citizenship' and that they should be encouraged to engage in formal volunteering, leading to a nationally recognised qualification that has been endorsed and recognised by higher education and employers.

Business companies should reconsider their commitment to the common good and move beyond current corporate social responsibility initiatives to joint ventures with others in the public, private and voluntary sectors that could also be regarded as corporate social opportunities.

I would make the case for a greater charitable commitment, meaning the giving of time as well as money as follows:

Giving is good for us because that is what we are supposed to do. The history of the human species tells us that we have evolved successfully by developing a biological need to help others because this is the best way to sustain and prolong life.

History also tells us that the most successful societies, defined by their sustainability as much as by their wealth, developed a concept of the common good and encouraged commitment to it.

Philanthropy laid the foundations of much of the civil society we have inherited. More philanthropy is needed now to sustain what we have and to invest to ensure that future generations inherit what we have today.

The amount of public money to support civil society is limited because the British people are not prepared to pay more tax.

There have always been limits to what the state can do and we must expect the state to do or provide less in future.

There are also limits to what the voluntary sector and charities can do so we shall always need an enabling state. Those who might believe that philanthropy could compensate for a smaller state are deluding themselves.

Although the top rate of tax has halved since the 1970s, the majority of those who have benefited are not charitable. Trickledown has not happened. There is statistical evidence to confirm that an increasing proportion of the wealth created in the last thirty years is going to a smaller number of people.

Whilst more charitable giving and volunteering cannot be the only solution to our financial and social problems, it needs to be said clearly that philanthropy can make a significant contribution because it can do what the state cannot do. In partnership with public funding and others, philanthropy can act as a catalyst to generate positive social change.

Philanthropy is not only for the rich and has the power to connect people to society and to their communities.

Philanthropy should be a moral force for good. More philanthropy is needed not simply because there is a need for more money. Philanthropy represents a commitment to the common good.

William Beveridge, the great Liberal and founder of the welfare state in the 1940s, reminded us that: 'The happiness or unhappiness of the society in which we live depends upon ourselves as citizens, not only the instruments of political power we call the state.'

In the twenty-first century, we must find a new narrative and new heroes to succeed the robber baron philanthropists of the past. They would help to create a broad social movement with a vision that inspires the many as well as the rich. They would persuade people that their participation matters and will make a difference to their own lives as well as their fellow citizens.

The new political message must be: there is such a thing as society and we are all responsible for it. Voluntary redistribution, the giving of time and money, is as important as tax in sustaining society for the sake of those who will follow us.

Will this happen?

The example of those I have written about should give us encouragement. Their leadership has demonstrated commitment, imagination, innovation and humanity. They are showing a way forward that could bring out the best in us. The future of our way of life depends upon whether sufficient numbers of us are prepared to follow their example, to commit to the common good by being prepared to put the needs of others before our own.

We live, apparently, in a post-factual and post-truth world. Despite the lies, deception, anger, hate, blaming, scape-goating, bullying and ranting, often amplified by social media, goodness and kindness are not yet extinct. We must, however, be on our guard to avoid stumbling into a new age of darkness.

If we are to aspire to a new age of optimism and enlightenment, we need to remind ourselves why and how humanity has flourished and hold fast to what matters most. Norman Stoller put it this way as I left him in his house overlooking Lake Windermere:

> I have been asked how others can be persuaded to follow my example and I find the question quite puzzling. If one does not feel uplifted by an act of unselfishness or gain enormous pleasure by offering help when there is a real need to, then one simply has not lived.

APPENDIX

WHERE ARE THE MORAL QUESTIONS IN TODAY'S ECONOMIC DISCOURSE?

Excerpts from a lecture given by Dame Zarine Kharas, co-founder of JustGiving, at the Royal Society of Arts in 2009, on being presented with the RSA Albert Medal for 'democratising fundraising'.

The theme I'd like to explore tonight is business itself. As the Archbishop of Canterbury so eloquently put it not so long ago 'I want to ask where the moral questions are in today's economic discourse'.

As a fundamentalist – a fundamental atheist, that is – I find it strange to be quoting the Archbishop, but he got it right when he mused that perhaps what we are shrinking away from is getting a new perspective.

The guiding principle by which most of us in the industrialised world live our lives today is a separation of our working and our personal lives. Work is the thing you do to make a living, while our 'good' life, our 'moral' life, is lived elsewhere – with family, friends and, quite often, charity or voluntary work. JustGiving users often echo this dichotomy – they talk about the things they do for charity as profoundly meaningful, while the world of business can sometimes be so meaningless.

Now that our financial system appears to be in ruin, and our politicians in disgrace, I believe we have an opportunity to re-open the debate and question the accepted wisdom that business must, and should, be 'a-moral'.

I believe we have not only an opportunity, but a duty to do so. Whilst we are so ready to point the finger at politicians and bankers, where is the acknowledgement of our own responsibility? I mean us, here, in this room, the people who run businesses and charities, who employ people, make investment decisions, and define the services and products that people consume every day.

As Amartya Sen argues, 'What is needed, above all, is ... an understanding of how a variety of organisations – from the market to the institutions of state – to which I would add: private institutions – can together contribute to producing a more decent economic world.'

And by private institutions I mean companies, large and small, that play such a significant role in our lives and, collectively, keep our economy alive.

I believe the time has come for those of us involved in corporate leadership – and I include charity leaders in this too – to adopt new forms of behaviours.

We must begin with the notion that business and ethics, rather than being incompatible, actually go hand in hand. By the way, I am not referring to corporate social responsibility here – a charade in my opinion because, in the vast majority of cases, it is so divorced from the real purpose of the business.

No, I am referring to the purpose of business itself. The debate is not a new one. In his history of the Reformation: *Religion and the Rise of Capitalism*, R. H. Tawney, the economic historian, described the origins of the idea that the 'business of business is business', the idea that all things to do with the business of finance were to be kept quite apart from the business of society itself.

But the very notion that 'the sole business of business is business', that maximizing shareholder value is the ultimate purpose of a company, needs to be thrown out once and for all.

Of course, I am not alone in believing this. In the most notorious conversion since the Damascene one, Jack Welch now calls shareholder value 'the dumbest idea in the world' – a result, not a strategy. 'Your main constituencies are your employees, customers and products.'

And here is the paradox: it is only when a company chooses *not* to make the maximization of profit its primary goal that it stands to create greater long-term value for shareholders. In other words, profit is a by-product of something much greater: creating a great product, developing employees, serving customers in brilliant ways; and let's not forget the poor old shareholders. A company needs to serve all these stakeholders in a balanced way.

Why then is there so little of it in evidence? Because the alternative calls for a radically new mindset. There needs to develop a general consensus that success is *not* measured only in profit and growth. It requires a painful change of behaviour, which most business people, not to mention politicians, are ill-prepared for. More specifically, it requires not only companies to change the way they behave, but shareholders, customers and suppliers, and employees.

Firstly, the investors. Shareholders must stop acting like lemmings; they must cease their folly in the relentless quest for continuous growth at unsustainable levels.

Running companies for long-term sustainability requires shareholders to understand that sometimes decisions that may have a negative impact on immediate profits may have longer-term value.

Here's an example. At JustGiving we have been in discussions with HMRC over a long period of time on the question of whether or not our fees should be subject to VAT. It has cost us large sums of money and a lot of time. We have finally obtained an initial ruling that they should not – pending a final ruling.

This means that, in future, JustGiving will be unable to set off the VAT we are charged by suppliers – this will cost us hundreds of thousands of pounds every year. To be precise, it will increase our costs by 8 per cent.

But I defy anyone to tell me that this is not in the long-term interests of shareholders. One of the most valuable by-products of consistently acting in the interests of clients has been the trust that our users say they place in us. And *that* surely must generate greater value to the Company and therefore to shareholders – in the long term.

Secondly, customers and clients. It requires customers and clients (even, dare I say it, charities) to stop seeking the lowest price rather than the best value – without any regard to the long-term impact. It requires them to view the companies that serve them as partners, and seek solutions that are mutually beneficial.

Thirdly and most importantly, the *real* change starts from within companies themselves, with the behaviour of all employees and how they choose to interact with each other.

I admire the many companies, most of them social enterprises, that generate huge social value through what they do. But I believe that innovation is possible on a larger scale, throughout the economy, if we consider it not from the angle of *what* a company does, but *how* it does it.

Thanks to a very unusual group of investors we, at JG, have been allowed to experiment and innovate not just with what we do but how we do it. Everyone is a co-owner of the business and is expected to act as such. There are no incentives based on bonus schemes; instead a proportion of our profit is shared by all. We have a flat structure without much hierarchy; we strive to work in true partnerships with our charity clients; all our profits are re-invested in the business; this is despite the fact that we are a for-profit company. But above all, we've more or less thrown away the rule book, we simply trust everyone to do the right thing.

Why did we make those choices? Because we believe it brings out the best in people and therefore works better for the company.

Look at the 'normal' way of doing things. When things go wrong, as they invariably do, what do we, in business and in society, tend to reach for? The answer is: rules, regulations, controls: better ones, more of them.

We've all succumbed to the temptation: as companies, we try and dictate how employees should work; as charities, we want to control what our supporters do and say about us.

But it's a vain delusion – especially as the internet continues to enable the fastest dissemination of information the world has ever known. Just ask the London Metropolitan police about that!

Listen to what Ricardo Semler of Semco, the Brazilian manufacturing company run along democratic lines, has to say:

> I believe the obsession with control is a delusion and, increasingly, a fatal business error. The more we grab for it, the more it slips away, and ever more desperate measures are applied, spawning Enrons, WorldComs, and hosts of lower-profile disasters. As the control mechanism grows harsher and harsher, what's lost is the central purpose of the business, any business – namely: a satisfying, worthwhile life for those involved and a reasonable (note the word reasonable) reward for their investment and hard work.

It is only in the absence of rules that a business can get the best out of people and become truly excellent.

At JustGiving we try but we're the first to acknowledge that we still have a long way to go. We dabbled in rules and regulations, and hierarchy, at first, as we grew – and quickly un-dabbled. We realised that, first, rules became obsolete almost from the moment we wrote them, and secondly, they brought out the worst in ourselves – a tendency to follow the rules somewhat blindly. To date, the only rule we have is to have as few rules as possible. So we have no hard and fast rules on holidays. We don't even have rules on expenses.

Last year we asked employees to set their own salaries. Much to our surprise almost all set their salaries at below market rates.

Bill Gore, the founder of WL Gore, the enormously successful multi-billion, multi-national, wanted to build a firm that was truly innovative. To this day, there are no rule books or bureaucracy. He strongly believed that people come to work to do well and do the right thing. Trust, peer pressure and the desire to invent great things, he said, would be the glue holding the company together, rather than the official procedures and rules other companies rely on.

Rules breed mediocrity, rather than excellence. I'm sure you all heard the Home Secretary being interviewed not so long ago on the question of her expense claim for her two homes. She said: 'I followed the rules. I sought advice and I followed that advice. I have done nothing wrong.'

Here's the point: it's not so much the obvious one that, like so many of her colleagues, what she was doing was blatantly wrong. No, the point is that she had no hesitation in declaring to the world that since she had followed the rules and had taken advice on the matter she was guilty of no wrong-doing. And politicians wonder why we have so completely lost our respect for them.

An innovative organisation does not need people who ask themselves whether they are following procedures. It needs people who are constantly looking for better ways of doing things, and constantly challenging what's been done before.

How that is achieved is quite difficult to articulate because, in truth, it *is* difficult, it's quite subtle.

I'll try and summarise it by saying that we, at JustGiving, aim to have honest conversations with each other, constantly debating how to serve our customers better. Far from being soft and quirky, ours is a tough and rigorous environment where decisions are made on facts, not egos; and innovation happens without fear of failure. But all these things can only emerge when you trust each other.

We do not have – wait for this – an organisational chart. I am often asked how this can possibly work. The answer is that we work in project teams to get our work done. An organisational chart is useless. What matters are the jobs at hand.

Effective teams are made up of people who are self-motivated and keep each other accountable. That, in turn, means everyone in the team is accountable to their team, not to so-called 'managers'. Management or leadership comes with experience and is there to provide guidance and direction, and to hold people accountable when team members fail to do so.

It sounds simple, but it is actually quite difficult in practice, because challenge requires courage, and most of us are conditioned by culture and education to be compliant rather than questioning at work.

But when people feel themselves to be highly accountable for what they contribute; are to be called to account by their peers for any shortcomings; where people are motivated by a deep sense of involvement and purpose, not because they have been told to do a job, or given the authority to do it; where they perform to the best of their abilities out of respect for, and commitment to, their team mates and customers; and where have a meaningful say in the business regardless of the nature of their job; then they do not need to be told what to do.

And if you do not need to be told what to do then the need for hierarchy disappears. The structures that were created for the industries of the Victorian era and the assembly lines of Henry Ford are no longer appropriate in the internet age.

There *are* other companies that operate on principles similar to the ones I've described. And yet it engenders cynicism and scepticism. One charity client of JustGiving's, for example, expressed deep mistrust in that it was apparent, as he put it, that our shareholders were clearly 'not in it for the money alone'.

But why the suspicion? After all, Adam Smith recognised 250 years ago that an economy requires other values and commitments such as mutual trust and confidence to work efficiently.

We don't need any more ethics workshops or corporate citizenship lectures – just plain, old-fashioned trust in the people we work with. It's amazing what happens when people feel they have the freedom to do the right thing.

In summary, social innovation is available to *all of us* in all the businesses that we are part of, and the organisations to which we belong, if we truly want it.